WAR
SUMMITS

WAR
SUMMITS

The Meetings That Shaped World War II
and The Postwar World

DAVID STONE

POTOMAC BOOKS, INC.
WASHINGTON, D.C.

Library of Congress Cataloging-in-Publication Data

Stone, David (David J. A.)
    War Summits : the meetings that shaped World War II
    and the postwar world / David Stone.— 1st ed.
    p. cm.
Includes bibliographical references and index.
ISBN 1-57488-901-X (alk. paper)
    1. World War, 1939–1945—Diplomatic history. 2. Summit
meetings—History—20th century. I. Title.

D748.S77 2005
940.53'22—dc22

                                        2004065029

(alk. paper)

Printed in Canada on acid-free paper
that meets the American National Standards Institute
Z39-48 Standard.

Potomac Books, Inc.
22841 Quicksilver Drive,
Washington, D.C., 20166

First Edition

10 9 8 7 6 5 4 3 2 1

Edited and designed by DAG Publications Ltd., London, UK.

CONTENTS

Preface   vii

Introduction   xi

PART ONE: SETTING THE STAGE

1 A World in Turmoil, 1939–1941   3

2 Genesis of the Warlords: Churchill, Stalin, and
   Roosevelt, 1874–1941   20

PART TWO: SHAPING THE WAR

3 The Road to "Arcadia": Placentia Bay and the Atlantic Charter   33

4 The "Arcadia" Conference and the Pacific Dimension,
   December 22, 1941, to January 14, 1942   43

5 Arcadian Aftermath: Europe or North Africa?   50

6 In the Bear's Lair: The First Moscow Conference, August 1942   58

7 End of the Beginning: North Africa and the Eastern Front, 1942   64

8 Global Strategy and Unconditional Surrender:
   The Casablanca Conference, January 14–24, 1943   70

9 Sicily, Italy, and the Second Front: The "Trident" Conference,
   May 12–25, 1943   78

10 Italy, the Pacific, and Operation "Overlord":
   The "Quadrant" Conference, August 14–24, 1943   85

11 **Toward the Power of Three:** Moscow and Cairo,
October to November 1943   94

12 **The Power of Three:** The Tehran Conference, November 1943 115

PART THREE: SHAPING THE PEACE

13 **The Fruits of their Labors,** December 1943 to July 1944   145

14 **Idealism and Realism:** The Dumbarton Oaks Conference,
August 21 to October 9, 1944   174

15 **Strategy, Economics and "Tube Alloys":**
The "Octagon" Conference, September 12–16, 1944,
and the Hyde Park Meeting, September 19, 1944   180

16 **The Bear and the Bulldog:** The "Tolstoy" Conference,
October 9–19, 1944   194

17 **Matters of War and Peace:** The "Argonaut" Conferences,
January 20 to February 11, 1945   208

18 **Götterdämmerung:** The Final Defeat of Germany,
March to May 1945   226

19 **Anatomy of a War Summit:** The "Terminal" Conference,
July 17 to August 2, 1945   237

20 **Quo Vadis?** War Summits and the Postwar World   264

Notes   281

Select Bibliography   296

Index   299

PREFACE

ROM THE OUTSET, writing an account and analysis of the war summits that shaped World War II invited me to fall into either or both of two very obvious but at the same time not entirely unavoidable traps. First, it would be all too easy to produce yet another history of World War II, but with the war summits highlighted rather than as a dominant focus. Second, there was the very real danger of writing yet another multibiography of Churchill, Stalin, and Roosevelt during the World War II period.

With regard to the first of these potential traps, I acknowledged that a reader who might not be familiar with the causes, lead-in to, or general course of World War II might find an account that began in mid-1941 somewhat out of place and lacking the essential historical context in which to set all that then followed. With that in mind, Chapter 1 attempts to provide, albeit only in summary form, an account of the salient milestones along the road to war. At the same time, my intent with this chapter is also to convey a sense of the growing turmoil that was progressively consuming the world through the two decades prior to the outbreak of the war; for from this turmoil was born the remarkable Alliance of Great Britain, the Soviet Union, and the United States—at the very core of which was the no less remarkable system of war summits by which the Allies planned how they would win the conflict and then how they would win and manage the peace that crowned their victory. Factual coverage of the course of the war in the subsequent chapters is by and large limited to summaries of events which indicate the success or otherwise of the various war summits, or to accounts of the events which later affected or placed these meetings in context.

Next, even with the second of these two perils still firmly in mind, it was indisputable that Churchill, Stalin, and Roosevelt were the key figures present at, or who influenced directly, all of these crucial meetings. Consequently, the inclusion of a certain amount of biographical or anecdotal coverage of the three Allied war leaders has been unavoidable; indeed, it has been essential. However, I have generally endeavored to restrict this coverage to those biographical or personal matters which bore directly upon the conferences which form the central theme of this work. Nevertheless, in order to provide a little more historical depth, and so assist the reader's understanding of the later motivation, actions, and decisions of all three Allied war leaders, I have included within Chapter 2 a brief summary of the lives of each through their formative years, up to the point at which their very separate careers began to converge in the 1940s. In doing this, I have attempted to distil out and emphasize those matters which later influenced, directly or indirectly, their participation in the Allied war summits. I would also commend to the reader the endnotes, by the liberal use of which I have attempted to amplify many secondary or peripheral aspects of the main theme without disrupting what is invariably a complex and often convoluted story. By this approach I hope that I have succeeded in my aim of providing a straightforward account and analysis of an international system of consultation, negotiation, compromise, and strategic decision-making which was every bit as unique as the scale and nature of the war it was developed to win.

I must now record my particular thanks to Col. (retd) Nigel Flower, a former colleague in the world of military intelligence. This work has benefited greatly from his considerable depth of knowledge and expertise on Russia and the Soviet Union, and he has also brought to the project a wealth of personal experience of the background to high-level military decision-making and strategic planning. His critical—but always well-founded and positive—observations regarding this work have proved invaluable, while his several anecdotal insights into Stalin and the Soviet Union have added depth and a human perspective to many parts of it. However, it is to my publishing editor Rod Dymott that I am especially grateful. First of all he sowed the seeds of the original idea, then throughout its development he maintained both his support for the project and an unswerving faith in my ability to bring it to a successful conclusion. Last of all, I owe a debt of gratitude to Jeremy Whitehorn of Heartland Old Books, of Tiverton in Devon, for allowing me unlimited access to the several important but long out-of-print works of reference from among his extensive stocks of military, historical, and political publications.

Finally, while this work relies upon a wide range of sources for its factual accuracy and for arriving at the conclusions and opinions indicated, it is in the main composed of original text, which in turn reflects the fact that it is an entirely new review and contemporary analysis of the subject rather than an account culled directly from official documents or other related works. While on the one hand this will, it is hoped, make some of the assertions and views expressed both contentious and thought-provoking, it also follows that any omissions that may be identified are the result of my own assessment of their importance or relevance, as well as of my consequent decision to summarize or exclude some events and material. It follows that any errors which may unintentionally have appeared in the text are my responsibility and mine alone.

INTRODUCTION

BERLIN, JULY 1945: a city traumatized and in large part destroyed by the savage fighting that had raged through it until just two months previously. Everywhere were the soldiers of the victorious Allies—British, American, and Russian—but those of Stalin's Red Army were by far the more numerous, understandably so, as it had been six armies of the 1st Belorussian Front, commanded by Marshal Zhukov, that had first broken into the heart of the capital of the Third Reich and raised their blood-red victory flag on the top of Hitler's Reichstag on May Day, 1945. Not that Adolf Hitler or any of the leaders of the so-called Thousand-Year Reich had witnessed this act which symbolized the end of Germany's National Socialist dream. The German Führer was already dead, killed by his own hand on April 30, along with his erstwhile mistress and wife of just one day, Eva Braun. Most of his closest associates, ministers, generals, aides, advisors, and supporters were also dead, or in hiding, or on the run. Meanwhile the Allied intelligence staffs, military police, and hundreds of thousands of ordinary servicemen in British, American, and Russian uniforms sought these members of the Nazi hierarchy in order to deliver them up to justice for the crimes they had inflicted upon the world—against Europe and the Soviet Union in particular—during some five years of total war.

However, Europe was finally at peace, for the first time since the summer of 1939—although many in Spain, Austria, Czechoslovakia and Poland might justifiably argue they had not been truly at peace since the mid-1930s—and the time had come, in the words of various politicians, to shape a "brave new world," a "land fit for heroes to live in," and similar, so that the wholesale death, destruction, desolation, and despair of the long years of conflict that had at last culminated in the Allied victory might not have been in vain.

So it was that the town of Potsdam, which lay about ten miles to the southwest of the ruined German capital, was selected to host the last of the landmark meetings of the Allied leaders of World War II, a final meeting that was intended to shape the new postwar Europe, but which in practice also laid the foundations for what became known as the "Cold War". In July 1945 all that was largely unforeseen and very much for the future, however, as the arrangements for the last of these great conferences were put in train. It was the final in a series of such summit meetings that had begun in the closing weeks of 1941, and then continued on a regular basis throughout the war, driven in equal measure by the progress of the conflict and by the national and international agendas of the leaders who participated, or by their high-level representatives or chiefs of staff. But just as the strategic-political world in 1945 was a very different place from that of 1941, so had the leaders also aged and changed since the first summit just three years earlier.

By the time that the Allied leaders gathered at Potsdam, Churchill's great ally and friend, President Roosevelt, was dead, having survived long enough to know that Allied victory was within grasp but unable to savor its fruits, and unable to witness the atomic devastation and final defeat of Japan. Harry S. Truman had succeeded him as president, and now led the U.S. delegation at Potsdam. In those late July days of 1945, Churchill's own enforced departure from the conference was also imminent, but this was not as a result of ill-health, although five years of war had undoubtedly taken their toll: in this case Churchill was constrained to leave Potsdam following his defeat in a British general election that was remarkable not only for its outcome—and for the British people's rejection of the war leader who had epitomized the fighting spirit of the nation when it had stood entirely alone against the might of the German Reichsheer, Luftwaffe, and Kriegsmarine during the dark days of 1940 and 1941—but also for the electioneering ploys adopted by a socialist Labour party whose activists were now determined to gain power as soon as possible, by any means and at any price. Churchill undoubtedly had a premonition of the Labour landslide—much of it thanks to the socialists' astute but opportunistic exploitation of the service vote—and he was in any event apparently less energetic and robust at Potsdam than he had been at the earlier summit meetings. It was nevertheless a most inappropriate time for the international community to lose the considerable experience, intellect, and ability of one of the two remaining architects of the triumvirate that had evolved over time to become the "Big Three." Ultimately, Britain, Europe, and the West undoubtedly paid a long-term price for the British socialists' relatively shortlived victory in the 1945 British general election.

The displacement of Churchill by Attlee in mid-conference at Potsdam must have been incomprehensible to Joseph Stalin, the other surviving member of the "Big Three". Here he witnessed a victorious nation rejecting its triumphant war leader in the very hour of its and his victory. Such a bizarre event assuredly could never have occurred in Stalin's Soviet Union, and Churchill's dismissal from office told the Soviet leader much about the quaint and sometimes flawed nature of political democ racy in a country that he had already assessed would undoubtedly confront the Soviet Union in the years ahead. No doubt Stalin also reflected with some satisfaction on the new U.S. president's preoccupation with, and aversion to, the former colonial empires of Great Britain, France, and other European nations, and on his administration's somewhat idealistic view of the nationalist and independence movements then emerging from the myriad armed resistance groups which had been set up by the Allies about the world. Stalin knew that the line between the nationalist and the communist was very fine, and all the finer where a nationalist movement's weapons, funding, and external support were being generously provided by the communist Soviet Union. Certainly, the naivety of the United States could be exploited, and, in the knowledge that the United States had just produced a viable atomic weapon, any political fault lines or weaknesses in what Stalin knew would, in the future, be the greatest military opponent of communism had to be clearly identified. Then, when the time was right, they had to be exploited exhaustively and, whenever necessary, ruthlessly.

So much of this, however, was for the future and another global conflict—one that would be very different from World War II that was just about to end in a flash of light, a pulse of radiation, and a veritable storm of blast and heat first above Hiroshima and then over Nagasaki. Just as Potsdam would provide the seeds of future conflict, this conference was also the political and strategic watershed that indicated the real end of the war against Germany. It also marked the end of an intricate process of consultation, negotiation, and planning that had begun in Placentia Bay, on the coast of Newfoundland, in August 1941. This process had then evolved during the subsequent months and years, and had consistently provided the strategic direction which had finally produced the Allied victory. Therefore, despite all its trials, tribulations, and aberrations, the meeting at Potsdam achieved closure for a war that had torn the world apart, and which had at one stage risked its domination by the triple evils of Nazism, fascism and Japanese imperialism. That these evils had not prevailed was due as much to the success—often against all the odds and following much debate—of the meeting of minds of the three great war leaders and of their subordinates and representatives at ministerial and chief-of-staff level. Potsdam was thus the final act in a process that was as much intellectual as it was political and strategic, and throughout which the personalities, agendas, experience, and foibles of the "Big Three" dominated. Consequently, Churchill's selection of "Terminal" as the coded title of the Potsdam conference was most apposite, for this last gathering of the leaders of the three great powers that had fought and won World War II ended not only that conflict, but also a three-year process of consultation and strategic planning unprecedented in the history of warfare—a remarkable process that had enabled the Allies not only to outfight the Axis forces that opposed them, but also to outthink and outsmart the Axis war leaders in Berlin, Rome, and Tokyo who had led their peoples on to the precarious and ultimately disastrous path to war.

Part One
SETTING THE STAGE

1
A WORLD IN TURMOIL, 1939–1941

T HE START POINT OF THE TURMOIL that was by 1941 escalating and flowing in an irresistible tide of chaos, death, and
destruction across virtually the whole of the world is usually set
as September 1, 1939, the date of Germany's invasion of neighboring
Poland. However, the real origins of the world war which followed lay
much further back in time and, as history has shown time and again, the
imperfect political resolution of an armed conflict will almost certainly
result in another clash of arms involving all or some of the earlier
protagonists. World War II was no exception, and in many respects the
Treaty of Versailles, signed in 1920 to set the seal on World War I of
1914–18, put in place a temporary armistice rather than a lasting peace.
It was an armistice that would endure for less than two decades, during
which an aggrieved, humiliated, and politically unstable Germany
looked forward to the next round of war in Europe, and from the 1930s
made its preparations accordingly.

Although Britain adopted an increasingly conciliatory foreign policy—
albeit one that eventually translated into the discredited policy of
appeasement—France remained firmly set against any such overtures.
Quite apart from the wholesale destruction that the "Great War" had
wreaked upon eastern France and Belgium from the North Sea to the
Swiss border, and the enormous numbers of casualties that France had
incurred, the government in Paris, together with a large proportion of
the French population, viewed the Versailles settlement as a much-
belated opportunity for France to avenge the humiliating defeat it had
suffered at German hands in 1870–71. Consequently, while Britain took
account of the need to take Germany—despite the war, still, potentially,
an economic and industrial powerhouse—fully back into the community

of European nations, any substantial progress was balked by French reservations and objections. The construction of the Maginot line of forts along France's eastern border exemplified the French attitude to Germany. At the same time, the government in Russia was less focused on the defeated Germany than upon subduing, consolidating, securing, and developing the enlarged Soviet Union in accordance with the ideology of Marxist-Leninism.

Meanwhile, on the other side of the Atlantic, the last of the four victorious great powers of 1918, the United States—a nation which had not long experienced the consequences of submarine warfare and had only relatively briefly been exposed to the horrors of trench warfare in the final campaign on the Western Front—subsided into isolationism, commercialism, and further developing its technological and industrial base. Elsewhere, in the defeated Germany, the punitive and humiliating effects of the terms set at Versailles combined with the world economic crash and recession of the 1920s (and the consequent hyperinflation) to destroy many of the seeds of commercial and personal wealth that had emerged during the post-1918 years. The instability this caused led to the rise of a number of extreme right- and left-wing political organizations— including the Nationalsozialistische Deutsche Arbeiterpartei (the NSDAP, or Nazis) and the communists—and in due course to the collapse of the Weimar Republic. Moreover, all the while there was a widespread belief in the country that the German army had in reality not been defeated in the field in 1918, but rather it had been betrayed by self-interested politicians and others at home. The post-1918 treatment of Germany, the chain of events within that country through the 1920s and early 1930s, and the misunderstanding or underestimation by many in positions of power and authority of what was truly happening within Germany contributed directly to the Nazis achieving political preeminence, and to Adolf Hitler becoming German Chancellor in 1933 and the leader—*Der Führer*—in 1934. From that time on, the route to the turmoil of the 1940s was well signed for those statesmen and politicians who chose to take note of these warning indicators.

After 1934, one of the first milestones on the road to World War II was the Spanish Civil War from 1936 to 1939, a classic clash between the forces of fascism or nationalism and republicanism, the latter in its widest sense. The bitter and protracted conflict in Spain provided Germany's revitalized and fast-expanding armed forces an opportunity to trial many of the new advances in military technology, and to practice some of the tactics that would maximize their effectiveness. In devastating air raids such as that against Guernica on April 26, 1937, the Heinkels, Junkers and Messerschmitts of Germany's Condor Legion, supporting General Franco's forces, perfected many of the bombing and fighter ground-attack techniques that would soon be a vital component of the *Blitzkrieg* concept. The scale of the German military involvement in Spain was more than matched by that of Italy, which was by then ruled by the fascist dictator Benito Mussolini. Many of the modern weapons used in the Spanish conflict were subsequently adapted as necessary in the light of combat experience, perfected, and then mass-produced and issued widely to the Wehrmacht.

Elsewhere, on March 7, 1936, Hitler denounced the Locarno Pact, as German troops reclaimed and occupied the previously demilitarized Rhineland. Then, almost exactly two years later, Hitler ordered the annexation of Austria—the *Anschluss*—followed by the announcement of his territorial claim on the Sudetenland in Czechoslovakia. The crisis in Europe gained in pace, and between September 29 and 30, 1938, the process of appeasement of Hitler reached its zenith, when British prime minister Neville Chamberlain and French premier Édouard Daladier met with Hitler and Mussolini and signed the Munich Agreement. Chamberlain and Daladier agreed Germany's annexation of the Sudetenland; but, with memories of World War I still very much alive in both France and Britain, both leaders considered that this was an acceptable price to pay for Hitler's guarantee of what Chamberlain famously termed "peace in our time" when interviewed shortly after his return to England. Meanwhile, in Nazi Germany the first deportations of its Jewish citizens took place on October 28; then, during the night of November 9—*Kristallnacht* ("Night of [broken] Glass")—groups of stormtroopers and civilian mobs attacked and burned Jewish synagogues and commercial premises throughout Germany. Three days later, the German Jewish community was collectively fined one billion marks. The expulsion of all Jewish pupils from German schools followed on November 15, and the compulsory "Aryanization" of all Jewish commercial enterprises from December 3.

On March 15, 1939, the Czech president, Emil Hácha, visited Hitler in Berlin, in the hope that he might be able to negotiate a continued independence for his country, which had by then been, for all practical purposes, abandoned to its fate by Britain and France. Hácha's mission was a total failure, and it ended with him signing an instrument of surrender. This capitulation was followed by the German occupation of Prague, the establishment of the German Protectorate of Bohemia and Moravia, with the cession to Germany and German occupation of Memel on March 23, and the end of Czechoslovakia as an independent sovereign state.[1] On March 31, 1939, Britain and France guaranteed the security of Poland; but on May 22 Germany and Italy (which had seized Albania six weeks earlier) concluded a military alliance, and the next day Hitler informed the most senior generals of the Wehrmacht high command that a war with Poland was now inevitable. Between May 31 and June 7, Germany concluded nonaggression treaties with Latvia, Estonia, and Denmark; then, more significantly, on August 23, the Soviet-German nonaggression pact was signed in Moscow, and this included a secret protocol on Poland. On August 25, a Polish-British treaty was signed, but, despite this treaty and a series of last-minute appeals made to Hitler by U.S. president Roosevelt, Pope Pius XII, and Daladier, on September 1, 1939, the German panzers roared into Poland. Long columns of vehicles, horse-drawn equipment, and marching infantry filled the roads in the border area, all moving eastward to exploit the successes of the rapidly advancing armored forces. On September 3, Great Britain and France declared war on Germany; but it was all much too late. The Polish capital, Warsaw, fell on September 27, signalling the defeat, occupation, and impending subjugation of Poland by German troops. Internationally, the world's twenty-year journey toward the ultimate turmoil of general war in Europe had moved on apace since 1934, and had almost reached its destination.

While these momentous events had been taking place in Europe, on the other side of the world, in China, another nation had been imposing its will upon others by force of arms. There, imperial Japan's extensive incursion into Chinese territory from 1937 would finally draw it into direct conflict with the United States and the western European colonial powers, and make inevitable its inclusion as the third member of the Berlin-Rome-Tokyo Axis in September 1940. The full-scale Japanese attack launched in 1937 was a further blow for a country that was already being gradually torn apart by the struggle between Chiang Kai-shek's Kuomintang forces and Mao Tse-tung's communists—despite the fact that the Japanese invasion forced Chiang into an uneasy if tempo-rary alliance with the communists.

The campaign conducted by the Japanese army in China was frequently characterized by mass killings, countless atrocities against civilians, a total disregard for the lives of prisoners of war, and the wholesale bombardment of Chinese towns and cities from the ground and the air. Such barbarisms provided a graphic preview of the sort of war that the Japanese armed forces would later wage against the Allies from December 1941, although few in the West took much note of this in the 1930s, indeed, in July 1939 the British government recognized Japan's special status in China, including its responsibility for main-taining the rule of law in the territory its forces occupied! However, apart from the Japanese sinking of the U.S. Navy gunboat USS *Panay* on December 12, 1937, a full-scale clash of arms between Japan and the Western powers was still very much for the future, and through the late 1930s China—notably the key industrial province of Manchuria—remained the focus of Japanese military action. The initial assault in 1937 had provoked extensive anti-Japanese demonstrations and civil unrest across China; this soon spread to Shanghai, and into the areas occupied by the international communities, who still maintained a sizable pres-ence in China, including detachments of troops to ensure the security of the various international settlements. In 1938, one of these military detachments—specifically that of the U.S. Marines stationed in Shanghai—became directly involved in suppressing riots in the city, in order to protect U.S. lives and property. As the decade drew on toward its close, many Americans had come to sympathize with the Chinese people, having by then become fully aware of the brutalities and excesses perpetrated by the Japanese war machine. Consequently, the arrival of Japanese troops in Shanghai considerably increased U.S.-Japanese hostility and tensions in the late 1930s, and was an important contributory factor in Washington's subsequent decision to impose an arms embargo and economic sanctions against Japan. International trade and commerce had traditionally been significant foreign policy issues for the United States, and Washington had long been committed to the policy of keeping China open to free trade with and by all, and to preventing its domination by any single country.

However, the home islands of Japan were not well blessed with strategic raw materials, and so the impact of the U.S. sanctions was much greater than it might have been for many other nations. Moreover, many of the political and military leaders in Japan already regarded the United States as their country's principal rival for commercial and military supremacy in the Pacific region. This, together with the vital need to obtain strategic resources sufficient to meet its civil and military needs, would eventually set Japan on its course of conquest in Southeast Asia, and would by default lead it directly into war with the United States, Britain, the Netherlands, and France. So, as Hitler and the Nazis achieved absolute power in Germany, and Mussolini and the Italian fascists consolidated their position in Italy, events in Japan and China were also moving inexorably toward the conflict which would in due course blaze across the Far East, Southeast Asia, and the Pacific, turning what had begun as a primarily European conflict into a full-scale world war.

Following Germany's invasion of Poland at dawn on September 1, 1939, Great Britain, France, and the dominions of Canada, Australia, New Zealand, and South Africa all declared war on Germany. Poland was quickly subdued, and a German onslaught against western Europe was judged imminent. In Britain, the inevitable, massive air bombardments such as those seen in Spain and now in Poland were awaited with trepidation. However, no attack came, and, although a British Expeditionary Force (BEF) was landed in France in anticipation of the German advance westward, a "Phony War" ensued during the winter months of 1939–40, at least on land. However, on the high seas it was a very different matter, as the Royal Navy sought to keep open the seaways against the very real threat posed by the German U-boats and surface raiders.

The Treaty of Versailles had permitted the German navy to have three "pocket-battleships," each of ten thousand tons displacement, and although their designers had not exceeded the limitations imposed upon them, they had produced a trio of very potent warships, each of which was well armored, capable of twenty-six knots, and armed with six eleven-inch guns. Technologically, these vessels outclassed every British cruiser then in service. The pocket battleships were complemented by a small number of modern cruisers mounting eight-inch guns, plus the U-boat fleet. These warships together represented a major threat against the sealanes to Britain, especially those from the United States, and the destruction of this German maritime capability attracted the highest priority during the closing months of 1939.

The most active and successful of the German pocket-battleships was the *Admiral Graf Spee*. She had first come to the notice of the admiralty through her operations in the South Atlantic, then in mid-November the raider was identified in the Indian Ocean. An Anglo-French task force of five warships operating from Freetown and Dakar was already seeking to intercept her, while two more Royal Navy cruisers patrolled the Cape of Good Hope. Meanwhile, off the coast of South America, another Royal Navy task group of four cruisers, commanded by Commodore Harwood, patrolled the South Atlantic off Rio de Janeiro and the mouth of the River Plate. Although the sinking by the *Graf Spee* of a tanker in the Mozambique Channel on November 15 had focused the hunt on that area, the ship's exposure in the Indian Ocean had been no more than a ruse by its astute and experienced commander, Captain Langsdorff. The German raider had in fact reversed her course and returned to the South Atlantic, successfully evading the British and French warships en route. Indeed, in late November, the lack of intelligence about the ship's whereabouts made it unclear whether one or two (the *Graf Spee* possibly in the company of a sistership, the *Admiral Scheer*) German raiders were loose in the southern oceans. The third of these pocket battleships, the *Deutschland*, was then known to be in port in northern Germany.

However, on December 2, the *Graf Spee* sank the merchantman *Doric Star*, and although this action took place more than three thousand miles from the South American coast, it nonetheless indicated to Commodore Harwood that the raider was heading toward his small task group, which was by then only three warships strong–HMS *Ajax*, HMNZS *Achilles* and HMS *Exeter*. At 6:14 in the morning of December 13, Harwood's force sighted the *Graf Spee*, and battle was joined shortly thereafter. With hindsight, Langsdorff's best course would have been to maneuver out of range of the cruisers' six-inch and eight-inch guns and destroy them with his eleven-inch guns at his leisure. However, Harwood's audacious tactics of closing with the German vessel as quickly as possible, and from several directions at once, denied Langsdorff the time and opportunity to do this. Over the next one and a half hours, the British cruisers inflicted considerable damage on the *Graf Spee*, but themselves suffered devastating damage in the course of doing so. Nevertheless, the cruisers forced Langsdorff to make for Uruguay, and the River Plate port of Montevideo. Although HMS *Exeter* was put out of action, and both HMS *Ajax* and HMNZS *Achilles* were severely damaged, they pursued the *Graf Spee*. There they blockaded the pocket-battleship, and during the night of December 14 they were joined by the fourth cruiser of the task group, HMS *Cumberland*. With the *Graf Spee* trapped, the admiralty dispatched other Royal Navy warships to join Harwood's battered but victorious force. Escape was clearly impossible for the *Graf Spee*, and at 6:15 in the evening of December 17, with virtually all of her crew already safely disembarked onto a German merchant vessel, the pocket-battleship weighed anchor and turned her bow toward the open sea–and the waiting Royal Navy warships. Then, at 8:45 in the evening, a series of large explosions tore the ship apart as she was scuttled by her crew—an action that had required the approval of Hitler himself. During the night of December 19, Captain Langsdorff shot himself, unable to bear the loss of his ship and the responsibility that he bore for the *Admiral Graf Spee*'s defeat at the hands of the Royal Navy.

In Britain, the population rejoiced at the news of the outcome of the Battle of the River Plate: perhaps the horrors of war they had by now awaited with trepidation for some three months would not be visited upon the British Isles? However, while it was indisputably a remarkable achievement in its own right, this early naval victory proved to have been something of a false dawn. In early April 1940 the "Phony War" on the mainland of Europe suddenly ended, with all the martial efficiency, violence, and destruction implicit in the German concept of *Blitzkrieg*—the "lightning war."

On April 9, German ground forces, supported by wave after wave of dive bombers, stormed into Norway and Denmark. Their strategic mission was to seize control of Norway's mineral resources, primarily the deposits of iron ore that were now so vital to the German industrial war effort. Neville Chamberlain was still the British prime minister, although his position in light of the flawed Munich Agreement of September 1938 was becoming weaker by the day. The focus of conflict moved to the Norwegian Sea, and both Britain and France sent landing forces to Namsos, Andalsnes, and Narvik in Norway. However, despite some initial successes against the German occupation forces, this campaign could never have been sustained militarily or logistically— especially as the main threat remained that posed to France.

Just one month after the invasion of Norway and Denmark, the Germans launched their attack on the low countries and France. Predictably, their armored divisions circumvented the now redundant Maginot line as the panzers struck into the Netherlands, Belgium, and Luxembourg. At the same time, the massive Belgian fortress of Eben-Emael—the key to the defense of the River Meuse—quickly fell to a daring *coup de main* by the 438 men of the Luftwaffe's gliderborne Fallschirmjäger (paratroops) of the "Sturmabteilung Koch," who landed right on top of the fortress. The uncertainty of September to April had already ended in Scandinavia, and now at 4:35 in the morning of May 10, 1940, western Europe began to experience the turmoil that would afflict it for the next four and a half long years.

In the evening of the same day as the German invasion of the low countries, King George VI summoned Winston Churchill to Buckingham Palace in London. Chamberlain's failing administration had run its course, he had resigned, and Churchill was invited to form a new coalition government, one with a multiparty composition appropriate to the crisis that now existed. Thus the third of the three key players (the other two were of course Stalin and Roosevelt, both of whom were already in place as leaders of the Soviet Union and the United States respectively) in what would later become the process of the war summits assumed his awesome responsibilities as the British prime minister on May 10, 1940. He did so with the grim but pragmatic promise that he had "nothing to offer but blood, toil, tears and sweat." His pronouncement was very apt, for the Netherlands quickly capitulated on May 14, with much of the great city of Rotterdam already lying in ruins; Brussels was occupied on May 17, and Antwerp fell on the eighteenth, the formal Belgian surrender following ten days later.

What of the battle for France and the three corps (comprised of ten divisions, with a total of 237,319 men) of the British Expeditionary Force under the command of Gen. Lord Gort, much of which had been occupying defensive positions to the east of Lille between the French 1st and 7th Armies since the previous October? With the Maginot line outflanked, the British and French positions on the border had become untenable, and a withdrawal was inevitable. As the panzer divisions sped westward, French and British units alike gave ground steadily as they withdrew toward the Channel coast and the port of Dunkirk. By the third week of May, the remaining Anglo-French forces in northern France held a perimeter around Dunkirk that was about six miles deep and not more than twenty-five miles long, with the sea at their backs and the military might of the German 9th, 10th, 14th and 26th Army Corps in front of them. The fate of these troops seemed to be sealed, but then, in the so-called Miracle of Dunkirk, the admiralty implemented Operation "Dynamo," under the direct control of Admiral Ramsay. Between May 26 and June 4, a mixed fleet of British, French and Belgian naval vessels, together with a disparate armada of privately owned craft of every type, embarked a total of 338,226 men and conveyed them to safety in England. Of these, 198,315 were British and 139,911 were from allied units, predominantly French. While Dunkirk was a remarkable achievement, it was in no sense a victory, and even those men who had been rescued brought with them little more than their personal weapons and some equipment—if that. A large part of the Miracle of Dunkirk was the Germans' failure to complete the destruction of the BEF, although it had certainly been well within their capability to do so. This turn of events was in part prompted by Hitler's hope that he could yet achieve a suitable political accommodation with Britain once France had been dealt with. With that in mind, the panzer divisions now turned away from the channel and struck southward, there to complete the collapse of what remained of the French army.

Elsewhere, Mussolini judged this an opportune moment for Italy to declare war on Britain and France. On June 14, Paris was occupied without any French resistance, and on the same day the Germans broke through the Maginot line to the south of Saarbrücken—in precisely the same area that the Prussian and Bavarian armies of von Moltke and Bismarck had begun the eight-month-long Franco-Prussian War which had defeated and humiliated France just over seventy years earlier, in 1870–71. On June 16, Marshal Henri Philippe Pétain succeeded Reynaud as French premier; this was followed by France's truce with Germany, signed at Compiègne on June 22, which in turn prepared the way for the creation of the Vichy government and its policy of cooperation with the German occupiers.

At the end of June 1940, Great Britain and its recently appointed but redoubtable prime minister truly stood alone against the might of the German-Italian military forces now arrayed against them from North Africa to the English Channel. This isolation was heightened by the air bombardment that the Luftwaffe now unleashed upon the British Isles from July 10, and by the start of the air campaign fought by the Royal Air Force (RAF) from August 13 in an attempt to stem the bombing onslaught. Battling against all the odds, and in spite of crippling losses among fighter pilots, the RAF finally won a notable strategic victory in the skies above a beleaguered England in mid-September, when the Luftwaffe's failure to achieve air supremacy above the English Channel and southeast England prompted Hitler to postpone the intended invasion of Britain, Operation "Seelöwe" (Sealion)—an invasion which had been daily anticipated by London ever since the end of May. Having fought and lost the Battle of Britain, from September and throughout the winter of 1940–41 Reichsmarschall Hermann Göring now directed the

Luftwaffe against British cities, in the hope that the policy of terror bombing (what every British city-dweller soon came to know as "The Blitz") would force Britain to sue for peace. Although great destruction was caused to these centers—London especially—together with many thousands of casualties amongst the civilian population, the strategic aim of the Germans was not achieved. This failure, coming only a few months after the RAF's victory, contributed directly to Göring's progressive slide from favor with Hitler from early 1941.

While these momentous events had been unfolding in Europe, in the Baltic the Soviets had taken full advantage of the situation to occupy Estonia, Lithuania, and Latvia during June 15 and 16, secure in the nonaggression pact that they had signed with Germany in August 1939. Stalin's recent war against Finland, which began with the Soviet invasion of November 30, had concluded just over three months later with the signing of a peace treaty in Moscow on March 12. In due course, Stalin would be a key member of the Western alliance and a contributor to the process of the war summits, but in mid-1940 the Soviet Union, while not an active ally of Nazi Germany, was at the very least a passive observer of German aggression—somewhat ironically, given the ideological divergence of bolshevism and fascism. At the same time, it was capitalizing on the international fallout from this in order to further its own national interests. The strategic defensive position of the Soviet Union on its western and northwestern flank had been hugely strengthened by the division of Poland, the occupation of the three Baltic states, and the Soviet military campaign in Finland.

So much, then, for two of the principal nations that would, in due course—and against all contemporary expectations, given the situation in the fall of 1940—come together as allies less than a year later. In the meantime, across the Atlantic in Washington, President Franklin D. Roosevelt and his advisors were watching the spreading conflict in Europe with growing concern, while assiduously guarding the neutral status of the United States. Roosevelt had, as early as April 1939, appealed to Hitler to respect the independence of the European nations. This appeal, together with a further plea on August 25 the same year, had been ignored by Hitler, who judged that the United States was not relevant to his plans for Europe and would certainly not go to war with Germany in order to frustrate them. Roosevelt's subsequent condemnation of Italy's declaration of war on France and Britain in June had also passed without Berlin or Rome identifying it as a matter of any particular consequence. However, in addition to having a significant German immigrant population of its own, there was also a not inconsiderable amount of support for Germany in several parts of America: many U.S. citizens admired and applauded the way in which Hitler and the Nazis had, apparently, brought order, security, and commercial prosperity to Germany in place of the chaos of the Weimar Republic. In late 1940, the Nazis' excesses and their escalating persecution of the Jews had gained little visibility beyond mainland Europe, and, where they had been reported beyond Germany, they had often been dismissed as exaggerated or simply untrue.

Then, on September 3, Roosevelt took one of the first substantive steps toward aiding Britain directly when he authorized the transfer to the Royal Navy of fifty obsolete U.S. Navy destroyers in exchange for the use by the Americans of a number of naval bases in British overseas territories in the Western Hemisphere. Six weeks later, on October 16, the president ordered a first draft of personnel for the U.S. forces, which involved the registration of 16.4 million men. Washington was certainly looking both west toward the Pacific (and the Philippines in particular) and at the continued Japanese aggression in China, and this move was a clear indication of U.S. intent and military preparedness following the creation on September 27 of the Berlin-Rome-Tokyo Axis (Hungary, Slovakia, and Romania all joined the Tripartite Pact between November 20 and 25, and Bulgaria joined on March 1 the following year). Ever conscious of Britain's still precarious situation in late 1940, on December 17 Roosevelt made the historic "lend-lease" proposal to provide all manner of military equipment, weapons, and vital strategic resources, just as the German bombing of British cities achieved its greatest intensity. Britain's acceptance of Roosevelt's proposal underwrote both the nation's current ability to fight on and its future ability to carry the war to the Germans. On January 10, 1941, the lend-lease bill was introduced into the U.S. Congress and on March 11 it was passed and signed off by the president. During these difficult months America and Great Britain drew ever closer, and in those months also the special relationship between the two countries and their war leaders was forged and reinforced. Within the year, the United States would become the third member of a great strategic alliance, and its president would become a key member of the triumvirate later accorded the title of the "Big Three."

By the end of 1940, the accelerating turmoil that had consumed Poland, Czechoslovakia, Scandinavia, France, the Low Countries, and Britain had spread to North Africa. There, the in-place force of British and dominion troops under the command of Gen. Sir Archibald Wavell had been reinforced in early December, in order to deal with the sizable Italian army then threatening the Suez Canal and British interests in the eastern Mediterranean from Italian Libya. Although the campaign carried significant risks, Wavell's British and Australian divisions smashed into the Italian armies at dawn on December 9. Victories at Sidi Barrani on January 9–10, at Tobruk on January 21–22, and at Benghazi on February 6 soon followed, with the capture of Marshal Rodolfo Graziano's army in Cyrenaica at Beda Fomm after it had been cut off by British armored units. However, following the arrival in Tripoli on February 12 of Lt. Gen. Erwin Rommel to assume command of the Deutsches Afrika Korps (DAK) and restore the Axis situation in North Africa, the British soon experienced the start of a series of setbacks that would not end finally until November 1942. The lead elements of the DAK arrived in Tripoli on February 14, and on February 24 the DAK clashed with the British forces for the first time when an advance unit encountered two troops of British armored cars and a platoon of Australian antitank guns; the German unit opened fire, destroying two armored reconnaissance cars, one truck, and one armored car, while disabling and capturing a further armored car. This minor clash marked the start of the DAK's desert offensive and the legend of Rommel.[2]

On March 24, El Agheila was captured by the Germans, and the British fell back to Mersa Brega. There, Rommel attacked on March 31, and, despite their strong defensive positions, once again the British withdrew. Wavell was professionally competent, but he had command responsibilities that encompassed all of North Africa and Egypt, and his subordinate field commanders—in succession, Generals Wilson, Neame, and O'Connor—were totally outclassed by Rommel. These senior commanders certainly did not provide the standard of leadership at the operational level that their British, Australian, Indian, and other dominion troops deserved. The DAK's pursuit of the retreating British proceeded apace: German armored units reached Agedabia on April 2, Benghazi on the fourth, Barce on the fifth, Mechili on the sixth, and Derna on the seventh. By April 7, the DAK was poised to strike into Egypt, and so threaten the whole of the British control of the Middle East. Only the 9th Australian Division and an *ad hoc* force of artillery and armor at Tobruk still guarded the British western flank in Cyrenaica, and on April 11 the DAK's 5th Light Division and two Italian divisions ("Brescia" and "Ariete") began the siege of Tobruk. However, as other units of the DAK reached Bardia on April 12 and Halfaya Pass on the fifteenth, the punishing effects of their lightning, four-hundred-mile advance began to tell on the men and machines of the DAK. Thereafter the desert war seesawed back and forth, although, on balance, the DAK and its Italian allies enjoyed more success than their opponents, despite giving ground where necessary. In mid-June 1941, General Wavell launched his last counteroffensive, Operation "Battleaxe," to the southwest of Halfaya Pass on the Egyptian border. Once again, Rommel emerged victorious, and this success on June 17—after which Wavell was removed from his command—confirmed in the minds of many British commanders and soldiers the myth that Rommel was unbeatable. Not until the arrival in the desert in August 1942 of Lt. Gen. Bernard Law Montgomery as the new commander of the British Eighth Army would that myth, and that of the invincibility of the Afrika Korps, be firmly laid to rest. In the meantime, the continued lack of a decisive British success in the desert sands of North Africa in 1941 gave rise to considerable concern in London, while every reverse suffered further reduced Churchill's confidence in the professional ability and offensive spirit of the senior commanders of the British and dominion forces in Egypt and Cyrenaica.

Elsewhere, the turmoil continued. On April 6, Germany invaded Greece and Yugoslavia. This forced a British withdrawal in Greece, followed by the evacuation of the Greek mainland between April 23 and May 1. On April 27, German forces occupied Athens. Then, on May 20, the Germans launched a massed airborne assault on to Crete. Although the losses amongst the paratroopers during the initial airborne assault were very heavy, Crete fell to the Germans on June 1. Only on the high seas were the British still enjoying some successes, with the Royal Navy's defeat of the Italian fleet at Cape Matapan on March 28 and the sinking of the battleship *Bismarck* in the North Atlantic on May 27. Meanwhile, in France, Marshal Pétain had, on May 16, formally approved the Vichy administration's policy of cooperation with Germany. This came just two days after thirty-six hundred French Jews had been arrested in Paris.

In mid-1941, the position of Great Britain and its dominions was indeed an isolated and lonely one—with hope rather than substance occupying the minds of many, as the conflict which had already engulfed mainland Europe, the Balkans, and North Africa seemed poised to sweep the British Isles into the ambit of the Third Reich. However, on the other side of the Atlantic, President Roosevelt had already judged that the eventual involvement of the United States in the spreading conflict was all but inevitable, and on May 27 he proclaimed a national state of emergency. This was followed on June 5 by U.S. secretary of state Cordell Hull's denunciation of Pétain's policy of collaboration with Nazi Germany. On June 14, Roosevelt ordered that all Axis funds held in the United States were to be frozen. Although it had not yet identified sufficient justification to go to war, these U.S. actions provided a clear signal of future intent to Churchill in beleaguered Britain, and they should also have provided an equivalent signal to Hitler in Berlin. But, in June 1941, Adolf Hitler was concerned with more weighty matters.

On the evening of June 21, more than four million Axis soldiers, 3,360 tanks, and seven thousand artillery pieces, with the support of two thousand combat aircraft, were preparing to launch Operation "Barbarossa" from eastern Poland. This campaign would, at a stroke, bring together Churchill and Stalin to defeat their common enemy, and would involve the United States directly in providing the material support for both, thereby making the future full-scale commitment of its military and industrial might to what would soon become the Allied cause a relatively easy matter. By his ill-judged invasion of the Soviet Union on June 22, 1941, Adolf Hitler facilitated the unlikely alliance of Stalin's communist Soviet Union with the two capitalist powers of Churchill's Great Britain and Roosevelt's United States. By doing so he ensured that Nazi Germany would eventually lose World War II and that his so-called Thousand-Year Reich would exist for only four more years. However, that was for the future, and in mid-1941 Hitler, Mussolini, and the Axis powers could derive considerable satisfaction from the vast amount of territory they now controlled, from all that they had achieved militarily thus far, and from the progress the Nazis had already made in solving what they had come to term the "Jewish Problem"—albeit that, in their wake, they had left a trail of death, destruction, and despair on a scale so great that it was virtually unquantifiable. In less than two years they had, indeed, created a world in turmoil, but now they were about to reap the consequences of all that they had sown: these consequences planned, developed, and implemented by their enemies through the process of the war summits, led by three of the greatest war leaders of the twentieth century— Winston Leonard Spencer Churchill, Joseph Vissarionovich Stalin and Franklin Delano Roosevelt, the "Big Three."

2
Genesis of the Warlords
Churchill, Stalin, and Roosevelt, 1874–1941

THE FOCUS THROUGHOUT THIS WORK is upon the war summits, the great meetings that shaped the course of the Allied response to the war that the Axis had inflicted upon the world. However, any account of the war summits cannot be separated from a consideration of the role played by the three men who led Britain, Soviet Russia, and the United States through, and out of, some of the darkest years of their existence. Even where their subordinates or representatives attended the lesser war summits, ministerial conferences, and chiefs of staff meetings in their place, the will and guiding influence of Churchill, Stalin, and Roosevelt was always in evidence. Consequently, although any attempt to replicate the contents of any of the many biographies already written on these men lies far beyond the scope of this account of a *process* (rather than an account of those who took part in that process), the central role of the "Big Three" in the war summits nevertheless demands a brief description of the very different lives and quite dissimilar pathways to political power experienced by these three remarkable men in the years before their countries' national interests converged in mid-1941. An understanding of the formative events of their genesis and some aspects of their resultant personalities may allow the later views and decisions of the war leaders within the summits to be better appreciated.

Winston Leonard Spencer Churchill was born at Blenheim Palace in Oxfordshire on November 30, 1874. Ever since the eighteenth century and the first Duke of Marlborough, Blenheim Palace had been the ancestral home of the Marlborough family, and so Winston was part of a family that was powerful and enjoyed a lifestyle that was both privileged and comfortable. Despite these advantages, and his later literary successes, the young Churchill's early academic prowess was unspectacular. He entered the Royal Military College, Sandhurst, from Harrow barely achieving the required pass in the entrance examination. However, he subsequently did well at Sandhurst and passed out eighth of one hundred and fifty in his intake. Already a competent horseman, he was commissioned as a second lieutenant in the 4th Hussars in February 1895. Everyday life for an officer in a British hussar regiment called for a considerable private income and, despite his illustrious antecedents, the death of his father, Lord Randolph Churchill, just a few weeks after Winston was commissioned presented the young subaltern with the joint financial challenges of meeting his military obligations and supporting his widowed mother. In October 1896, Churchill and his regiment disembarked at Bombay at the start of an eight-and-a-half-year tour of duty in India, although Churchill himself remained with the regiment for less than two years of this period. Based in Bangalore and with limited opportunities for action or other diversions, he acquired a love of literature, in particular the great works of history and empire. In short order he read the works of Macaulay and Gibbon and thus established a wider understanding of the fundamentals of imperial power—and of the weaknesses that were also inherent in these. His reading gave Churchill a breadth of understanding of military history and its interrelationship with statesmanship and politics that far exceeded that of most of his young contemporaries; it also opened for him a literary career that ran in parallel with all that he did during the rest of his life, and provided him with what soon became a lucrative means of supplementing his army pay. His first book, *The Story of the Malakand Field Force*, was eighty-five thousand words in length and earned Churchill some £600 (more than $50,000 by today's values) when it was published in 1898. This work signaled the start of a literary output—nonfiction except for the novel *Savrola*—that developed rapidly and was by any standards prodigious. *The River War*, two hundred and fifty thousand words in length, was published in two volumes in November the following year. Books, newspaper articles, and letters all flowed from his pen. It is impossible to write history effectively without becoming aware of its lessons or to enjoy reading it without empathizing with those who lived in former times, and Churchill's enjoyment of, and proficiency with, the written word shaped his later ideas and perceptions, particularly regarding the nature and role of the British Empire, and contributed to his adventurous (and often romantic) view of the business of imperial soldiering and warfare. This attitude to life led to the young Churchill participating in the battle of Omdurman in the Sudan on September 2, 1898—where, while attached to the 21st Lancers, he took part in the British army's last full-scale cavalry charge—and then, a year later, found him in South Africa as a war correspondent for the *Morning Post* during the Boer War, where he was captured by the Boers but then escaped after four weeks of imprisonment in Pretoria.

Although Churchill had reveled in the military life, and more specifically in the excitement and personal challenges of active service, he resigned his commission in 1899, having by then lived more dangerously and experienced more adventures than many of his military peers and most of his civilian contemporaries. Indeed, his short period of service in the army of Queen Victoria had provided him with personal resilience and an abundance of experience of warfare and military life that he would draw upon time and again in the days of conflict that were then still well in the future. This knowledge, his understanding of leadership, and the personal self-confidence that this experience conferred on him at a formative stage of his life were significant. This significance is self-evident, and it is questionable whether, in more modern times when such opportunities are no more, a politician or aspiring statesman who lacks any firsthand military experience can ever understand the real nature of war and those who are called upon by their country to prosecute it. With his military credentials well recognized and his status as a published author and journalist established internationally, Winston Churchill at last began his political career on October 1, 1900,[1] when he was elected as the Conservative Party's member of parliament for Oldham, Lancashire. He was then in his twenty-sixth year. In 1904, he crossed the floor of the House of Commons and joined the Liberal Party, and in 1908 he married Clementine Hozier, a confirmed Liberal.

At Tbilisi[2] in Georgia on December 21, 1879, Ekaterina, a washerwoman, and Vissarion Djugashvili, a shoemaker, were delivered of a son—Joseph Vissarionovich. He was born into relative poverty at a time when the life expectancy in Russia of the children of all but the rich was minimal. Disease, malnutrition, injury, and a savage climate all took their toll, and Joseph was the only one of his siblings to survive beyond childhood, having himself experienced smallpox, as well as being afflicted with a disability of the left hand and lower arm which in due course made him unfit for military service. Despite the lack of success of his father's business enterprises and the family's social position, Joseph received an adequate early education at the church school of Gorni, which enabled him to prepare for, and gain, a scholarship to the ecclesiastical seminary at Tbilisi. Despite, or perhaps because of, its religious provenance, the seminary provided a focus for Georgian nationalism in a part of the Russian empire which maintained strongly its individual character and whose citizens were aware of the economic (oil) wealth of Georgia, as well as of its strategic situation as a bulwark against the Islamic nations to the south.

The differences between Churchill's origins and those of the young Georgian could not have been starker. Nevertheless, Joseph Djugashvili shared with Churchill a love of literature, and in 1895, the same year that Churchill was commissioned from Sandhurst, Joseph's first poem was published in the liberal journal *Iberya*. However, Joseph's literary tastes were directed more toward great novelists such as Victor Hugo and Thackeray than toward the more weighty histories read so avidly by Churchill in the late 1880s. His interest in such foreign works attracted the displeasure of others, and paved the way for his increasing politicization as the years passed. He was expelled from the seminary in 1899 for failing to attend for his examinations, and took a clerk's appointment. His political involvement and socialist inclinations attracted a police raid on his accommodation in 1901. In 1902, his arrest was followed by imprisonment and deportation to Siberia for three years, although within two years he had escaped and returned to Tbilisi. At that time he became a committed bolshevik and an advocate of the socialist principles expounded by Lenin, whom he met for the first time in December 1905 at a bolshevik conference in Finland. In 1905 also, he married his first wife, Ekaterina Svanidze, who died two years later. Thereafter, in company with other leading bolsheviks, he adopted a name that better suited his political aspirations—Stalin (literally, "man of steel"). With Joseph's election in 1907 as a member of the Party's executive committee in the Azerbaijani city of Baku, in the oil-producing region, the course of his political career was set. However, its progress would not be straightforward by any means.

In several ways the early life of Franklin Delano Roosevelt was similar to that of the young Churchill, already in his eighth year when Franklin was born at the Roosevelt family home, the estate at Hyde Park on the banks of the Hudson river, on January 30, 1882. Certainly the Roosevelts were wealthy, privileged, and one of America's well-established and leading families. An only child, Franklin was at first educated at home and then at Groton school in Massachusetts, a small and exclusive private establishment which maintained and taught the principles and standards of an earlier age. Academically, he did moderately well at Groton, although his achievements were by no means exceptional. Understandably perhaps, since he was an only child, the influence of Franklin's parents was strong, and he subsequently abandoned his own wish to train as a naval officer and instead went to Harvard. Notwithstanding his future political successes, the fact that he did not follow his inclination to serve in the navy on leaving Groton was always a matter of some regret to Roosevelt; in later years, there were several clear indications that he would have made a particularly good U.S. Navy officer. However, at Harvard he did not excel and failed to take his masters degree, resulting in the only (albeit tenuous) parallel with the literary lives of Churchill and Stalin—his involvement as the editor of Harvard's daily university newspaper. A further unremarkable period of study followed his time at Harvard when the young Roosevelt attended the three-year Columbia Law School course in New York. In 1910, he entered politics and was that year elected as the Democratic party's state senator for Dutchess County, New York. Five years earlier he had married Eleanor, the niece of the former Republican president Theodore Roosevelt.

Thus, by 1910, the future war leaders had embarked upon the very different sorts of political careers that would eventually, and at virtually the same time, sweep each of them to the pinnacles of power in their respective countries, and on a global scale.

The political fortunes of Churchill, Stalin, and Roosevelt through the early decades of the new century were very different. Churchill held various offices in the Liberal and (following his return to the Tory party in 1924) Conservative governments. He was first lord of the admiralty at the time of the Gallipoli landings in 1915—a disastrous operation that he had strongly advocated, and following the failure of which he felt constrained to resign. The true effect of the Dardanelles operation upon Churchill would be seen again almost thirty years later, during the war summits of World War II.[3] Churchill's departure from office in 1915 in turn opened the way for him to make a temporary return to soldiering, when he commanded an infantry battalion in France for six months in 1915–16. There was a certain irony in this, as it had specifically been to break the stalemate in the trenches of the western front that Churchill had originally proposed, and so strongly supported, the Dardanelles operation. However, Churchill's return to military duty was indeed shortlived, for both he and others had recognized that his particular talents and ambitions now lay elsewhere. He returned to political life but, as a frequent, eloquent, and strident critic of several of his party's policies—and having twice changed his political allegiance within two decades—he remained isolated from the centre of political power until the failure of Neville Chamberlain's policy of appeasement and Germany's invasion of the Low Countries on May 10, 1940. Then, his isolation from the government and the whole business of appeasement served him well in practice, for he was one of very few British politicians of experience and stature who had not been tainted by association with Munich and Chamberlain's naive miscalculation of Hitler's aspirations and intentions for Europe and the Third Reich.

On May 10, 1940, in his sixty-sixth year, Churchill was a man who was widely read and intellectually astute, with a sound knowledge of the history of the world. He was a man committed to promote, apply, and sustain the British principles and qualities that had facilitated the development and preeminence of one of the greatest empires in the history of the civilized world. He was already a seasoned politician with more than three decades of political experience and statesmanship, having held all but the highest national offices; and, just as importantly, he was a man who had experienced the horror and reality of war at first hand, and had commanded and directed men in battle. As the panzer divisions raced through the Netherlands and Belgium, and across the French fields en route toward the English Channel, Winston Churchill became the prime minister who was destined to lead the British nation and its dominions through what would soon thereafter develop into World War. II; in the course of which he would also fulfill a wider and equally crucial role as the British member of the "Big Three," thereby contributing directly not only to the progress of the war but also to the international shape of the world that would follow it.

How unlike a Western political career was that experienced by Stalin! Yet his rites of passage as a bolshevik socialist in Russia in their own way prepared him for the destiny that he found from 1941, and arguably somewhat earlier. From 1905, Stalin experienced an almost uninter-rupted cycle of persecution, imprisonment, exile, and escape. Throughout, he moved ever higher up the party ladder, while also managing to travel extensively within eastern Europe. In February 1913, after many lesser banishments, Stalin was sentenced to deportation to Siberia. There he languished—albeit in conditions that were far less severe than those of the post-revolution gulags—until February 1917, when the fall of the czar allowed him to escape. A month later he was in Petrograd, where he took temporary control of the party's affairs until Lenin arrived to assume command in April. In 1918, Stalin married his second wife, Nadezhda Allilueva, the daughter of a bolshevik who had kept him well supplied with books and other comforts during his four-year exile in Siberia.

From 1918 to 1920, Stalin was political commissar of the southwest group of armies during the bitter civil war between the bolsheviks of the Red Army and the White Russian forces. Although not truly a military commander, he was certainly involved in the conflict at firsthand, as well as in advising on some of the strategic decisions that were taken. One of these led to the Treaty of Riga in 1921, whereby the western provinces of the Ukraine and Belorussia were ceded to Poland—a decision that would in due course resonate with the "Big Three" time and again as the always difficult issue of the Soviet-Polish border was raised by Stalin.[4] While his preoccupation with this particular issue was also motivated by strategic considerations, his personal involvement in the loss of Russian territory to Poland in 1921, however well justified it may have been at the time, certainly remained at the forefront of Stalin's consciousness up to and during the 1940s.

With the death of Lenin in January 1924, a contest for leadership of the party—and therefore of the Soviet Union—developed between Stalin and Trotsky.[5] However, whereas Stalin's vision was to build the new bolshevik state as a model that would, in due course, inevitably be followed by the rest of the world, Trotsky was the archetypal revolutionary, and his time was already past. In 1925, Trotsky resigned as commissar for war, in 1926 he was expelled from the politburo, in 1927 he was expelled from the party, and in 1929 he was deported from the Soviet Union. Although by then hardly a threat to Stalin, Trotsky was subsequently assassinated by the NKVD in Mexico in August 1940. In the meantime, Stalin, as the unchallenged leader of the party and the Soviet Union, set out in 1930 to put his great plans for the new Soviet state into effect, starting with what quickly proved to be the disastrous policy of the collectivization of Soviet agriculture and the wholesale industrialization of the nation. In the face of widespread resistance by the rural peasant population to these policies, Stalin ordered that they should be imposed by the state—the party, the police, and the Red Army. Between 1929 and 1932, terror, repression, and famine engulfed the Russian countryside. At the same time, enforced industrialization and urban expansion proceeded at a breathtaking pace, with predictable consequences to the quality (as opposed to the quantity) of industrial output and to the quality of the life of the workers in the newly built plants and factories. Just as these tumultuous changes were taking place under his leadership, Stalin experienced a great personal tragedy when his wife shot herself in November 1932. The failure in large part of a core socialist policy and bolshevik ideological belief occurring at the same time as the death of the mother of his beloved daughter Svetlana, who had been a moderating influence in his life, were blows that hardened and embittered Stalin. However, while on the one hand this boded ill for the domestic future of the Soviet Union, given the coming ideological and bitter battlefield struggle between Nazism and bolshevism, the desensitizing effect of these great tragedies shaped the man who was destined to oversee the response to what was from mid-1941 always the greatest part of the armed threat exerted by Germany. If ruthlessness and unswerving determination were the result, these were undoubtedly qualities that were entirely appropriate for the savage war in which the Soviet Union would shortly find itself engaged.

By 1934, the Soviet Union that Stalin had created was undeniably a totalitarian, monolithic, and ideologically dogmatic state, ruled by a communist party whose policies and power were maintained by the party, its commissars, and officials, and enforced by the OGPU (the forerunners of the NKVD) and the Red Army. At the top of the pyramid of power were Stalin and his immediate supporters, all of whom knew that their own positions were always precarious, as Stalin's ruthless purges in 1937 of many of his longstanding bolshevik colleagues and of many thousands of other Soviet citizens demonstrated. Of Lenin's original politburo, only Stalin and Trotsky (who was by then living in exile overseas) survived the 1937 purges, as the leaders of the Red Army, the upper and middle tiers of the communist party, and the members of the Red Partisans were all culled. By the end of the decade, Stalin's secret police had created the "chief administration of corrective labor camps and labor settlements," a chain of work camps—prison camps, in reality—that stretched across northern European Russia and well into Siberia. Thus was born the infamous gulag (a very different facility from its predecessor of Czarist times), which would for almost half a century be used as a repository for thousand upon thousand of men and women whose views or actions conflicted with those of Stalin, the ruling communist elite, and those who served them. Simultaneously, the gulag provided an inexhaustible and indispensable source of forced labor to take forward Stalin's dream of modernizing and industrializing the Soviet Union in line with communist ideology.

As the decade drew to its close, Stalin observed the twin failures of appeasement of Germany and of any form of collective security as the

West distanced itself from the Soviet Union. This in turn shaped and reinforced Stalin's view that national interest was all, and that any foreign policy action could be justified by the needs of the Soviet Union. This philosophy would in due course underwrite Stalin's thinking throughout the war summits process. But more immediately, during the night of August 23–24, 1939, it allowed Vyacheslav Molotov, the Soviet people's commissar for foreign affairs, and Joachim von Ribbentrop, the German foreign minister, to conclude the Soviet-German Frontier and Friendship Treaty—in effect, a nonaggression pact. This historic arrangement foreshadowed the partition of eastern Europe, the invasion and dismemberment of Poland, and Hitler's invasion of the low countries and France, secure in the knowledge that no threat to Germany would emanate from the east. Consequently, this pact in many ways actually expedited World War II, and thus Stalin's action was unforgivable in international terms. However, from the perspective of the Soviet leader, it made perfect sense. It not only enabled him to regain some of the territory lost in an earlier age—specifically that in Poland, a matter close to Stalin's heart given his indirect involvement in the loss of Russian territory to Poland in 1921—it also provided a breathing space for a Soviet Union much weakened by the organizational turmoil and purges of the 1930s, before the mighty armed clash between bolshevism and the fascist Nazis, an ideological and military clash that Stalin well knew was absolutely inevitable.

On the other side of the globe, within the very different world of U.S. politics, Roosevelt's career had progressed steadily. Certainly, he had capitalized upon his privileged start in life, but he had nonetheless progressed on merit and by using his undoubted interpersonal skills to good effect. In 1913 he was made assistant secretary of the Navy, an appointment that was somewhat ironic given his earlier leanings toward the sea, but also one to which he consequently brought an empathy with the naval service and a natural awareness of the capabilities and nature of sea power. Roosevelt's subsequent career was characterized by reliability and quiet competence rather than brilliance, and in 1920 he was nominated as the Democratic party's candidate for the post of vice-president. Significantly, the Democrats lost the election, having placed great emphasis on the need for U.S. involvement with the League of Nations. Roosevelt's unshakable and idealistic belief in the need for an international security organization such as this remained at the very heart of his personal political philosophy and would reemerge most strongly during the war summits of the coming conflict—occasionally affecting, and to the detriment of, more immediate matters.[6] Despite the 1920 election failure, Roosevelt's political star was still rising when, in August 1921, he was suddenly struck by polio (in those days an all-too-common disease), which crippled him and meant that he would thereafter have to rely upon the use of a wheelchair. What would, for most men of thirty-nine with a burgeoning career ahead of them, have been a total disaster, conferred upon Roosevelt a new determination and inner strength to confront and overcome his disability. In 1928 he was elected governor of the state of New York, in 1932 he was nominated as the Democrats' presidential candidate, and in March 1933 Theodore Delano Roosevelt became president of the United States of America. His election campaign, conducted during some of the darkest days of the Depression, had emphasized the "New Deal" policies of the Democrats, and these sat well with a man whose higher ideals, integrity, and concerns for the ordinary citizens of America were always evident. Despite his personal background, this approach to U.S. domestic policies complemented his views on international security matters, and would later assist Roosevelt to comprehend, if not necessarily agree with, Stalin's declared socialist vision of equality of wealth and opportunity for the people of Russia—a vision that was in any case of somewhat doubtful sincerity, given Stalin's repressive actions within the Soviet Union ever since he had achieved absolute power in that country.

As the 1930s moved on, and the growing economic and political turmoil in Germany threatened first the stability of that nation and then that of Europe, Stalin and Roosevelt were firmly in place as the leaders of the Soviet Union and the United States, respectively; only in Great Britain would the third member of the "Big Three" have to wait until the very beginning of the next decade to assume at last his crucial role in the business of forging a great alliance, and then winning both a war and the fragile peace that would follow it.

Part Two
SHAPING THE WAR

3
The Road to "Arcadia"
Placentia Bay and the Atlantic Charter

THE FIRST OF THE GREAT ALLIANCES of World War II was not that forged by the Allies, the United States, Great Britain and the Soviet Union; rather it was the Tripartite Pact made by Germany, Italy, and Japan on September 27, 1940. By that pact the Berlin-Rome-Tokyo Axis was formed, and, arguably, all that followed was therefore in response to the improbable alliance of national socialist Germany and fascist Italy with imperial Japan. The apparently invincible military strength of the German war machine and the global reach of the wider Axis by late 1940 were undoubtedly factors in Hitler's decision to attack Russia in June the following year, while also influencing the decision by the Japanese to launch their bid to dominate Southeast Asia and the Pacific region in December 1941. During the six months from June to December 1941, these two events—Operation Barbarossa on June 22 and the attack on Pearl Harbor on December 7—drove almost every twist and turn in the great alliance that would develop in response. Moreover, at all stages, this evolution reflected the personalities and determination of the men who headed the three-nation Alliance, Roosevelt, Churchill, and Stalin, whose iron wills and clarity of purpose were modified only occasionally by the often larger-than-life military and diplomatic figures who supported and advised them and, ultimately, did their bidding.

Soon after 3:15 in the morning of June 22, four million Axis soldiers (of which more than three million were German) and three thousand three hundred and fifty tanks burst across the Third Reich's frontier with the Soviet Union. They advanced on more than a dozen major axes, from the shores of the Black Sea in the south to Finland in the north. This huge force was supported by the fire of some seven thousand artillery pieces and more than two thousand combat airplanes.

Perversely, Hitler's invasion of Russia—thereafter always the main focus (in terms of scale) of the German war effort—was the catalyst that ensured that Britain and the British Empire would no longer stand alone against the Axis powers, and thus it also ultimately became the instrument of the Third Reich's defeat. But the inevitable alignment of the Soviet Union with Britain—and therefore with the United States as well—against Germany was itself perverse, for it involved the alliance of a totalitarian and communist Russia, headed by a ruthless bolshevik dictator, with a democratic British nation for whose own war leader bolshevism was anathema. Nevertheless, in late June, as a German attack on Russia became ever more likely (even though Stalin, and therefore the rest of the Soviet leadership, had continued to adopt a state akin to denial), Britain and the United States had determined that they would support Moscow if the invasion took place.

Churchill held the pragmatic view that the overriding priority was to defeat Nazi Germany, and that need necessarily outweighed his reservations concerning the nature and ideology of the Soviet regime. Consequently, the joint U.S.-British strategy was developed on June 20 at a meeting at Chequers, the British prime minister's country house, at which the principal participants were Churchill, Sir Anthony Eden (the British foreign secretary), Sir Stafford Cripps (the British ambassador to the Soviet Union), and John Gilbert Winant (the U.S. ambassador to Great Britain). The outcome of this timely meeting enabled Churchill to respond immediately to the German invasion of Russia with a radio broadcast during the evening of June 22, when he stated unequivocally that the single focus of the British nation's effort was the defeat of the Nazi regime, and that therefore it would henceforth provide whatever assistance it could to Russia for its fight against what was now the common enemy. Churchill already knew from Winant that President Roosevelt supported this line, and would by implication authorize the provision of substantial material support for the war against Germany. This aid would well exceed a simple relaxation of the restrictions on U.S. trade exports to Russia, despite the U.S. state department's unease over the recent, somewhat dubious status of Russia consequent upon the provisions of the Molotov-Ribbentrop nonaggression pact.

Churchill's broadcast made public the embryo existence of the great Alliance that was destined on the one hand to win World War II and on the other to create a somewhat imperfect postwar world. In the succeeding days, Roosevelt, who concurred with Churchill on the need to do everything to achieve the early defeat of Nazi Germany, moved to enable and accelerate the process of providing war material to Russia. An important figure in those weeks following June 22 was Harry Hopkins, Roosevelt's roving diplomat, representative, and fact-finder in London, and then in Moscow.

In furtherance of Roosevelt's desire to advance the program of U.S. support for Russia, Hopkins visited Stalin in Moscow on July 30 and 31. Although American forces were not at that stage directly engaged in the war, Stalin took the opportunity not only to welcome the anticipated U.S. support, but also to indicate his belief in the eventual and inevitable need for German forces to be directly engaged by American troops. By extension, the Soviet leader was already firmly of the opinion that only by forcing Germany to fight on two fronts in Europe could the pressure on the Russian forces on the eastern front be alleviated and a German defeat guaranteed. This view underlined Stalin's almost obsessive preoccupation with the need for a second front to be launched in western Europe, a subject that dominated most of his later meetings with the U.S. and British leaders or their representatives. Nevertheless, during that July meeting, Stalin undoubtedly impressed Hopkins, who reported back to the U.S. president what was subsequently shown to be an excessively favorable view of the Soviet leader's affability and of his apparent willingness to cooperate with his new allies. But, most significantly for the future development of the war summits, Hopkins had also broached the need for the heads of the three allied governments to meet in order to determine the strategic way ahead, and to expose and discuss the multiplicity of often complex national interests involved—in other words, to establish their joint strategic priorities for the rest of the war against Germany, and for whatever followed the German defeat. Stalin already had very clear views on his priorities and territorial aspirations for the postwar Soviet Union, and, while of course not exposing these to Hopkins at that stage, he therefore welcomed the proposal to hold such a conference. Thus was born the concept of what later became the war summits of the "Big Three," although the first of these meetings to be attended by all three leaders, that at Tehran in November 1943, was still more than two years away. In the meantime, Churchill and Roosevelt were moving the summit process ahead bilaterally, and between August 9 and 12, 1941, the two leaders met at Placentia Bay,[1] on the Atlantic coast of Newfoundland. Churchill had traveled to the meeting on the battleship HMS *Prince of Wales*, which he had boarded at Scapa Flow.

The prime minister's sea passage was not uneventful, and the *Prince of Wales* had on several occasions to alter course following reports of two U-boats in the waters ahead of the warship, which also had a dedicated destroyer escort throughout the crossing. The *Prince of Wales* arrived off Placentia Bay shortly before 6:00 in the morning on August 9, and about an hour and a half later it made its rendezvous with the USS *Augusta*, on board which was President Roosevelt. As the *Prince of Wales* passed the various U.S. warships lying at anchor in the bay, its Royal Marines band played "The Star Spangled Banner," and the USS *Augusta* responded with a rendition of "God Save the King." Churchill and his senior advisors went aboard the *Augusta*. Roosevelt, supported by his son, Col. Elliott Roosevelt, greeted Churchill at the rail as both national anthems were played once again. Churchill presented the president with a personal letter from King George VI. During the days that followed, the two leaders met, dined, and were entertained variously on both of the warships. Typical of the harmonious and generally relaxed nature of this historic Anglo-U.S. summit meeting was the presentation to every man of the crew of the *Prince of Wales* of a small box containing two apples, an orange, half a pound of cheese, and two hundred cigarettes, together with a note stating, "The Commander-in-Chief, United States Navy, sends his compliments and best wishes—Franklin D. Roosevelt, President of the United States, August 9th, 1941." Such were the shortages in Britain at that time that these items were luxuries indeed, and the American gesture was very much appreciated.[2]

The meeting between Churchill and Roosevelt at Placentia Bay focused primarily on the future program of material support for the Soviet Union, but already Stalin had communicated to Churchill his hope that British forces would imminently stage a landing in western Europe to open a second front.[3] The British leader had indicated that this was simply not feasible, and Stalin's perception that Russia was bearing the full brunt of the German onslaught, with Britain doing nothing to alleviate this, hardened considerably as the panzer divisions thrust ever deeper into Russian territory. Meanwhile, Roosevelt and Churchill reinforced their support for the Soviets by deciding to send W. Averell Harriman to Moscow for the Americans and Lord Beaverbrook for the British, with the task of moving the aid program forward apace.

However, the long-term international importance of the Placentia Bay meeting well exceeded its consideration of the aid for Russia program. Over dinner in the evening of August 9, Roosevelt suggested to Churchill that it would perhaps be useful to set out their longer-term aims and aspirations for the great venture upon which they had embarked; there can be no doubt that Roosevelt knew, even then, that it was only a matter of time until the United States became directly involved in the war. Churchill registered the president's proposal, and that night he drafted a proposed text for what eventually became the Atlantic Charter. The publication of this document was, in terms of policy, a defining moment of World War II. It also laid down many of the standards of international behavior and modalities that the postwar world sought to achieve. As such, although the charter was produced initially as the U.S.-British strategic policy guidance and rationale for the future prosecution of the war, it eventually provided the wider international community with the foundation on which was built the postwar world.

In summary, Churchill's proposed text of August 9 stated that the allied nations sought to gain neither territory nor other advantages from the war. He proposed that, with the future liberation of occupied territories in mind, there should be no territorial changes without the freely expressed acquiescence of the peoples concerned; and, linked to that, the right of all peoples freely to choose their nation's form of government should be respected. In an early indication of what would much later prove to be one of the more naive aspects of post-1945 U.S. foreign policy, Roosevelt inserted wording to the effect that "self-government" had to be restored to those nations in which it had been usurped. With an eye always to the future circumstances of the postwar British Empire, Churchill agreed to this text, but added that "sovereign rights" should enjoy an equal priority with "self-government." Stalin was of course not involved with this drafting activity, although had he been so he would no doubt have had some trouble agreeing with any of these three funda-mental principles without major modification, as none of them accorded with his perception of the postwar world or with the practical aspira-tions and objectives of the Soviet communist movement.

Further to these high-level ground rules, the subject of a framework and system for postwar international security was considered. Churchill favored an international organization that would achieve this, but Roosevelt identified in this the resurrection of the ghost of the failed former League of Nations—something that would be entirely unaccept-able to the American administration and people. In order to achieve a workable compromise, Churchill proposed a revised text that indicated an intention in the short term to disarm any nation that might threaten the future peace, but with a longer term aspiration to establish a wider (but not necessarily all-embracing international) and permanent system of general security. This text was finally agreed by Roosevelt, who understood very well that, notwithstanding the obvious difficulties of maintaining adherence to such ideals throughout an international alliance, the nature of American public and official opinion was such that it could only be induced to sanction the further involvement of the United States in the war if its actions were in support of clearly stated moral principles such as these. At that early stage of the war Roosevelt undoubtedly viewed the security of the postwar world as one that would be dominated almost entirely by the United States and Great Britain, albeit with the Soviet Union now emerging as a third major player, so that in late 1941 the chance that the postwar world would follow the course devised by these two leaders must have appeared good. In later times, Washington's view of Britain's role was modified somewhat, while this rather simplistic and (some might say) arrogant view of America's global destiny survived long after Roosevelt's death. This, in turn, all too often lost America friends and allies, provoked major armed conflicts in the postwar years, and not infrequently conflicted directly with the laudable principles expressed in the three main clauses of Churchill's and Roosevelt's initial draft.

Nevertheless, the significance of the document that emerged from the Anglo-U.S. meeting of minds at Placentia Bay was historic, and provided a policy touchstone or point of reference for virtually everything that was decided and planned thereafter. The Atlantic Charter was duly signed by all parties on August 12, 1941.

Two follow-on activities took place in the immediate aftermath of Placentia Bay. First, Beaverbrook and Harriman carried out their planned visit to Moscow from September 28 to October 10. They participated in a series of meetings with Stalin and Molotov—the "people's commissar for foreign affairs"—in the course of which the broad level and nature of military aid for the Soviet Union was agreed. The aid package was substantial, and between October 1, 1941, and July 1, 1942, the following items were to be shipped to the Soviet Union:

Category	Quantity / Remarks
Tanks	500 per month.
Other armored vehicles	Monthly quota unspecified.
Cargo vehicles	Monthly quota unspecified.
Antiaircraft guns	Monthly quota unspecified.
Antitank guns	Monthly quota unspecified.
Combat and transport aircraft	400 (of which 100 to be bombers) per month.
Communications equipment	Monthly quota unspecified.
Medical supplies	Monthly quota unspecified.
Textiles	Wool and made-up cloth. Monthly quota unspecified.
Raw materials	Lead, tin, copper, steel, magnesium, nickel, rubber, leather. Monthly quota unspecified.
Footwear	Monthly quota unspecified.
Oil	Monthly quota unspecified.
Wheat	Monthly quota unspecified.

Of course, the U.S. commitment to this virtually open-ended package of material assistance as a part of its existing lend-lease aid program was made at a time when the nation was not yet at war with Germany, and before the Japanese attack on Pearl Harbor had taken place. Although Beaverbrook and Harriman had originally been careful not to commit their nations to deliver these items to Russia, but merely to guarantee their availability, in the course of the negotiations Stalin finally secured U.S. and British agreement to "give aid to the transportation" and "help with the delivery" of this material. Thus was born the subsequent operational nightmare for the Royal Navy of conducting the Arctic convoys to Murmansk and other ports on the littoral of northern Russia, together with a hostage to fortune that Stalin readily exploited against Britain in general, and Churchill in particular, during the coming months whenever the operational or climatic situation in the North Atlantic and Arctic region resulted in these convoys failing to achieve these agreed levels of aid.

The second follow-on action from Placentia Bay stemmed from Churchill's concern over Stalin's perception of the principles contained in the Atlantic Charter. Churchill was already aware of the Soviet leader's suspicions over British postwar ambitions, and his concerns over what he viewed as the disproportionate weight of the war with Germany then being borne by the Russians. Churchill, ever the experienced and astute statesman, was also aware of the potential danger to the developing Alliance of any misunderstanding or rift between the three major players. No doubt he was also sensitive to Stalin's cultivation of Roosevelt and the United States at the potential expense of British interests. In view of this, it was arranged that Sir Anthony Eden visit Moscow in mid-December with the task of clarifying and explaining to Stalin the scope, implications, and practical effects of the Atlantic Charter. The desired result was to be the amelioration of Stalin and his acceptance of the Atlantic Charter, but without any U.S. or British concessions being made. Despite his views on bolshevism, Churchill knew that, without gaining a large measure of Stalin's trust (or at least ensuring that he understood British aspirations and the limits of these, thereby minimizing his obsessive suspicion of Britain and its empire), the alliance against Germany would be fundamentally, and possibly fatally, flawed.

Eden's mission to Moscow was conducted between December 16 and 28, and therefore took place in the period shortly after the Japanese attack on Pearl Harbor of December 7, which brought about the formal entry of the United States into the war. Despite the historic events then unfolding in the Far East and the Pacific, the meetings in Moscow focused upon the Atlantic Charter as planned, underlining Stalin's preoccupation with the postwar map of Europe and, in particular, with what would in a future era become the Soviet sphere of interest in eastern Europe. The talks were complex, and centered upon Stalin's vision of a postwar western frontier of the Soviet Union that incorporated much of the territory of the Baltic States, Finland, Poland, East Prussia, and specific facilities in Romania—all of which, clearly, diverged from the principles of no territorial gain and of national self-determination laid out in the Atlantic Charter. Soviet intentions toward Poland were particularly sensitive, in light both of its previous imperfect relations and erratic dealings with its western neighbor and of the fact that the German invasion of Poland was the final act that had precipitated Britain's entry into the war. However, always the pragmatist, Stalin did suggest that the terms of the Atlantic Charter might be circumvented by British agreement to Soviet wishes being made in a secret protocol to the alliance treaty. While such secret agreements had featured extensively in European diplomacy over the centuries, this course was directly contrary to the new way for such matters envisaged by Roosevelt and Churchill. Accordingly, Eden adopted the time-honored tactic of politicians and diplomats when faced with an impasse over a vital issue: he proposed that further consultation and discussions should take place. He therefore promised to take Stalin's proposal back to the British government in order that it might receive further consideration both in London and Washington. Although Stalin accused Britain of seeking, through the terms of the Atlantic Charter, to weaken the postwar Soviet Union by failing to agree its proposed frontiers, he must have known that such agreement was unlikely at that stage. Consequently, Eden's visit enabled the principles produced at Placentia Bay to stand, but with many of the practical territorial issues they raised remaining unresolved until their consideration by a postwar conference (at which Stalin no doubt considered that he would be a key player).

Thus Stalin's suspicions of British motives were hardly allayed by Eden's visit, and at one stage he voiced the opinion that the Atlantic

Charter was more anti-Soviet than anti-Axis in its application. However, the simple fact that this high-level dialog was ongoing was itself a success of sorts, and while neither Eden nor Churchill were able to derive much satisfaction from the meetings, Eden had at least been able to present and define the unity of purpose that underwrote the future actions of what had, on December 7, truly become the "Big Three" alliance of war leaders. At the same time, Stalin had been required to expose the full extent of his postwar plans to his two major allies, a revelation that must have confirmed many of Churchill's concerns over the expansionist policies of the Soviet communists.

While Eden had been in Moscow, Roosevelt and Churchill had been meeting in Washington for a series of talks codenamed "Arcadia." While all of the high-level meetings and conferences would prove to be of varying historic significance, the "Arcadia" conference was undoubtedly the next defining moment in the process of developing the Allies' strategy for the conduct of the war, and, although it was conducted bilaterally between Roosevelt and Churchill, its decisions impacted very significantly upon the wider war. This was not least because, since Placentia Bay, Japan had fully committed its forces to combat against the Allies, and the United States had at last become a full participant in the business of defeating the Axis powers.

4

The "Arcadia" Conference and the Pacific Dimension

December 22, 1941 to January 14, 1942

THE JAPANESE AIR ATTACK against the principal base of the U.S. Pacific Fleet at Pearl Harbor, Hawaii, is almost without exception described as a "surprise attack." For the occupants of Schofield Barracks, at Hickam Field airbase, the navy yard, and the harbor complex, as well as for the crews of the battleships, cruisers, and many other warships moored there, the Japanese operation was undoubtedly a complete surprise, and the wholesale devastation wreaked upon the base was testament to that—although its long-term strategic impact was much reduced both by the fact that the U.S. fleet's aircraft carriers were not at Hawaii that day, and because of the large number of disabled vessels that were subsequently salvaged and rendered seaworthy once more. But, despite the operational surprise inflicted upon the sailors, marines and soldiers based at Hawaii, there had for many weeks been little doubt in Washington and London that war with Japan was both unavoidable and imminent; and Roosevelt, together with the chiefs of staff and his political advisors, had therefore been considering their strategic options and priorities for some time.

Some twelve months earlier, on November 12, 1940, when war with Japan was still judged much less likely, Admiral Stark, the chief of naval operations, had defined the first priority for U.S. maritime forces as the defense of the continental United States and its interests in the western hemisphere. Next was U.S. support for Great Britain and the defense of the Atlantic sealanes. Third and last was the defense of U.S. interests in the Pacific. These priorities were subsequently formalized and translated into the so-called ABC-1 plan during a series of joint Anglo-U.S. staff meetings in Washington from January 29 to March 29, 1941. However, as that year drew on, more and more intelligence indicators suggested that Japan was adopting an increasingly combative position in its dealings with the United States. Consequently, on November 5, following an urgent request from the Chinese for U.S. assistance against Japanese aggression in southern China, Roosevelt caused the ABC-1 plan to be reviewed by the U.S. chiefs of staff in light of the developing Japanese military threat to the Pacific region.[1]

However, despite the steadily increasing amount of intelligence which indicated that Japan was moving ever closer to war, the review of ABC-1 was concluded with no significant change of emphasis being proposed, and the chief of staff of the army and the chief of naval operations concurred in recommending to Roosevelt that the plan was valid and should therefore remain, despite the increased tension between America and Japan. Thus the updated military analysis continued to be entirely in agreement with the general policy that Churchill and Roosevelt had defined some six months earlier, for the U.S. chiefs of staff confirmed that any dilution of the U.S. military (but principally naval) effort in order to conduct an open-ended offensive war against Japan would risk the defeat of the Japanese being achieved only at the expense of the campaign against Germany in the Atlantic. At the same time, a realignment of U.S. priorities in favor of the Pacific theater would almost certainly compromise the chance of opening a second front in Europe, thereby risking a German consolidation and indefinite dominance of that continent. This, then, would in turn allow Berlin's military might (its ground forces in particular) to be directed almost exclusively against the Soviet Union. At the same time, any such U.S. maritime strategic realignment would undoubtedly reduce or negate the ability of Britain and America to provide the Soviets with the vital material support that had already been promised.

Despite these sound arguments against any reorientation of U.S. policy, as Churchill and his military advisors—some eighty in all—traveled aboard HMS *Duke of York* to the "Arcadia" conference in late December, they were understandably troubled that the certainties in place prior to Pearl Harbor, and the U.S. commitment to the established priorities of the Alliance that had already been expressed unequivocally in a joint memo provided to the president by Admiral Stark and General

Marshall on November 5, might well have been overtaken by the event that had taken place at Hawaii on December 7, 1941. The British leader had already experienced the dark days of 1940, when Britain had stood alone against Nazi Germany. Now Churchill had to consider the very real possibility that an American populace demanding early revenge against Japan for what Roosevelt had publicly termed "a day of infamy" might so affect U.S. policy that the British could find themselves providing the only defensive bulwark against the German western front, while the Soviets would be constrained to fight the main conflict in the east largely unsupported by their Western allies.

In fact, Winston Churchill's fears proved unfounded, although the issue was certainly debated closely by the leaders and their advisors at the "Arcadia" conference. Indeed, "Arcadia" exemplified the art of nego-tiation, compromise, and rational discussion of world-shaping matters at the highest level, and the true strength of the Anglo-U.S. relationship— a direct consequence of the closeness of that between Churchill and Roosevelt—at that time.

In the immediate aftermath of the Japanese attack, the U.S. leadership had indeed broached with the Soviet government the perceived advan-tages of a combined U.S., Soviet, British, and Chinese campaign against the increasingly dispersed Japanese forces in the Southeast Asia region. The U.S. military chiefs also expressed to Moscow their concern that Japan might launch a preemptive attack against the Soviet maritime territories that lay close to Siberia. Had Stalin been less focused upon the more immediate German threat, he might well have been tempted to support such action, which would almost certainly have led by default to the Pacific theater's assuming primacy amongst the U.S. strategic priorities. But Stalin's agenda was already firmly established, and, far from joining the war against Japan, he simply restated the pressing need for a second front to be launched in Europe. Consequently, the "Arcadia" conference was important both for its reaffirmation of the Alliance's existing strategic policy (the Japanese entry into the conflict notwithstanding) and for its further consideration of the key issue that would dominate "Big Three" meetings and negotiations for the next two years—the time and place at which a second front should be established.

The need for a second front to be opened against Germany in due course was not in doubt, although the way in which this was to be done attracted a great deal of debate. Churchill was clear that an early landing in northern France was unrealistic, and therefore proposed a joint Anglo-U.S. campaign against the Axis forces in North Africa, with the strategic aim of tightening the ring about Axis-held Europe while also capitalizing upon a hoped-for British victory in Libya. This option would also enable U.S. ground forces to be seen to be engaged directly in combat at what was generally viewed as a relatively low level of operational risk. As such, it was a politically attractive option for the U.S. president. The arguments advanced by Churchill and his advisors were persuasive, and by the end of the main conference session of "Arcadia" the Allies had agreed that a second front—but not one that would have been recognized as such by Stalin—would be launched against the Axis forces in North Africa, with a view to securing control of the entire coastline of that territory. In the meantime, the level of Anglo-U.S. air attacks against Axis targets would be increased, while material aid to Russia would continue to be provided by all available means. At the same time, however, "Arcadia" identified the fact that any large-scale ground offensive against Germany itself in 1942 was unlikely (other than by the Soviets on the eastern front), although such an operation might be possible in 1943: launched directly into western Europe, or from the south via the Mediterranean, or through Turkey and the Balkans. The general policy for the second front had been set, but even these fairly conservative timelines soon proved overoptimistic as the British suffered defeat at the hands of Gen. Erwin Rommel in the North African desert, and the war in Southeast Asia raged on with ever greater ferocity and a succession of reverses for the Allies.

Therefore, although "Arcadia" was dominated by the second-front deliberations, the whole issue of the new enemy that had finally unmasked itself in the Pacific was by no means relegated to irrelevance. Certainly the pre-December 7 "defensive" posture in the Pacific was now changed to one in which the Allies were committed to regaining the initiative during the period until Germany was defeated, although this action would be mounted on a scale that fell well short of the strategic level, and was never to be to the detriment of the campaign against Germany. Thus were the American people and certain of their military leaders appeased; and, indeed, General Marshall, whose advice and influence often proved decisive at these meetings, held firm to the Alliance's established strategic concept and championed it throughout "Arcadia." In any case, as it was argued time and again during those meetings in Washington, the best guarantee of success against Japan would be the prior defeat of Germany, which would allow the full military weight of the Alliance to be brought to bear in the Pacific, Far East and Southeast Asia. Furthermore, an ill-thought-out deployment of Allied forces in the region, together with the strategic gains already made by the Japanese forces, militated against any quick or easy campaign in the Pacific. At the same time, although clearly very much a two-sided advantage, it was undeniable that every territorial gain by the Japanese took them ever further from the home islands. Each Japanese victory dissipated their forces, extended their lines of communication and imposed an increasing operational and logistic burden upon their air and maritime forces—which gradually reduced their ability to defend their homeland against an eventual invasion by the Allies.

However, despite the general consensus achieved at "Arcadia," the Pacific-versus-Europe issue was inevitably resurrected as the Japanese campaign gained ever more momentum during early 1942, with a succession of notable achievements. Just three days after Pearl Harbor, on December 10, Japanese aircraft had sunk the battleships HMS *Prince of Wales*[2] and the battlecruiser HMS *Repulse* off the coast of Malaya; then, after a defensive battle lasting only eighteen days, Hong Kong—the "jewel in the crown" among Britain's Far Eastern imperial territories—had fallen on Christmas Day to the forces of Major-General Sano's 38th Division, under the overall command of Lt.-Gen. Takaishi Sakai, the Japanese commander-in-chief in south China. Meanwhile, Japanese forces had invaded and quickly overrun Malaya, Burma, the Philippines, and the Dutch East Indies, all of which territories had just been identified at "Arcadia" as places that would be denied to the Japanese invaders. Just over two weeks after the fall of Hong Kong, on February 15 the allegedly impregnable British island base of Singapore capitulated to those Japanese forces under the command of Lieutenant-General Yamashita that had fought their way southward along the length of the Malay peninsula.[3]

This catalog of reverses at the hands of the Japanese for Great Britain and the United States alike resulted in only about fifteen percent of the one hundred and thirty-two thousand U.S. soldiers deployed overseas during January, February, and March 1942 being sent to Iceland and Northern Ireland in support of the European theater: almost all of the remainder were dispatched to the Pacific theater, including Australia.

The Pacific-theater lobby in Washington understandably gained strength in early 1942, and it was probably only Roosevelt's determination, supported by General Marshall's certainty, that kept the Allies' strategic plan on track. However, the wisdom of this course was generally irrefutable, and Brig.-Gen. Dwight D. Eisenhower, one of Marshall's protégés and an assistant chief of staff in Washington, encapsulated the argument in a staff paper dated January 22 that formed the basis of a key presentation on February 28. Eisenhower was absolutely clear that the Allied focus had to be in Europe: anything else would result in a dissipation of resources and a potentially disastrous loss of time. He identified that it would also risk a German victory against Russia, and the loss of the Middle East, Burma, and India. Implied but not stated in his assessment was the political fallout for an alliance that now needed the Soviet Union and could not afford to risk the Moscow leadership seeing the European theater relegated to secondary importance by the United States and Great Britain. Eisenhower also demonstrated that, although Germany had the stronger military capability, Japan was in reality strategically stronger, due to the fact that it was not then at war with the Soviet Union: Germany was already committed to what would soon become a war on two fronts. Moreover, while all of the Allies could physically commit their forces against those of Germany and Italy— Stalin had ordered a major counteroffensive just a month earlier—this could simply not be achieved against the Japanese. Finally, he had assessed that the necessary U.S. Navy resources to support offensive operations in the Pacific would be up to four times greater than those for the Atlantic, and that the former option was therefore unsustainable, no matter how emotive the arguments for an unrestricted offensive against the Japanese might be.

Eisenhower's deep personal commitment to what might be termed the European project, even as early as 1941–42, was of special significance in light of his subsequent elevation, on Marshall's recommendation, to command the future campaign in northwest Europe from 1944—the true second front that Stalin had called for. An early indication of Marshall's faith in this rising star was the joint chiefs of staff's endorsement of Eisenhower's recommendation, developed from the strategic generalities of "Arcadia," that the Anglo-U.S. military staffs should develop a joint plan of operations against German-occupied northwest Europe that would permit a steadily increasing scale of counter-air operations from May, and of joint ground force offensive operations by the late summer.

Thus, from "Arcadia" and its decisions, had flowed a strategic policy that was militarily credible, enabled detailed planning to take place for the next stage of the war, and even, by and large, survived the impact of the attack on Pearl Harbor and all that occurred in the weeks and months that followed. However, while Roosevelt, Marshall, and others were satisfied with the rightness of maintaining the Europe option, its adoption opened an entirely new debate, as Churchill's enthusiasm for a landing in North Africa was by no means shared by many in Washington (including General Marshall), who viewed anything other than a landing in northwest Europe as a distraction and an unnecessary dissipation of the Allied forces that should as soon as practicable engage directly the German armed forces in Europe. This was, of course, a view that Stalin would also applaud. Although "Arcadia" and its reaffirmation of the Allies' priorities and purpose had undoubtedly represented significant progress, the process of discussion and negotiation had much further to run, and the evolving system of the Allied war summits was still at an early stage of development.

5

Arcadian Aftermath

Europe or North Africa?

THE SERIES OF HIGH-LEVEL MEETINGS arranged to take place between March and late July 1942 were particularly important, as the final decisions that emerged from them directly shaped much of the course of the remainder of the war up to the invasion of France two years later. These discussions also revealed the then relatively parlous military capability of the Western allies when set against their strategic aspirations. The reverses that the Allies had already suffered in the Far East, Pacific, Mediterranean, and Libya were at the same time salutary and timely indicators of the work that needed to be done before a landing in continental Europe would be feasible. This subject and the broader second-front issues involved provided the focus for a flurry of visits, meetings, and conferences that took place during the six months after "Arcadia."

From the outset, the Americans were of the opinion that all efforts should be directed toward the invasion of mainland Europe. Certainly logic supported this view, especially when seen from Washington. Eisenhower, ever the astute and competent staff officer, developed his stated position by highlighting the advantages of concentrating all U.S. resources on the buildup to this invasion in Britain prior to the cross-Channel invasion, rather than on their diversion to what many senior members of the U.S. administration—notably secretary of war Henry L. Stimson and General Marshall—regarded as an unnecessary adventure in North Africa. Eisenhower pointed out that the former prioritization would ensure that German forces had to be maintained in northwest Europe, thereby preventing their redeployment against the Russians on the eastern front. This in turn meant that the Germans would be unable to defeat the Soviet Union before the onset of the next winter, by which time both the weather and the considerable amounts of Western aid being sent to the Soviets would impact significantly upon the war on that front. At the same time the sea route to Great Britain was self-evidently shorter than that to North Africa, which meant that U.S. maritime assets traveling to and from the former were being used to maximum efficiency; these vital sea routes had to be kept open in any case, so the continued need to deploy U.S. warships along them, and in effective numbers, was not in question. Moreover, given that aid to the Soviets remained a strategic priority for the Allies, this could only be achieved if the North Atlantic sealanes remained open and operating at full capacity. Eisenhower's last point took specific account of British circumstances and needs. He pointed out that in a cross-Channel operation the Allies would enjoy air superiority, due to the nearness of the British airbases (although, of course, the presence of the Luftwaffe in northern France and the Benelux countries was also considerable), while at the same time the proximity of the cross-Channel operation would mean that the overall strength of Britain's homeland defenses would not be depleted.

Not surprisingly, Roosevelt was attracted by the strength of these arguments, and in late March the U.S. military staff developed the plan for an invasion of France scheduled for April 1, 1943. Next, on April 1, Roosevelt directed Marshall and Harry Hopkins to brief Churchill in London on what had by then been codenamed Operation "Bolero."

Full of enthusiasm, the U.S. briefing team explained the scope and scale of "Bolero" to the British leader and chiefs of staff. While Britain would provide at least two thousand five hundred combat aircraft and eighteen divisions of troops, the United States would commit some thirty divisions and more than three thousand combat aircraft. Although the English Channel was the point of main emphasis, the plan also allowed for a lesser operation to be mounted in late 1942, either to exploit an unforeseen collapse of the Nazi powerbase within Germany or to assist the Soviet forces in the event that they should suffer a strategic reverse. This contingency operation was codenamed "Sledgehammer."

The Operation "Bolero" meeting in London proved unsatisfactory. Although Churchill and the chiefs of staff indicated their agreement in principle to the U.S. plan, together with their enthusiasm for what was by any standards a huge U.S. commitment to the war against Germany and the liberation of Europe, this session exposed the fundamental cultural differences between the British and the American approach to the war. Inevitably, the political and military leaders of both nations were influenced by their history, their experience, and their national character. In spring 1942, the Americans lacked war-fighting experience: they had suffered a direct attack on U.S. territory only in far-off Hawaii, and they were eager to embark upon the great crusade in Europe which, once won, would permit them to settle accounts with the Japanese. The British, however, had already been fighting for more than two and a half years: much of London, and of many other British towns, cities, ports, and industrial areas, lay in ruins as a result of air bombardment; British forces were in many cases exhausted, and were universally in need of reconstituting, reequipping, and retraining following a series of disastrous defeats in France, Norway, North Africa, and the Far East. While Churchill did not for a moment doubt the need for the eventual invasion of France, both he and the British chiefs of staff were of the opinion that any sort of cross-Channel operation in 1942 was not feasible and, although the Americans departed with the clear (but misplaced) impression that their proposals had been endorsed by the British leadership, it later transpired that Churchill had significant reservations about the practicability of Operation "Bolero" being launched in 1943. The energetic and enthusiastic, but somewhat naive, approach of the Americans to the invasion of Europe stood out in stark contrast to the cautious approach of the British—whose judgment had already been shaped by the hard experiences of 1939–42. In simple terms, Churchill knew very well that, the scale of U.S. resources notwithstanding, the combat power necessary to invade, hold the bridgeheads, and then liberate Europe from a German war machine still flushed with the successes of 1940 could not be generated in 1942, probably could not be generated by 1943, and even might not be available by 1944—although it was hoped that, by then, Germany would have been considerably weakened through attrition. However, in a bid to ameliorate Roosevelt, maintain the momentum of the U.S. buildup in Britain, and avoid prejudicing Washington's commitment to Europe, Churchill was probably guilty of intentionally allowing Marshall and Hopkins to believe that their mission at the "Bolero" meeting had been successfully accomplished. Certainly, irrespective of the eventual date of the invasion, he wanted the Anglo-U.S. staff planning for it to proceed uninterrupted.

In any event, this Anglo-U.S. mismatch of perceptions about the timing of the second front was highlighted when Molotov visited London, and then Washington, in May. While Churchill was indefinite and cautious about the possibility of an invasion in 1942, Roosevelt indicated that such action was positively likely. In practice, this visit was particularly timely, as it forced the issue into the open and also allowed Churchill to restate his belief in an Allied first landing in North Africa. Finally, it enabled the principles of the original Operation "Bolero" concept to be reviewed, with the British concerns and modifications taken fully into account. This in turn ensured that the overall plan for the invasion of Europe was much more soundly based than had been so with its first iteration. In order to present the British position to Roosevelt, Churchill traveled once again to Washington. The date was June 19.

This summit meeting was critical. Marshall and Stimson defended their position strongly, and in particular expressed their concern about the possibility of a Soviet collapse before the end of the year—something that, they argued, could only be avoided by launching a second front in western Europe. Stalin's influence upon the U.S. leadership—founded upon Hopkins' initial meeting with the Soviet leader—was still deeply ingrained within the Washington hierarchy. But Churchill doubted that the Soviet situation was so dire, and in any case argued that an invasion of northwest Europe in 1942 was doomed to fail for clearly identifiable military reasons. In principle, Churchill argued, there should be no such landing unless the intention and capability to remain were both in place; the ghosts of Dunkirk were still very much in his consciousness and those of his military commanders. The prime minister reiterated that the landing should only be made when the wider German forces had been sufficiently weakened through the attrition of their forces on the eastern front. He was also very aware that time would permit Italy to be excised from the Axis in due course, and key to the achievement of this was a first landing by the Allies in North Africa rather than northwest Europe.

The meetings were difficult. By June 21, all that the Americans had conceded was an intention to review "Bolero" in September, having developed it in detail by then, thus implying that no Operation "Sledge-hammer" would be entertained before that month. However, as is so often the case in war, the strategic debate was suddenly affected by oper-ational events elsewhere: on that very same day, the major British base of Tobruk in Libya capitulated to the troops of Gen. Erwin Rommel's Afrika Korps.

The fall of Tobruk had an almost immediate impact upon the "Bolero" debate. In order to restore the situation in North Africa, Churchill asked that a U.S. division be sent to Libya as soon as possible—the U.S. 2nd Armored Division had already been earmarked to join the Allied forces defending Libya. However, with continued successes by the battle-expe-rienced and apparently unstoppable Afrika Korps likely, Washington opted instead to provide the British forces in North Africa with a signif-icant amount of additional matériel, while not at that stage sending U.S. troops. Quite apart from doubts regarding the combat readiness of the American troops to confront Rommel at that point in the war, trans-porting a U.S. division to Libya would have seriously depleted the amount of shipping available for the priority movement of U.S. troops to Great Britain. This would have been anathema to General Marshall and others, whose sights were still firmly set upon their own concept for Operation "Bolero." However, even though the flow of cross-Atlantic movement to Britain was preserved, this reallocation of much essential war matériel to the North African campaign of itself inevitably weak-ened the chances of an early cross-Channel operation. And from these actions the respective U.S. and British positions on the second-front landing, henceforth retitled Operation "Roundup," were clarified.

The Americans, having seen their preferred course of action against the Germans weakened by the unavoidable Anglo-U.S. response to events at Tobruk, decided to initiate substantive offensive action against the Japanese in the Pacific theater, at Guadalcanal. Although this had the potential to reduce U.S. support for the war against Germany,

Churchill recognized that it also meant that his reticence over a possible landing in 1942 or 1943 had been appropriate. Consequently, in early July he advised Roosevelt that the British view was that the Operation "Sledgehammer" contingency option was now a nonstarter. At the same time, he once more promoted his proposal for the second front in 1942 to be launched against North Africa rather than continental Europe—an action which would directly engage U.S. ground forces in the war against the Germans.

By his response to Churchill's communication Roosevelt showed his qualities as a world-class statesman rather than simply as a politician. Despite the forceful opposition of Marshall, Hopkins, Stimson, and the J.C.S., the president effectively put the needs of the Alliance before the recommendations and views of his U.S. military and political advisors. Following a fairly acrimonious meeting between the respective chiefs of staff in London in late July, Roosevelt overrode all U.S. objections to what was by then an unshakable British position, and indicated his belief (and decision) that Operation "Torch"—a landing in North Africa—should take place not later than October 30. Marshall and Stimson took the president's decision with fair ill-grace and continued to argue the case for their original plan for "Bolero." However, the die had been cast, and Roosevelt ensured that the top priority he now accorded to the direct involvement of U.S. ground forces against the Germans in North Africa was made crystal clear to the J.C.S. Meanwhile, Churchill and the British chiefs of staff could derive considerable satisfaction from the fact that they had finally secured a negotiated acceptance of their plan against the persuasive arguments of no lesser advocates than General Marshall and Secretary of War Stimson. They had also done so notwithstanding their awareness of Stalin's views on the pressing need for an Anglo-U.S. cross-Channel invasion of France to alleviate the Russian position on the eastern front.

Many in Washington undoubtedly viewed this as a triumph for British hesitancy and caution over American enterprise and enthusiasm. However, in reality what would undoubtedly have been a highly risky and probably abortive attempt to invade northwest Europe in 1942 (or possibly 1943) had been supplanted by a viable operation against North

Africa, and one that would, albeit indirectly, match the Alliance's strategic aims, with the notable exception of providing Stalin with an Anglo-U.S. second front in mainland Europe in the near future. But the greatest significance of Roosevelt's acquiescence in the British case was its effect on the Western Alliance and the vital relationship between Roosevelt and Churchill. The already strong bonds of understanding—the meeting of minds—between the U.S. and British war leaders were further reinforced, together with the wider bonds of the Anglo-U.S. Alliance.

Thus had the process of the war summits matured and moved forward once again, even though Stalin was no doubt less convinced of the benefits that this conferred upon the campaign being waged by the Red Army at that stage—especially as the Soviet leader had been given the impression by Roosevelt in April that a second front in Europe during 1942 was a distinct possibility, even though this had been a largely unsuccessful attempt by the president to divert Stalin from his preoccupation with Soviet postwar frontiers by suggesting an early relief for his forces on the battlefield. Consequently, the next challenge for the three-power Alliance was to maintain Soviet cooperation and the principles of the Atlantic Charter against the conflict of its key features with Stalin's postwar territorial aspirations. At the same time, the Anglo-U.S. part of the Alliance had to ensure that the Russians were able to continue their telling attrition of the German forces in the east.

The potentially irreconcilable issue of territory was the subject of much Anglo-U.S.-Soviet activity, many communications, and many meetings through the spring of 1942. However, just as the fall of Tobruk had forced a resolution of the "Bolero" issue, so German battlefield successes against the Red Army in the Ukraine and the Crimea weakened Stalin's bargaining position, as he was very aware that unbending insistence upon his territorial demands could actually prejudice U.S. resolve to launch the second front; and there was already a groundswell of concern in Washington and London over the implications for the peoples of a number of Baltic and eastern European states if Stalin's requirements were met. In any event, the Wehrmacht's successes on the battlefield forced Stalin and Molotov to moderate their original demands, in that they were content to sign, on May 26, a twenty-year

Anglo-Soviet treaty that bound the allies together in their common cause while avoiding any specific mention of the territorial issues. Stalin had not forsaken his aspirations, but, just as had Roosevelt over "Bolero," he had recognized the greater need to achieve a negotiated accommodation with his allies. At the same time, Churchill had accepted that the omission of these matters was no more than their postponement; but this postponement did mean that, at least for the immediate future, the Allies could together advance the business of defeating Germany.

Throughout this period of negotiation, Roosevelt had maintained, via Molotov, the impression that the second front would be established in 1942 and, by implication, that this would be in Europe. On June 20 the Soviet media announced that this was so. However, the next day Tobruk fell, and the demise of Operation "Bolero" followed, together with any possibility of a second front in Europe in 1942. The potential impact of this turn of events was momentous: no longer could the prospect of a second front in Europe in 1942 be upheld for Stalin's benefit, and, furthermore, the balance of Anglo-U.S. activity was about to be switched positively to North Africa. At the same time, coincidentally, the maritime operational situation about the North Cape meant that a reduction in Anglo-U.S. aid to Russia was about to be implemented. With the potential for a disastrous rift between the Western allies and their Soviet partner a very real possibility, Churchill determined to visit Moscow and talk directly to Stalin, a man who already harbored considerable suspicions over British imperial motives and who also suspected (from his various dealings with U.S. personnel) that the Anglo-U.S. Alliance was perhaps not as seamless as it purported to be.

6

In the Bear's Lair

The First Moscow Conference, August 1942

ALTHOUGH THE WAR HAD BEEN ONGOING for some three years by the late summer of 1942, and the German invasion of Russia was by then more than a year old, what became known as the First Moscow Conference was the first occasion on which Churchill and Stalin met face to face. It was an historic occasion. Although this meeting from August 12, 1942 was ostensibly bilateral, inasmuch as Roosevelt was not involved, there was nonetheless U.S. representation, as Averell Harriman attended in order to support Churchill in what both he and Roosevelt knew would be a difficult session for the British leader. Far from being an intrusion, Churchill had welcomed Harriman's presence as a clear demonstration of the close harmony that existed between the U.S. and British view of affairs.

Not surprisingly, Stalin had accorded the management, control, and hosting of this meeting the highest priority. This was a first opportunity to demonstrate the success and the power of the communist system to the Western world. From the moment that Churchill's aircraft landed at an airport near Moscow during the afternoon of August 12[1] until his departure for Tehran at the end of the program of guards of honor, conferences, banquets, and lavish entertainment that the Soviets had organized for their Western allies, the stage-management of the Moscow meeting was impressive. Just as impressive were the security arrangements that impinged upon the visitors throughout their stay in Moscow—arrangements that were clearly designed just as much to observe and constrain the activities of the Western delegates as to assure their safety. On a personal level, Stalin gave Churchill the use of his personal *dacha* at nearby Kuntsevo throughout the conference period. Despite the privations and significant food shortages by then being suffered by the population of Moscow—this being readily observed on the streets of the city, despite the fact that the visitors' official motorcades invariably traveled everywhere at sixty miles per hour, irrespective of the road conditions—Churchill's detective noted that the final banquet, an event of more than three hours' duration, comprised some ten courses of exquisitely prepared food. Such a feast would have been regarded as luxurious even in peacetime, let alone in time of war. Prodigious amounts of accompanying alcohol were consumed, with about twenty-five toasts being drunk at that banquet alone.

Against the wider canvas of the war, the First Moscow Conference might all too easily be relegated to insignificance, as it delivered no document or agreement of the status of the Atlantic Charter, an Operation "Bolero" initiative, or similar. However, its actual importance was immense, for it was during those days in August that the embryo three-power Alliance solidified, and the mutual understanding—if not a complete meeting of minds—that had for some time existed between Churchill and Roosevelt was expanded to include the thoughts and perceptions of the Soviet leader. Thus the Alliance truly became one that comprised the "Big Three," rather than one of a "Big Two" and the Soviet Union.

Churchill's time in Moscow and meetings with Stalin fell into three distinct phases, each ostensibly unrelated to each other, with the whole program utilized by Stalin to showcase the international image of the Soviet Union to the best advantage. In order to understand the phases of the negotiations it is necessary to look in particular at Stalin's wider motives and, despite his omnipotence within the Soviet Union, the need for him to measure any international or foreign policy pronouncement against the national interest of the Soviet Union in general and of the communist party of the Soviet Union (CPSU) in particular.

In the outwardly pessimistic form adopted by military briefers since time immemorial, Stalin first of all explained the worrying extent of German progress and his concerns over the ability of the Red Army to hold at Stalingrad and about Moscow; but he then adopted a more optimistic view of the capability of the Red Army and the probable outcome of the war on the eastern front. All the while he emphasized the numbers of German troops that had been removed from the west in order to conduct operations against the Soviets, thereby indicating fairly unsubtly his critical view of Anglo-U.S. inaction against a depleted Axis capability in the west. Churchill rehearsed the usual arguments about the risks involved in a premature landing in northwest Europe, and the two leaders in effect agreed to disagree over the British assessment that no invasion was practicable in 1942. In response to the implied accusation that the British had no stomach for a fight against the Germans, Churchill showed remarkable restraint: he was very aware of the stakes involved if there should be a seismic split between Stalin and himself at this stage of the war.

Churchill was able to rebut Stalin's criticism by explaining the dramatic increase in bombing of Germany that would shortly be set in motion, and by providing details of the Anglo-U.S. plans for Operation "Torch" in North Africa. The strategic implications of Anglo-U.S. control of the North African littoral were clear to Stalin, and its potential threat to the Germans in occupied Europe offset to some extent the more straightforward advantages to the Russians of an Anglo-U.S. cross-Channel invasion of France. Churchill also introduced the possibility of Anglo-U.S. air support for the Soviet southern front, further improvements to the Lend-Lease arrangements and their movement to Russia, and the possibility of future action against the German forces in Norway. The first session with Stalin ended with Churchill and Harriman both cautiously optimistic over the generally calm way in which the Soviet leader had accepted what both knew was (in Stalin's eyes) bad news about the second-front issue. However, twenty-four hours later Stalin's mood had changed, and an optimistic report provided to Roosevelt by Harriman at the end of the first day's discussions proved somewhat premature.

During the second day of the talks, on August 13, Stalin returned to the original Soviet arguments for a second front in 1942. He castigated the two Western representatives for reneging on the earlier understanding provided to Molotov (by Roosevelt in particular). He also took the opportunity to reemphasize the role of the Red Army in drawing away German forces from the west, thereby facilitating just such an operation. Finally, Stalin highlighted the shortfall in the amount of aid promised to the Soviet Union in recent weeks, a reflection in fact of the devastating effects of the German U-boat campaign against the Atlantic and Arctic convoys rather than of any Anglo-U.S. intention not to meet their obligations to their ally. In the face of this barrage of criticism both Churchill and Harriman held firm: the former did not rise to Stalin's blatant assertion that the British Army (unlike the Royal Air Force!) lacked the will to fight the Germans, while the latter emphasized that the decisions and courses of action explained the previous day were indivisibly those of the British and American leadership taken together.

In retrospect, the change of tack adopted by Stalin on the second day was probably for three reasons. First, he may have felt the need to reassert his dominance of what was patently a meeting on his own ground—in the very lair of the Russian bear. Next, he had always to take account of his domestic audience, and to have been seen not to have attacked the representatives of the noncommunist, capitalist West (notwithstanding that they were his vital allies) would probably have been unthinkable if he was to maintain intact his domestic powerbase. Thirdly, following Molotov's meetings with Roosevelt and his own dealings with the U.S. president, it would probably have been a major omission had Stalin not taken the opportunity to test the true strength of the Anglo-U.S. Alliance, in order to understand both the reliability of the two nations and their leaders as joint allies in the short term. No doubt he was also assessing Anglo-U.S. potential cohesiveness in advance of the time when the German threat no longer existed and a new sort of conflict—a "Cold War"—imposed itself upon East-West relations. Based upon the outcome of this second part of the conference, it is fair to say that Stalin achieved the aims of his secondary agendas, while the primary strategic positions of the Allies remained unchanged. During the latter part of these negotiations, Stalin's attitude softened again, and there is little doubt that he had by then gained the measure of Churchill to his satisfaction, just as Churchill had determined his own opinion of the Soviet leader.

This led naturally into the third part of the visit—one that was entirely informal in nature—for, on the night of August 15, Churchill took dinner with Stalin and his family, and in that cordial atmosphere the two men continued to discuss issues well into the small hours of the following day. Amongst the many topics discussed, Stalin indicated his enthusiasm for a future meeting of all three Alliance leaders.

It would be wrong to suggest that the nature and conviviality of the August 15 evening meeting was indicative of some remarkable new relationship between the two leaders—their so different backgrounds and political ideologies were simply unbridgeable—but, at the very least, by the end of Churchill's groundbreaking visit to Moscow each man had formed an opinion of the strengths, the character, and the national imperatives of the other. Both men were of necessity good judges of such things, and this new understanding—which was one that could only ever have been achieved face to face—was the foundation of a satisfactory working arrangement thereafter, even though both parties were well aware that on certain matters agreement would always be impossible, and that an ongoing suspicion and mistrust of each other would be an unavoidable and ever-present part of their relationship. The world of diplomacy and international relations has ever been so.

During the two months that followed the Moscow conference and preceded the Operation "Torch" landings, Churchill and Roosevelt engaged in an unremitting dialog with Stalin to alleviate his concerns and suspicions that the two Western allies were not meeting what he believed to be their strategic Alliance obligations. Stalin's criticism and complaints centered as always upon the issues of the second front and the amount of Anglo-U.S. aid provided to the Soviet Union. With regard to the latter, the quantity of aid had indeed (unavoidably) suffered shortfalls during the summer, when the treacherous seas, virtually unending Arctic daylight and often appalling weather about the North Cape of Norway, together with the U-boats and Luftwaffe attacks, had combined to decimate several of the large convoys that set out from Iceland to Archangel. The situation had reached a crisis in late June. On that occasion, a convoy designated PQ.17 had been attacked, command and control had broken down, the ships had scattered, and, of thirty-four merchant vessels (twenty-two of them American), no fewer than twenty-four had been sunk. This disaster had taken place despite PQ.17's having had a large escort of Royal Navy warships.[2] The heavy toll of Allied shipping in the Arctic waters was almost matched by that suffered in the Atlantic, and Churchill and Roosevelt therefore informed Stalin that the large convoys which had been dispatched through the summer and early fall would have to be suspended, not least because large numbers of Allied ships were now also required to support the impending Operation "Torch." Although, at the end of the year, convoy PQ.18 did manage to fight its way through to Russia having lost only thirteen of its forty-three vessels and having claimed forty-one Norway-based Luftwaffe aircraft shot down, by the end of 1942 the Allies had lost some 1,664 ships—a tonnage approaching almost eight million—of which eleven hundred and sixty had been sunk by U-boats.[3]

However, although the Western leaders had curtailed the level of support provided via the Arctic convoys, they had at the same time offered Stalin the prospect of direct Anglo-U.S. air support (Operation "Velvet") for the Soviet southern flank in the Caucasus,[4] an ongoing (if much reduced) level of material aid by the established northern sea route, and the provision of aircraft to the Soviets by means of additional supply routes, notably via Persia and the Pacific. Predictably, Stalin was unimpressed, but in practice he had little choice but to accept the facts as they were presented to him, while using them as propaganda to blame the significant curtailment of Anglo-U.S. material support by sea for the lack of significant progress then being made by the Red Army. However, the tide of war was about to turn on several fronts, and the patience, diplomacy, and perseverance of Roosevelt and Churchill—often in the face of blatantly unfair and ill-advised criticism by their Soviet ally—were about to prove their value as the days of October 1942 drew on.

Although sometimes imperfect, and still by no means a three-way meeting of minds, the great Alliance was about to produce some tangible results, as the Soviets continued to engage the greater part of the Wehrmacht on the eastern front and the Anglo-U.S. part of the partnership at last launched its planned offensive action in North Africa. Linked inextricably to the outcome of that campaign had been the arrival in Cairo on August 12, 1942 of Lt. Gen. Bernard Law Montgomery, the new commander of the British Eighth Army.

7
End of the Beginning
North Africa and the Eastern Front, 1942

I N 1942, MONTGOMERY WAS FIFTY-FOUR YEARS OF AGE. He had served as a regular officer since 1908. He was a consummate professional, and was one of the relatively few senior commanders to have emerged from the Dunkirk debacle with his reputation largely unscathed. Ironically, Montgomery was not Churchill's first choice of Eighth Army commander, but Major General Gott, who had already been selected for the post, was killed in an air crash the day before he was due to be appointed. Thus the next in line become the new army commander—a fortuitous turn of fate as subsequent events would prove, because Montgomery's subsequent actions soon produced for the Western allies the long-awaited turning point in the war against Germany.

In short order, Montgomery revitalized the Eighth Army, removing many tired and less competent commanders and ensuring that all of his subordinates had both the ability and the determination to defeat Rommel's Afrika Korps. At the same time, he impressed his own partic-ular style of command upon all parts of the army, meeting, briefing, and being seen by all those under his command right down to the smallest subunit and to the individual soldier and airman. The energy, profes-sionalism, and confidence that he imparted soon pervaded all parts of an army that had thus far enjoyed little success—certainly when it had been confronted by Rommel. Montgomery's ability and approach soon bore fruit, when the Afrika Korps, while attempting to outflank the Eighth Army to the south and reach Cairo, was lured into a trap on the Alam Halfa ridge.

Between August 31 and September 3, Rommel's elite 15th and 21st Panzer Divisions, their lines of supply and communication already severely overstretched, tried unsuccessfully to break through blocking positions held by the British 22nd, 23rd and 8th Armoured Brigades and 7th Armoured Division. Meanwhile, apart from a period of inactivity caused by a sandstorm, the British Desert Air Force carried out effective bombing sorties against the attacking German armored formations. Soon after dawn in the morning of September 3, the German armor was forced to withdraw. Montgomery and the Eighth Army had together won their first victory against the Germans in North Africa, Rommel's alleged invincibility had been disproved, and no longer could Stalin accuse British soldiers of being reluctant to fight, and defeat, the Germans. It was true, nevertheless, that Alam Halfa had been a defensive victory, and as such it was but the precursor to the twelve-day offensive battle of El Alamein which demonstrated to Allies and Axis alike that the tide of the war had at last begun to turn in the former's favor.

Montgomery's preparation and planning for El Alamein were meticulous. Although the battle was hard fought from its very beginning on October 23, and subsequently included a major modification of the British point of main emphasis for the crucial breakout operation on November 2, by November 4 it was apparent that the German and Italian forces were broken. Ironically, due to ill health, Rommel was not present to witness the demise of his Afrika Korps divisions, but had he been so it is doubtful that the British victory would have been any less decisive.[1] Thirty thousand Axis prisoners were taken, including nine generals, and the way was opened for the victorious Eighth Army to pursue the withdrawing Axis forces, to advance westward into Libya and on to Tobruk, Benghazi, Tripoli and Tunis, and eventually to link up with the Allied forces engaged in Operation "Torch." For the Alliance as a whole, and for Churchill in particular, the impact of the British success at El Alamein far exceeded its more obvious operational implications.

On the western side of North Africa, more than a thousand miles away, across the beaches of French North Africa at Algiers, Oran and Casablanca, American soldiers took their first offensive action in the western theater alongside their British allies when, on November 8, Operation "Torch" at last took place. The landing craft nosed up to the shoreline and the troops of the Anglo-U.S. force, commanded by General Eisenhower, spilled out of their landing craft, waded ashore, and raced up the sandy beaches to establish what Churchill had long viewed as an acceptable compromise solution to the second-front issue. The invasion force met little or no effective resistance from the Vichy French forces. The lack of counteraction was perhaps fortuitous, as various aspects of the U.S. coordination, control, and organization of "Torch" left a certain amount to be desired. The extent of American military inexperience was very evident from this, their first such joint amphibious operation, and it was therefore also particularly fortunate that neither German troops nor any of the North African-based Spanish forces of Franco's fascist regime were deployed against the landing sites—although, in the follow-on operations, many of these same U.S. troops would soon find themselves engaged in combat with German forces.[2]

However, for the Allies, "Torch" was but a start point, and Eisenhower in particular learned a great deal from the foray that he would apply to good effect less than two years later. Nevertheless, while "Torch" generally met its objectives and paved the way for later successes, it also demonstrated all too clearly Churchill's wisdom in counseling Roosevelt against a premature and undoubtedly catastrophic attempt by the Allies to land in northern France during 1942. Operation "Torch" also exposed the difficulties inherent in war-fighting governed by ideals and principles such as those expounded by the Western allies, when Eisenhower chose to negotiate a local security arrangement with the Vichy government's vice-premier, Admiral Jean-François Darlan.[3] This arrangement attracted significant operational benefits for the Anglo-U.S. force operating in Tunisia and elsewhere in the French territories in north and west Africa, but, despite Churchill's and Roosevelt's support for Eisenhower's pragmatic action, this dealing with a close associate of the Nazi enemy generated considerable unease in the United States. It also provided an early indication of some of the difficulties that would arise over the precise status of France and the administration of its overseas territories in the Allies' future planning—both for France's role during the remainder of the war and in its aftermath. Thus the Americans began to understand that the military victory against Germany would be neither quick nor easy, and that its achievement would almost certainly involve compromising of some of the high ideals for which the Alliance fought. Stalin had no such qualms about matters of principle, and endorsed Eisenhower's action unreservedly, applauding its favorable impact upon the Allies' campaign.

While events had been unfolding in North Africa, the Soviet Army had also been gaining ground. Much of its equipment had been updated or replaced, its manpower had been reinforced, and several new senior commanders of proven ability were in post; and, thus prepared, it launched a new general offensive against the weakened German forces. Most importantly, by November 22 the Soviets had successfully encircled and trapped the German Sixth Army—some twenty German and Romanian divisions—under General Paulus at Stalingrad. The issue had been in the balance during September and October, but Hitler's ill-judged order that Stalingrad was to be taken at all costs sealed the fate of the Sixth Army and played directly into Stalin's hands.[4] Just as El Alamein had marked the turn of the Allies' fortunes on the western front, so the approaching disaster for the Wehrmacht at Stalingrad signaled the fact that the process of rolling back and defeating the invaders in Russia was also well under way. However, the greater part of the ground war against Germany was being conducted by the Soviet Union, and Stalin ensured that this fact was highlighted whenever the opportunity to do so presented itself, just as he explained any reverses suffered by the Red Army as yet another consequence of the failure of his Western allies to mount the second front in Europe. At the same time, of course, he continued to emphasize the cohesiveness of the three-power Alliance, albeit stressing the scale of the Soviet Union's role within it.

Nevertheless, as Churchill had already observed in an historic broadcast to the British people on November 11, shortly after Montgomery's victory over the Afrika Korps: "This is not the end. This is not even the beginning of the end. But it is, perhaps, the end of the beginning." As subsequent events proved, the prime minister's measured assessment on that November day was both prophetic and accurate. By the end of 1942, even the remorseless German attrition of Allied convoys to Russia was gradually being reduced. More and more RAF Coastal Command airplanes, with ranges of eight hundred miles, were produced and deployed to protect the convoys, and aircraft based on the convoy escort carriers now provided almost immediate air protection. Meanwhile, advances in technology provided the Allies with shortwave radar and new, heavier depth charges. These capabilities together dramatically improved the ability of the Allies to deter, detect, inhibit, and destroy increasing numbers of the more than one hundred U-boats that the Kriegsmarine routinely had at large in the Atlantic, North Sea, and Arctic waters on anticonvoy operations. On land, on sea, and in the air, the "end of the beginning" had surely been reached.

There was still a long road to be traveled by the Allies, however, and, in the aftermath of Operation "Torch," and with a full-scale invasion of mainland Europe now clearly not feasible in 1943 (although General Marshall still favored and promoted this course of action), the Western allies found their more immediate strategic options focusing almost by default upon the Mediterranean region, while the J.C.S. in Washington, as ever, sought to divert resources to the war against Japan in the Pacific. This debate provided the preparatory work for what became known as the Casablanca Conference (codenamed "Symbol") in January 1943.

Even a cursory review of the issues prior to Casablanca showed how little they had really changed since the meetings at Placentia Bay and Washington in late 1941 and early 1942. The relative flexibility of Roosevelt and his ability to understand the wider picture contrasted with that of his principal military advisors, many of whom continued to support planning options that should by late 1942 have been ruled out. No doubt a considerable amount of military staff time was wasted developing and promoting what were patently national rather than Alliance objectives, but, fortunately, both Roosevelt and Churchill were able to rise above such parochial and potentially divisive matters. However, Churchill was well aware of the national pressures that bore upon the president, and it was he who sought another Anglo-U.S. summit meeting at an early date so that he could preempt the considerable arguments within the J.C.S. for the United States now to concentrate its efforts on the Pacific. In late 1942, both leaders must have been increasingly irritated by the ongoing friction between some members of their military staffs, with each pursuing what they perceived to be the correct objectives, but with each agenda still very much based upon the very different national imperatives that had been so evident at the "Bolero" meeting between the U.S. J.C.S. team and the British chiefs of staff in London in April that year.

Roosevelt was against a bilateral Anglo-U.S. meeting and favored one that would also be attended by Stalin. Despite his reservations—he felt that there were still matters that the United States and Britain needed to resolve before a three-power summit took place—Churchill acquiesced, and the Soviet leader was duly invited to attend what would have been the first "Big Three" summit, in North Africa. However, despite three separate invitations from his Western allies, Stalin declined to leave the Soviet Union at that time: the battle at Stalingrad was reaching its climax, and there were signs of a weakening German position in the Caucasus. Thus, despite the fact that Roosevelt viewed another bilateral and exclusively Anglo-U.S. summit as a less than ideal solution, it was decided that the two leaders would meet in Casablanca in mid-January 1943. Notwithstanding Stalin's absence, the meeting of Roosevelt and Churchill at Casablanca ranked as one of the key war summits, and one that had a considerable impact upon the rest of the war.

8

Global Strategy and Unconditional Surrender

The Casablanca Conference, January 14–24, 1943

WHEN ROOSEVELT AND CHURCHILL MET at Casablanca the fortunes of war had at last changed in the Allies' favor. In Russia, the German Sixth Army was encircled and doomed to defeat, in Libya the British forces were racing west toward Tripoli and the Mareth Line, and in Tunisia the Anglo-U.S. forces were consolidating and moving eastward following their earlier landings in Operation "Torch." Thus the Casablanca summit was underscored by a degree of cautious but certainly justified optimism.

This historic meeting was characterized by three issues or outcomes. First, and most importantly, it was at the post-summit press conference that Roosevelt announced that the Allies would accept nothing less than the "unconditional surrender" of the Axis powers. Next, it exposed yet again the continued preoccupation of General Marshall and others with the need for a second front in France and with Pacific-theater issues. Finally, it confirmed and amplified the Allies' policies for the rest of the war, as well as addressing aspects of the future course of the campaign against the Japanese in the Pacific and the Far East. However, despite the many other issues discussed and advanced at Casablanca by the two leaders and their staffs, it was for the "unconditional surrender" pronouncement that this particular summit was assured of its prominence in the history of World War II.

At the conclusion of the summit, a joint press conference was convened by Roosevelt and Churchill on January 24. Having summarized the other decisions that had been taken, which now formed the agreed way ahead for the West's conduct of the war, Roosevelt stated that "The elimination of German, Japanese, and Italian war power means the unconditional surrender by Germany, Italy and Japan." He prefaced this by indicating that world peace could only be achieved by the elimination of German and Japanese (but without mention of Italian) war power. This momentous statement was qualified by Roosevelt's amplification of it, when he made it clear that this did "not mean the destruction of the population of Germany, Italy, or Japan, but it does mean the destruction of the philosophies in those countries which are based on conquest and the subjugation of other people." The message for the National Socialist regime in Germany, the fascist regime in Italy and the imperial Japanese regime was clear, as was that for those of their people who heard it. However, the divisive or propaganda impact of Roosevelt's amplifying remarks upon the populations of the Axis countries was probably limited at that stage of the war, while the separate Allied commitment not to make isolated peace deals meant that its later effect was also much diminished. Nevertheless, these remarks accorded absolutely with the fundamental principles enshrined in the Atlantic Charter, although, as ever, their precise interpretation in Washington, London, and Moscow differed somewhat. Similarly, the practical import of "unconditional surrender" was perceived differently by the Allies, and particularly by Stalin.

Nevertheless, the issue had been considered beforehand by the Allies' political and military advisors alike. For the United States, the matter was quite clear: Germany had been able to rise again as a military power after 1918 primarily because of the failure of the then Allies to impose an "unconditional surrender" upon the country at the end of World War I. The "lesser" form of its defeat allowed the German people, encouraged by the various postwar national political movements— notably the Nazis—to believe that their army had not been defeated and that the nation had been betrayed from within. The U.S. pressure for the perceived mistake of the past not to be repeated was articulated by the state department's subcommittee on security problems in spring 1942, when its chairman, Norman Davis, presented the proposal that the Allies should this time demand the unconditional surrender of the Axis states, rather than merely an armistice. On January 7, just before the Casablanca conference, Roosevelt advised the J.C.S. of his intention to support the concept of unconditional surrender. Apparently, although he had certainly broached the subject with Churchill beforehand, Roosevelt's decision to announce it at this press conference took the British leader by surprise. However, this would appear to have been more a question of presentation and timing rather than an indication of any disagreement over policy, and Churchill immediately endorsed and reinforced Roosevelt's announcement at the January 24 press briefing.

Indeed, there were clear advantages to its exposure at that time. Quite apart from the U.S. view of the potential difficulties inherent in an armistice, the announcement sent a powerful signal to Stalin regarding the resolve of his Western allies to pursue the Axis defeat to the end, while at the same time it mitigated to some extent the unease in Washington over the potential precedent set by Eisenhower's accommodation with the late Admiral Darlan in French North Africa following Operation "Torch." Roosevelt and Churchill were both very aware of the presence of French Generals de Gaulle and Giraud at Casablanca, and the curtailment of any such future agreements with Vichy or similar Axis or Axis-sponsored governments would have been duly noted. Thus was the concept of "unconditional surrender" enshrined irrevocably within the war aims of the Alliance at Casablanca—a statement of policy that had short-term advantages, but which would also pose a number of difficulties for the Allies in the longer term.

During the main planning sessions at Casablanca, the way ahead for the campaign in the Mediterranean theater had been addressed. Predictably, General Marshall viewed anything other than a cross-Channel invasion as a distraction, whereas the British recommended that the Allies' success in North Africa—which campaign was, in any case, now to be pursued to its conclusion—should provide the springboard for an invasion of Sicily, prior to the direct attack of Italy with the strategic aim of forcing that country out of the war. In any case, the British chiefs of staff pointed out, the forces that had by then been deployed to North Africa could not now reasonably be used for a cross-Channel operation in 1943,[1] and therefore their use for an invasion of Sicily was the best option. Marshall, albeit reluctantly, accepted the logic of this argument and gave the plan his support. This first step toward continental Europe would be codenamed Operation "Husky."

The U.S. position with regard to the second front and way ahead in the Mediterranean may not have been accepted, but the American negotiators were more successful in reopening the issue of the war against Japan. Although it was still understood that an increase in Allied activity in the Pacific and Far East should not be allowed to compromise any unexpected opportunity to defeat Germany in 1943, the British, having secured agreement to Operation "Husky," were forced to agree an increase in the tempo of the war with Japan. This would include upgrading U.S. air support for the Chinese forces, including a significant increase in the transport of matériel by air to China from India over the Himalayas ("The Hump"). A new campaign to recapture Burma in 1943 was also mooted and provisionally agreed, but subsequently this was much curtailed for practical reasons. Finally, despite British concerns, the U.S. team argued with some justification that it was necessary to take action against the Japanese forces in the Pacific, and in the Philippines especially, before they became too well established. Notwithstanding a possible diminution of U.S. maritime support for the European and Mediterranean theaters, this argument was militarily sound and laid the foundation of the Allies' (but predominantly American) Pacific naval and amphibious campaign of "island hopping" which began with the hard-won victory at Guadalcanal and finally took the Allies on to Japanese sovereign territory at Okinawa. It also facilitated the eventual success of the British campaign in Burma. Consequently, the Casablanca conference represented the point in the war at which the original prioritization accorded the cross-Channel second front was modified somewhat, as Churchill's long-held aspiration to launch an invasion into Italy came to fruition, and the similarly long-held U.S. aspiration to take substantive offensive action against the Japanese was agreed.

At Casablanca, Roosevelt, Churchill, and the Anglo-U.S. staffs also dealt with the way ahead for the cross-Channel operation and related matters. It was agreed that the security of the sealanes to Britain remained the highest priority. Upon this depended the success of the cross-Channel invasion, irrespective of when it might actually take place. It was noted that, as at the end of 1942, the losses of Allied shipping had exceeded new construction by some one million tons and that this situation was a serious constraint on the Allies' offensive capability. Closely linked to this, it was confirmed that the existing commitments and arrangements to provide the Soviet Union with matériel would be maintained. In furtherance of their earlier commitment to increase the scale of air attacks on Germany, it was agreed that the strategic bombing campaign should now be conducted on a twenty-four-hour basis, with the RAF bombing Germany by night and the U.S. Army Air Forces (USAAF)[2] bombing the country by day.[3] Finally, planning and preparation for the cross-Channel invasion moved ahead at Casablanca. While the existing commitment to the general buildup of U.S. forces in Great Britain as a matter of priority was reaffirmed, the summit also directed the establishment of a joint Anglo-U.S. planning group (titled Chiefs of Staff, Supreme Allied Command, or COSSAC) in London with the task of planning the invasion of northern France, whether on an opportunity basis in 1943, or as a major planned operation in 1944. Although the overall principle of the cross-Channel invasion was of course not new, the setting up of COSSAC was the first tangible step toward its achievement and paved the way for the development of the command structure that would direct the Allied landings in France in June 1944.

It was probably helpful to their progress at Casablanca that Roosevelt and Churchill had not been joined by Stalin. Had the Soviet leader been present at what would have been a first meeting of the "Big Three," it is probable that a debate about the location and timing of the second front would have overshadowed all else. As it was, the summary of conference deliberations and decisions sent jointly to Stalin by the two Western leaders told on the one hand of their intentions in the Mediterranean and Pacific, while on the other still indicating the possibility of a cross-Channel invasion in August or September 1943. Although such an invasion might have taken place in the event that Germany had comprehensively collapsed from within, in practice to suggest that it might yet be mounted in 1943 was little short of blatant deception; and yet this was undoubtedly necessary in order to placate Stalin and so preserve the strength of the Alliance.

Although Stalin's reaction to the outcome of Casablanca was no more or less critical of Anglo-U.S. intentions than had been so in earlier days, and the Allies' progress against the Germans in North Africa was undeniable, by mid-March his concerns and suspicions were once again very apparent. There was little evidence that either the campaign in North Africa or the forthcoming invasion of Sicily were drawing German divisions away from the eastern front; in fact, Stalin informed the two Western leaders that the German high command had just reinforced its forces there. With some two hundred Axis divisions—among them some of the best German and Italian combat troops—engaged against the Soviet army, Stalin's position was perhaps less favorable than his allies judged it to be. Certainly he resisted all U.S. attempts to gain direct Soviet military support against the Japanese. He was also probably very aware that those in Washington who favored a massive increase in the Allied effort in the Pacific would not have been disappointed if their overtures to the Soviets and suggestion that Japan was about to attack Siberia had precipitated just such an attack, thereby leaving Stalin no option but to enter the war against Japan.

The situation for the Allies worsened at the end of March, when a combination of inadequate merchant tonnage, a lack of available warships for convoy escort duty, the need to build up resources for Operation "Husky," and a significant strengthening of the German fleet at Narvik together forced a suspension of the convoys to Russia until September. Remarkably, but due primarily to the closely coordinated way in which this bad news was passed to Stalin by Roosevelt and Churchill, the Soviet leader accepted the situation with fairly good grace. However, as at the end of March 1943, he still clung to the belief that a cross-Channel invasion was a definite possibility for August or September that year. Had he been present at Casablanca, there is little doubt that Stalin would have quickly understood that this was simply not practicable; but, although the Alliance held true, the meeting of minds between the war leaders had still only been possible bilaterally, and it would not be until the final months of 1943 that the "Big Three" would finally meet as an entity. Before then, Stalin would learn that his aspiration for a second front in northern Europe in 1943 was, and in practice always had been, a nonstarter.

Following Casablanca, much intermediate work and negotiation was carried out by the Allies. This included Churchill's visit to Turkey for the Adana conference immediately after the Casablanca summit, when the prime minister met the Turkish leaders with a view to bringing Turkey into the war on the Allied side. However, the Adana meeting did not go as Churchill had hoped, and an assurance of Turkey's continued neutrality was the best that he could achieve.[4] Subsequent to Casablanca also was Anthony Eden's visit to Washington from March 12 to 30, when the British foreign secretary engaged in a detailed consideration of many of the key issues and principles that had emerged during the earlier summits and at Casablanca. In addition to his meetings with Roosevelt, Eden discussed these matters with Harry Hopkins and Sumner Welles, the latter of whom represented, and provided a conduit to, the U.S. state department. Interestingly, Eden's U.S. equivalent, Cordell Hull, rarely attended these sessions, but did conduct separate meetings with Eden. Hull's view of the postwar world exemplified the American line on international security and the future of the prewar European colonies which had already been exposed in the Atlantic Charter, and the British foreign secretary soon found himself under considerable pressure to agree to concepts that would have involved all matters of importance in the postwar world being dominated by the United States, the Soviet Union, Great Britain, and China. France was notable by its absence, and relegation to secondary-power status or less by Hull. In parallel with this, the old colonies would be enabled to proceed to independence, under a process that would, presumably, be regulated and overseen by the same four powers.[5]

The U.S. secretary of state's exposition on the future political shape and management of the world showed the extent of Washington's belief that it would be able to work effectively with the Soviet Union after the war, together with a view of China that of course preceded the communist revolution and Chinese civil war from 1945 to 1949. Not surprisingly, Eden, ever the diplomat, indicated broad agreement in principle while expressing various reservations over the detail of that which was put to him. These talks were broad-ranging, and covered the minutiae of the future international scene as envisaged by London and Washington. Predictably perhaps, given the functions of those ministers involved, the thrust of these talks was political rather than military; therefore, Eden's time in Washington that March tended to complement the war summits by broadening Anglo-U.S. awareness of each other's international perspectives and agendas, rather than adding significantly to the conduct of the war.[6]

Following Eden's visit to Washington and the announcement to Stalin of the unavoidable suspension of Anglo-U.S. aid by sea to Russia, Churchill judged that the time had come for another face-to-face meeting with the president. Accordingly, on April 29, he suggested that he and his military advisors should once again journey across the Atlantic to meet Roosevelt in Washington. Thus was born the next of the war summits, and this, the "Trident" conference, was scheduled to begin on May 12. On this occasion, Churchill traveled across the Atlantic in style aboard the *Queen Mary*, accompanied by the chiefs of staff and by Lord Beaverbrook among his other advisors.

9

Sicily, Italy, and the Second Front

The "Trident" Conference, May 12–25, 1943

T HE "TRIDENT" CONFERENCE advanced the Allies' planning
for the next year of the war and at the same time threatened the
cohesion of the Alliance because of the implications, or
perceived implications, of its outcome for the Soviet Union. The meeting
began on May 12, which coincided with the receipt of Eisenhower's
report that the Allies' campaign in Tunisia had been successfully
completed. Some one hundred and sixty thousand Axis prisoners were
in Allied hands, and, for the British, the benefits of reinforcing their
successes in the Mediterranean theater by concentrating on eliminating
Italy from the Axis appeared irresistible, despite U.S. reticence over any
move to carry the campaign beyond Sicily (and possibly Sardinia). Yet
again, it was argued, an invasion of the southern European mainland
would distract from the cross-Channel assault that all agreed must now
take place in 1944.

For Churchill and his military chiefs, the practical benefits of
launching a full-scale invasion of Italy once Sicily was in Allied hands
were both clear and achievable. Furthermore, Churchill argued, this
extension of the Mediterranean campaign would not affect the ability of
the Allies to invade northern France in 1944. With Italy removed from
the war, the Germans would have to weaken their forces elsewhere in
order to shore up their southern-flank defenses and to replace the
Italian units then operating in the Balkans. These enforced redeploy-
ments could also benefit the Soviets, as German formations would probably also need to be removed from the eastern front. The neutralization
of Italian naval power in the Mediterranean would enable RN warships
to redeploy to the Pacific and Far East theater, a matter that was, no
doubt, very much in Churchill's mind following a military conference on

the Pacific campaign that had taken place in mid-March. Similarly, following the less than satisfactory outcome of his meetings with the Turkish government at Adana in January, Churchill believed that Italy's defeat might yet induce Turkey to enter the war on the Allies' side. Finally, in addition to all the wider political and strategic arguments, the simple fact remained that the most efficient use of the considerable assets that the Allies now had in North Africa was their continued use in the Mediterranean theater.

Predictably, "Trident" produced a strategic planning compromise, but one that did, nevertheless, permit the military chiefs to develop their future operations. Significantly, "Trident" set a date of May 1, 1944, for the Anglo-U.S. invasion of northern France. Remarkably, as events turned out in 1944, this date was delayed only by a few weeks in fact. The Americans regarded the May 1 date as inviolable, although the British viewed the commitment as flexible and negotiable if circumstances merited it. Based on all that had gone before, these different views were entirely to be expected; but, in practice, they were not mutually exclusive. Setting a firm date allowed COSSAC to move forward its planning against clear timelines, although if major, unforeseen obstacles to the invasion had arisen prior to the summer of 1944 it is inconceivable that Roosevelt and the J.C.S. would have allowed the invasion (now codenamed Operation "Overlord") to proceed irrespective of these factors.

Next, Eisenhower was directed to plan for offensive action against Italy as soon as Sicily was secure, as well as expanding the Allies' air campaign against Germany's southern flank and in the Balkans. While it might seem that the British line had thus been entirely accepted, seven of the Allies' divisions currently in the Mediterranean theater were debarred from further involvement there after November 1, 1943, when they were earmarked for redeployment to Operation "Overlord." This constraint would subsequently limit the extent and effectiveness of Allied operations in Italy. As always, the directive to Eisenhower stipulated that his operations were not to be allowed to prejudice preparations for the cross-Channel invasion. Although an expansion of the U.S.-led campaign against Japan in the Pacific was endorsed at "Trident," the continued close control of the combined chiefs of staff over this campaign would ensure that the invasion of northwest Europe remained the principal focus of the Allies' plans and resources.

In order to explain his concept and the need for an invasion of Italy with the men who would be required to implement it, Churchill flew from Washington to meet with the key Allied military commanders at Eisenhower's headquarters in Algiers on May 29. At Churchill's request, General Marshall accompanied him to this meeting, which was attended on the British side by Gens Alan Brooke, Alexander, and Montgomery, plus Admiral Cunningham and Air Marshal Tedder. Eden was also present throughout, while the French Generals de Gaulle, Giraud, and Catroux also attended certain of the discussions, which were of course taking place on territory that Paris had always regarded as part of metropolitan France.[1] The Algiers meeting ended on June 3, with Churchill confident that his case for the invasion of Italy had been well made, and that it would subsequently be matched by the appropriate action.

Although Marshall still had reservations about the Italian campaign, he did not frustrate Churchill's briefing and, given the close relationship between Marshall and Eisenhower, the prime minister had once again demonstrated his political acumen and willingness to take a calculated risk in having General Marshall with him in Algiers. Certainly his presence—and, therefore, Roosevelt's implied endorsement of that which Churchill presented—would have been duly noted by Eisenhower and the other U.S. personnel present. However, just as matters seemed set fair for the Alliance following the "Trident" conference, other events combined with one particular aspect of its outcome to threaten the harmonious relations that had obtained between the Western allies and their Soviet partner ever since Churchill's first visit to Moscow in August the previous year, the difficulties over the Arctic convoys notwithstanding. Predictably, the aspect of "Trident" that created the potential for this disunity was the Anglo-U.S. plan to engage Italy directly and to delay the cross-Channel invasion until mid-1944 in consequence; and Stalin's criticism of this plan came just as Roosevelt was attempting to engineer a face-to-face meeting with the Soviet leader.

For some time the president had been very aware of the fact that Churchill had already managed to establish a personal rapport with Stalin during his visit to Moscow the previous August, and although Churchill and Stalin had certainly achieved a sound mutual understanding, Roosevelt was convinced that he could achieve an even better meeting of minds with the Soviet leader, especially on a one-to-one basis. While Roosevelt and his advisors may also have believed that, in contrast to Great Britain, the United States was losing ground in its dealings with Stalin, some officials in Washington also believed that the president's close relationship with the British prime minister had resulted in Churchill exerting an excessive influence over Roosevelt. If this were true, it might be countered and balanced by the development of a similar level of personal relationship between Stalin and Roosevelt. In view of all this, in May Roosevelt had dispatched Joseph E. Davies, an ambassador to the Soviet Union in the 1930s and a man with strong leanings toward the Soviets and their leaders, to prepare the way for the president to meet Stalin informally, possibly on either the Soviet or U.S. side of the Bering Strait—a deliberate device that would make Churchill's attendance impracticable.

Notwithstanding a remarkably inept presentation of his pro-Soviet case and Roosevelt's proposal for the bilateral meeting, Davies secured from Stalin agreement in principle, but no firm commitment. As ever, Stalin made his ability to meet Roosevelt consequent upon the progress of the Red Army on the eastern front, which of course, in its turn, depended upon the level of Anglo-U.S. material aid and, more importantly, upon the cross-Channel invasion that Stalin still believed would take place in late summer or fall of 1943. It was no accident that Stalin intimated to Davies that a meeting with Roosevelt might be possible in July or August. Although no firm date had been set, Roosevelt was satisfied with the progress that Davies had made during his short time in Moscow. However, just then, during the first week of June, the news of the "Trident" planning decisions reached Stalin. His reaction was unsurprising and robust, and it set back much of the work already accomplished—by Churchill in particular—to soften his views on the second-front issue. However, given that Roosevelt and Churchill had deliberately allowed the prospect of a cross-Channel invasion in 1943 to perpetuate in their dealings with the Soviets (whether or not Stalin truly believed this was operationally viable), the storm that now broke within the Alliance was probably inevitable.

Despite a very carefully crafted summary of the "Trident" decisions having been sent to Moscow—but nonetheless one that was accurate and fully argued—Stalin now accused the Western allies of a deliberate act of bad faith and of having ignored entirely his pleas and arguments for the second front in northern France. While a flurry of heated messages and the equally heated responses to them flowed back and forth between the Allies, on June 25 Churchill expressed to Averell Harriman in London his personal reservations about Roosevelt's attempts to set up a bilateral U.S.-Soviet meeting with Stalin. No doubt he saw his own influence threatened, not least because he knew that many in Washington concurred with Stalin's views about the need for an early cross-Channel invasion. If Roosevelt adopted the Soviet line, all Churchill's plans for Italy and the Balkans might be thrown entirely into disarray. Having considered the matter further, the prime minister proposed a compromise solution that might both prepare the way for a meeting of Roosevelt and Stalin, or indeed of all three leaders, while at the same time clearing up the matters of concern that were then causing such friction between the Allies. He suggested that a working-level meeting of the three foreign ministers, Molotov, Hull, and Eden, should first take place, in order that an historic meeting between all or some of the "Big Three" should not be marred by such potentially difficult and divisive matters.

Earlier that month the Alliance's affairs had been further compounded by Molotov's agreement with de Gaulle at a meeting in London that the Soviet government would henceforth recognize de Gaulle's faction as representative of the French republic—a pronouncement soon followed by a declaration by the French communist resistance movement of its support for de Gaulle and the Free French. This move in June 1943 was not a new departure for Moscow, as its formal links with de Gaulle had been developing ever since September 1941, when the Soviets had disassociated themselves from the Vichy regime.

However, despite Soviet pressure, neither Churchill nor Roosevelt trusted de Gaulle's motives. They therefore refused to follow the Soviet line, and did not accord his faction full and exclusive Anglo-U.S. recognition at that stage. Perhaps sensing that any further disharmony within the Alliance was wholly undesirable, and in the knowledge that there was, in any case, no urgency to settle the French issue, Stalin acquiesced—on the understanding that Moscow should be kept informed of, and fully involved in, any subsequent developments.

The early summer of 1943 was a watershed for the Alliance, for it marked a low point in the relations between the two Western allies and their Soviet partner. It also temporarily revealed some divergence of perception between Churchill and Roosevelt. However, the Anglo-U.S. Alliance was already too strong to be shaken by such matters, and Churchill, very aware of the vital need for continued Anglo-U.S. unity, ensured that his bond with Roosevelt remained as strong as ever. Meanwhile, what had from the outset been the greatest stumbling block to the unity of the Alliance and the cause of endless controversy both between Washington and London and between the Western allies and Moscow had finally and definitively been exposed to all parties, and thus had henceforth to be accepted as a fact. Although the cross-Channel invasion would not now be launched into northern France in 1943, it had been firmly—irrevocably, in U.S. eyes—scheduled for May 1, 1944. In the meantime, a spirited campaign in Sicily and Italy would eliminate Italy from the Axis and, hopefully, cause substantial numbers of German forces to be diverted from operations on the eastern front and in the Balkans to meet the new threat now posed to them from across the Mediterranean. While all this fell far short of the hopes, aspirations, and demands expressed by Stalin ever since August of 1941, he had little choice other than to accept the decisions taken in Washington at the "Trident" conference, together with the Anglo-U.S. policy concerning French issues. No doubt he sensed that this was not the time to risk the cohesion of an alliance that was, albeit slowly, at last moving toward a final victory over the Axis powers. Moreover, this victory would subsequently enable the Soviet Union not only to eject the German invaders from Soviet territory and punish the nation that had attacked Russia twice within the previous three decades, but also to achieve an even greater prize—Soviet communist domination of the greater part of postwar eastern Europe.

So it was that the Alliance's crisis of May to early July 1943 was generally overcome, as the "Big Three" once again looked to deal with the more immediate matters of defeating Germany, Italy, and Japan, with all three leaders confident in the knowledge that, by mid-1944, British and U.S. ground forces in very substantial numbers should, from that time, be fighting their way toward Hitler's Germany from the landing beaches of northern France.

10
Italy, the Pacific, and Operation "Overlord"
The "Quadrant" Conference, August 14–24, 1943

O N JULY 9, 1943, Allied forces stormed into Sicily in accordance with the plans that had been developed for Operation "Husky" following the Casablanca summit. The island was soon subdued, and, on July 25, Benito Mussolini, *Il Duce*, was deposed as the Italian head of state. This augured well for an invasion of the Italian mainland, and tended to reinforce Churchill's long-standing aspiration for Anglo-U.S. forces to embark upon a full-scale offensive in Italy—one that would at the very least secure its capital, Rome, for the Allies—and so remove that country from both the Axis and the war. However, in Washington, the usual reservations about any action that might bear adversely upon the cross-Channel invasion existed still; and it must be said that, as of July 1943, there was still only one complete U.S. division in Britain, much effort and many resources having already been deployed to support operations in the Mediterranean theater. Nevertheless, when Eisenhower proposed an amphibious landing at Salerno near Naples as the next stage after a successful conclusion of the Sicily campaign, the J.C.S. and Roosevelt approved this plan and also authorized an increase of U.S. forces for this new operation of some sixty-six thousand men. However, Churchill's attempts to increase these numbers even more, and to retain in the Mediterranean those forces that, it had been agreed at the "Trident" summit, would be released to Operation "Overlord" from November 1, 1943, were unsuccessful.

Thus, with Mussolini deposed, an invasion of mainland Italy imminent, and a clear timeframe for the preparation of the cross-Channel invasion in being, it was once more time for Churchill and Roosevelt and their respective staffs and advisors to meet. Yet again the British team headed across the Atlantic, this time to Quebec in Canada, for a war summit that bore the codename "Quadrant." Once again the party embarked on the *Queen Mary* for the voyage to Halifax, Nova Scotia, and this time the prime minister was accompanied aboard by his wife, Clementine, and daughter, Mary. Once in North America, the British delegation traveled on to Quebec by train. In the meantime, the chiefs of staff had moved there ahead of the Churchills, who carried out various other engagements before attending the latter part of the conference with Roosevelt. By then, their respective military staffs had analyzed and assessed the global military situation and were thus able to provide the necessary advice and recommendations to the two leaders once they had arrived in Quebec.

In the European theater, the overriding priority for the Allies remained Operation "Overlord." Although Churchill's former caveats[1] and notes of caution over the timing and form of the invasion were rehearsed yet again, the Americans were in no doubt that nothing should be allowed to affect the May 1, 1944, date, and it was clearly stated at "Quadrant" that resources would be allocated to "Overlord" even at the expense of future operations in the Mediterranean. Nothing was to be allowed to prejudice or delay Washington's goal of the invasion of France in mid-1944, and, for the purposes of COSSAC's planning, an Allied invasion force of some twenty-nine divisions was agreed at Quebec. While a repetition of the unequivocal U.S. line on this issue was entirely predictable, the real significance of its restatement was the commitment of Roosevelt, Marshall, Stimson, and the J.C.S. to a position and policy that had remained generally unaffected ever since the "Arcadia" summit, and which had, if anything, hardened in light of recent Allied successes. The line between maintenance of the aim and a flexible approach is always finely balanced in strategic matters, but Churchill might perhaps have been forgiven if the thought crossed his mind at the "Quadrant" meeting that some of his U.S. allies lacked his wider international vision—a vision that he had learned to understand from the inherited experience and study of some three hundred years of British national, imperial, and international history. Certainly, the collapse of Italy and the prospect of the former Axis state becoming a member of the Allies could open up a multiplicity of opportunities.

Nevertheless, the U.S. focus on the need for the cross-Channel invasion in order to defeat Germany was unequivocal, and there was a continuing need for Stalin, in particular, to hear this message time and again and not doubt its veracity, if the cohesion of the Alliance was to remain intact—and if his intentions toward postwar eastern Europe were not to be thwarted by a major Allied thrust into southern Europe via Italy and onward into Austria, the Balkans, and the heart of Germany itself, with the Soviet army still holding a line against the bulk of the Wehrmacht far to the east, on Russian territory. Such possibilities need not have concerned Stalin, for "Quadrant" limited the scope of future operations in the Mediterranean to the capture of Rome and the islands of Corsica and Sardinia, to be followed in mid-1944 by an Allied landing in southern France to complement the main "Overlord" landings in the north. Indeed, the massive commitment of Allied maritime assets to "Overlord" and to the Pacific meant that operations in the Mediterranean realistically could never have displaced the cross-Channel invasion, other than in the event of an entirely unexpected and sudden collapse of the Nazi regime in Germany.

But Europe was by no means the only theater of war considered at the "Quadrant" summit: the two leaders and their delegations also considered the future development of the war in the Pacific, the Far East, and China, and set a target of victory over Japan within one year of the defeat of Germany. The next stage of Gen. Douglas MacArthur's ongoing "island-hopping" campaign—a progressive series of interrelated amphibious actions—was also endorsed by the summit. This would take the U.S. forces ever nearer to their goal of recapturing the Philippines, then toward the various Japanese island territories, and finally, by mid-1945, to the two main islands that comprised the Japanese mainland. "Quadrant" also endorsed the decisions taken at "Trident" for an offensive in Burma and a substantial increase in the amount of aid provided to Chiang Kai-shek's forces in China. However, for practical reasons, Churchill had already expressed his reservations about these particular matters, and in due course they were in many cases extensively modified or rescheduled.[2]

Indeed, apart from one very significant aspect, the "Quadrant" summit was in many respects a review and endorsement of the "Trident" conference, rather than a war summit notable for any new initiatives or policies. The one very significant aspect which was not exposed to wider scrutiny was the signing by the two leaders on August 19 of the Quebec agreement on the "matter of tube alloys"—the Anglo-U.S. agreement on the vital subject of the development of the atomic bomb.[3] By this top-secret agreement both countries agreed to collaborate jointly in the production of the atomic weapon—the innocuously titled "tube alloys" of the title—and laid down their joint policy for its future use and control. It was agreed that the United States and Great Britain would never use these weapons against each other, nor against third parties without each other's consent. This meant that the United States and Great Britain had, in effect, agreed that each had a veto over the use of atomic weapons by the other. Furthermore, neither nation would permit the communication of information about atomic weapons to third parties without each other's permission.[4] Looking to the future, both parties also agreed that the policy for and parameters of the subsequent exploitation of atomic power should be determined by both jointly. Finally, the agreement specified the arrangements—including the estab-lishment and composition of a supervisory combined policy committee—to ensure "full and effective collaboration between the two countries in bringing the project to fruition." Understandably, this agree-ment received none of the exposure that had been accorded to the other issues dealt with at "Quadrant"; nevertheless, the significance of the Anglo-U.S. commitment jointly to produce the atomic weapon with all dispatch was enormous. Its successful outcome would in due course not only bring about a speedy end to the war with Japan, but it would subsequently provide the atomic (and later nuclear) threat that domi-nated "Cold War" strategy from 1945 to 1990, and which today still represents a major threat to the peace and security of nuclear and nonnuclear nation states alike.

However, apart from such weighty affairs of strategy and policy, it might be added that the "Quadrant" summit also fulfilled a quite sepa-rate, but nonetheless important, purpose. In the course and aftermath of the conference, Churchill, who had experienced a bout of pneumonia in late February 1943, and upon whom the punishing program of meetings and travel was already exerting its toll, took time to rest and recuperate during a short fishing holiday at Snow Lake in Canada. Prior to the conference, the Churchills had also taken time out to visit Niagara Falls and the Roosevelts in the United States. Thus, suitably refreshed and ready for the next phase of the Allies' war, Churchill once again returned to Britain, this time aboard HMS *Renown*.

With Sicily secure—notwithstanding the fact that most of the German defenders of the island had withdrawn successfully to the Italian mainland—between September 3 and 18 the Allies launched their anticipated assault on the Italian peninsula. From September 3, British forces landed in the Gulf of Taranto, while the main landings took place at Salerno from September 9. The subsequent battle to establish the beachheads lasted until September 18. In fact, the Italian government had already signed an armistice on September 3, although this fact was not made public until the eighth. The momentous events in Italy were seen by Churchill as a vindication of his earlier beliefs and urgings, and so they provided a tailpiece to what had been one of the major areas of Allied operations.

For the British prime minister, this collapse of the Italian fascist regime was encouragement for his concept of striking toward Germany from the south. At a stroke, Churchill saw an opportunity for the Allies to undercut Axis influence in the Balkans, in Hungary, in Romania, in Bulgaria, in Greece, and in Yugoslavia. Consequently, full of enthusiasm, at a meeting in Washington at the end of the first week of September he suggested that Allied successes could now bring about a crumbling of Axis authority in these countries just as they had in Italy, and that—just as he hoped would be so in Italy—the forces of these nations could be turned and employed in the Allied cause against Nazi Germany. However, despite the energy and certainty with which he stated the pressing need for the Allies to exploit the potentially enormous gains that might now be derived from events in the Mediterranean region, the U.S. military leadership remained unmoved in their resolve not to increase the scope of Allied involvement in that theater. Moreover, with each week that now passed, the sheer scale of the U.S. war effort was increasing the strength of American influence over Allied policy. Consequently, the principal focus was to remain, as ever, the Anglo-U.S. cross-Channel venture in mid-1944. The ongoing Italian campaign was of secondary importance, and a possible opportunity to change not only the course of the war to the Allies' advantage but also the future political status of much of postwar Europe was rejected by the U.S. military decision-makers in Washington.

In any event, such a visible diversion of the military power of the Western allies and an apparent abrogation in respect of Italy and other Axis powers of the concept of "unconditional surrender" espoused by Roosevelt and Churchill at Casablanca would certainly not have found favor with Stalin. Indeed, at the very end of the meeting in Quebec, a message was received from Stalin indicating his displeasure at the way in which the U.S. and British authorities had been negotiating, without Soviet input or involvement, a suitable armistice with the post-Mussolini Italian government of Gen. Pietro Badoglio. To reinforce his point, Stalin proposed the establishment of a new military-political commission of the three allied powers specifically to deal with issues involving the defection of Axis governments in the future.

Perhaps Stalin was to some extent justified in feeling excluded by his allies, but Moscow had been fully apprised of all that was happening in the Mediterranean region—both the political and the military events—and, in any case, these particular Anglo-U.S. successes were of relatively little strategic consequence to a nation that had, between July 5 and August 23, fought the Germans to a standstill during the Kursk-Orel campaign, and so ended the last great German offensive on the eastern front. Kursk was the greatest tank battle of the war, and the German panzer divisions lost some six hundred tanks during the first week of the battle alone, many of these being destroyed by the large numbers of Il-2 Shturmovik ground-attack fighters that were by then available to the reorganized, reinvigorated, and greatly reinforced Soviet air force. Then, on August 26, the Soviets launched a major new offensive along a front that ran from Smolensk to Rostov, and in the Caucasus and the Crimea—an offensive that was sustained successfully for the next nine weeks. By the end of the year, Smolensk in the north and Kiev in the south were once more in Soviet hands. This was war-fighting on the grand scale. How relatively insignificant must the Anglo-U.S. capture of Sicily and an Allied landing in Italy have seemed from Moscow's standpoint as, across the vastnesses of Russia, hundreds of divisions of armor and infantry were locked in a desperate and titanic struggle for supremacy and survival—a struggle that, it was now increasingly clear, would eventually be won by the Red Army, almost irrespective of whether or not the Western allies provided the second front that remained, nevertheless, the main focus of Stalin's dialog with his American and British allies.

So it was that by the late fall of 1943 the differing natures and scale of the military campaigns being waged by the Anglo-U.S. forces and those of their Soviet allies were, in practice, quite marked. To underline (and, possibly, provide a degree of justification for) Stalin's ongoing, perhaps obsessive preoccupation with the second-front issue, from Moscow's standpoint the strategic impact of the Anglo-U.S. military operations thus far no doubt appeared to be relatively limited; except inasmuch as their continued matériel support remained essential to the Soviet war effort. Indeed, while a Soviet collapse would undoubtedly have severely prejudiced the outcome of a cross-Channel invasion by releasing many German divisions for redeployment to France,[5] the real effect of the Allies' Italian campaign on the battles then in progress in Russia was not great; although, in a message to Roosevelt and Churchill on September 14, Stalin did acknowledge the successful Anglo-U.S. landings at Salerno, together with the significance of the detachment of Italy from Germany. Only a successful cross-Channel invasion of France had the potential to draw German divisions away from Russia, and force a significant refocusing and dilution of the Wehrmacht's matériel resources to meet the threat posed on two widely separated fronts, and it was this fundamental truth that lay at the heart of Stalin's argument for the operation.

Meanwhile, as the Red Army continued its westward advance on a broad front, as Anglo-U.S. forces developed their plans to capture Rome, and as planning for the much-discussed cross-Channel operation moved ahead apace, the subject of a summit of the "Big Three" was raised once again. The need for Roosevelt, Churchill, and Stalin to meet together rather than bilaterally was being driven by events, especially by the various political issues that were now arising with increasing frequency concerning the dismemberment and crumbling of the Axis. Only if the participants came face to face could a meeting of minds come about, and, at least, a fuller understanding of the relative positions and imperatives of the "Big Three" be facilitated. Quite apart from the many strategic and political matters that required resolution, the separate experiences of the Soviet Union, Great Britain, and the United States in the war thus far had been very different.

The Soviet Union had been invaded, many of its towns and cities besieged and laid waste, and millions of its citizens killed. In the meantime, Great Britain had been severely damaged by Luftwaffe bombing attacks, while it had also suffered the ignominy of the BEF's ejection from France in 1940 and the loss of many of its imperial possessions to the Japanese in the Far East from 1941. However, with the exception of the German occupation of the Channel Islands, none of the territory that comprised Great Britain had experienced an enemy invasion or occupation; and Hitler's decision to abandon Operation "Seelöwe" (Sealion) meant that the resurrection of this operation was now unachievable (so long as the campaign on the eastern front continued). The experiences of the Soviet Union since mid-1942, and of Great Britain and the British Empire since early 1940, contrasted with those of the United States, a country geographically secure from invasion and which had suffered a significant direct air assault on U.S. territory only in the distant Pacific islands of Hawaii in December 1941. Apart from U.S. involvement with the Atlantic convoys, throughout 1942 the American military focus had been on countering the Japanese in the Pacific theater, and it was only with the "Torch" landings in North Africa in November 1942 that U.S. ground forces had at last become fully engaged against the Axis forces in the west. With such divergent recent histories, and experiences of the war, it was inevitable that the perspectives of the three national leaders were colored and influenced by that which their countries had experienced and by their secondhand perceptions of the experiences of their allies.

While the frequent meetings already achieved by Roosevelt and Churchill meant that any sort of misunderstanding between these two was virtually nonexistent, between Stalin and his Anglo-U.S. partners, divided as they were by ideology and culture, there was undoubtedly a gulf of misperception and suspicion which needed to be bridged if the Alliance were to hold together and achieve its objectives. As Roosevelt and Churchill had already proved time and again, personal contact at the highest level was the key, and the time was now fast approaching when a trilateral summit involving all of the leaders would be essential if the Alliance were to remain intact, if it were to fulfill its short-term purpose of defeating the Axis powers—and, just as importantly, if its leaders were eventually to achieve a workable and equitable policy for managing security in Europe and in the wider postwar world.

Accordingly, just as American and British soldiers were preparing to land at Salerno on September 8, Stalin at last acquiesced in Roosevelt's and Churchill's urging of such a meeting. Prior to then, the Soviet leader had indicated that he was unable to leave the Soviet Union owing to the combat situation on the eastern front, and a meeting of foreign ministers in Moscow had been scheduled for late October in lieu of a "Big Three" summit. However, thanks to rapidly improving Soviet fortunes, Stalin now felt able to change his mind. Roosevelt had proposed a November meeting, which date Stalin agreed, although he was not prepared to travel further than Persia. Thus, at long last—almost two years after the United States had entered the war, and almost two and a half years since Churchill and Roosevelt had met at Placentia Bay and set in train the program of aid to Russia—formal planning for what would be the first of the "Big Three" summits began. However, with such a momentous meeting in prospect, it was prudent to clear as much of the lesser business beforehand as possible. Consequently, it fell to the three countries' respective foreign ministers to deal with a number of these matters in Moscow during October, and then for Roosevelt and Churchill and their chiefs of staff to gather in Cairo immediately prior to what became the Tehran summit, in order to agree upon and coordinate the Western allies' approach before the "Big Three" finally met in Tehran at the end of November 1943.

11
Toward the Power of Three
Moscow and Cairo, October to November 1943

THE TEHRAN SUMMIT ranks as one of the defining meetings of World War II, together with Placentia Bay, "Arcadia," and Casablanca, and, much later, with Yalta and Potsdam. The fact that it at long last brought together all of the "Big Three" leaders was but one historic aspect of this meeting, and as such it demonstrated the coming together of minds that was the great strength of the Allies—notwithstanding the enormous political and ideological differences that characterized the Soviet Union vis-à-vis its Western allies—compared with the lack of any such close harmony that had existed between the Axis leaders. The genuine unity of purpose and approach demonstrated by Roosevelt, Stalin, and Churchill at Tehran sent a clear and an unequivocal message to the Allied nations, the neutral countries and the Axis powers alike. But, quite apart from such presentational messages, the Tehran conference, together with the complementary meetings of the foreign ministers and of Churchill and Roosevelt just before the "Big Three" summit, dealt with, and resolved, a number of key and potentially difficult issues that had been raised during the previous eighteen months or so. The Tehran summit, together with the various discussions that immediately preceded it, was indeed a defining moment in the history of World War II.

The Meeting of Foreign Ministers in Moscow

Just as important, in its own way, as the "Big Three" summit was the meeting in Moscow of Eden, Hull, and Molotov that took place from October 18 to 30. Foo Ping-sheung, the Chinese foreign minister, also attended this meeting. Although the gathering was essentially political rather than military in nature (albeit that several specifically military issues were also dealt with), by late 1943 political and military matters had become virtually indivisible at the strategic level.

As well as their detailed deliberations on the specifics of the political road to victory and the subsequent management of the postwar world, the ministers advanced the process begun by Churchill and Roosevelt at Placentia Bay with a further consideration and amplification of the principles that should inform and direct these actions. Secretary of state Cordell Hull had come to Moscow with proposed draft texts for a declaration which he hoped would be endorsed by all of the Allies. The preparatory work on these had already been approved by Roosevelt and Churchill, although a preliminary draft forwarded to Moscow had not been received with much enthusiasm. Nevertheless, Eden believed that the U.S. proposals did provide a useful start point for the upcoming meetings. Predictably, the draft declaration reflected the broad thoughts already espoused by Roosevelt and Churchill concerning national self-determination and the need for a coherent system of international security postwar—one in which the United States, the Soviet Union and Britain would have a leading role.

In the course of discussion, Hull's proposed declaration underwent some modification, in the main in order to satisfy Soviet concerns about aspects of the original text. The phrase that implied exclusive domination of the postwar world by the United States, the Soviet Union, Great Britain, and China was removed. Text that could have been interpreted as permitting each signatory a right of veto over bilateral security arrangements subsequently carried out by each with lesser states either during or after the war was edited out, as was a clause that might have seen Allied forces occupying, as of right, parts of the territories that had been liberated by each others' forces—a most unlikely situation in practice, but one that could nevertheless have created huge political difficulties if implemented. In addition, what finally became known as the Declaration of the Four Nations on General Security reaffirmed the existing broad principles for the conduct of the war by the Allies and their interaction with the Axis powers, while carefully avoiding any specific policy direction on the issue of postwar frontiers in Europe. While Eden's experience and diplomacy were evident throughout, the ministers' meetings were dominated by Stalin's future agenda and his singleminded aspirations for the Soviet Union and eastern Europe, expressed through Molotov, and by the U.S. national interest and Washington's idealized view of the nature of international relations and security in the postwar world, expressed and strongly promoted by Cordell Hull. China was viewed by Moscow as a lesser power, and Hull had also had to contend with Soviet opposition to that country's being included as a signatory to the declaration. However, with Allied military successes now being reported on all fronts, Stalin no doubt saw no reason either to be troubled by a weakening Japan or to incur his allies' displeasure by opposing Chinese involvement—something that was, arguably, a paper transaction in any case. Consequently, on October 30, 1943, with all four nations agreed on its text, the Declaration of the Four Nations on General Security was signed.

The declaration was clearly an historic document in its own right, but its more immediate and important function had been its role as a backdrop to the detailed discussions of the foreign ministers: the process of the declaration's development had established a practical framework of principle and policy against which the rest of the Moscow conference was set. One example of this was the accord reached over the control and political future of Italy, a country about which, because of its recent history of fascism and because Italian units had been actively engaged against Soviet forces in Russia, Stalin and Molotov had particular concerns. Although the Western allies and Moscow had approached the question of Italy with significantly different proposals, in the course of their negotiations a common line emerged, due to the general agreement already achieved on the principles that should drive and shape the way in which the Allies would deal with former Axis powers and with liberated countries.

As always, the main focus of the Moscow conference was upon Germany, Austria, and the rest of central Europe, and here the ministers representing the "Big Three" found much to discuss. Here also, they achieved almost total agreement. At the outset, they reaffirmed the principle of no separate negotiation with the Axis powers, and of the immutable principle of nothing less than unconditional surrender, both of which matters were absolutely fundamental to Soviet participation in the Alliance but which eventually created a number of practical difficulties for the Western allies, not least the strengthening of German resistance in 1945 when Goebbels was provided with the useful propaganda argument that their forces had nothing to lose by this action. Hitler's propaganda statement in November 1944 that "capitulation means annihilation" was a clear and powerful motivator, and one that the propagandists of an alliance driven by the aim of achieving an unconditional surrender could not quite as easily refute. Moreover, the war in Europe probably lasted some months longer than necessary, due to a discrete surrender by major German forces to U.S. and British forces in the west being totally against the principles governing the arrangements for a surrender that had already been agreed by the three allies—principles that were monitored and policed rigorously by the Soviets. There is little doubt, and a fair amount of evidence,[1] that much of the Wehrmacht would have welcomed a chance to surrender to the Western allies well before May 1945, once it had become abundantly clear that a German military defeat was inevitable; some German generals had even assumed that their forces would then join U.S. and British troops against the Soviets. While this was clearly unrealistic (although Stalin no doubt feared such an eventuality), the unilateral Anglo-U.S. acceptance of a German surrender in the west could have enabled Anglo-U.S. forces to capture Berlin and occupy most of Germany before the Red Army could do so—a situation that would in turn have resulted in a very different postwar Europe from that which finally emerged in 1945, but which would at the same time have been identified by Stalin as a clear and present threat to the security of the Soviet Union, and so would certainly have prejudiced the (albeit imperfect) peace achieved in 1945. But such matters and speculation were still almost two years away when the foreign ministers dealt with the future of Germany in Moscow in October 1943, and when, together, they agreed upon the basic principles that all three Allies were to apply to a German capitulation.

The agreed principles ensured that Germany would have no room to deny that it had suffered a total defeat. The lessons of Germany's denial of the fact of military defeat following the 1918 Armistice and subsequent rise of National Socialism were, clearly, in U.S., British, and Soviet minds here. Further to this, every aspect of Nazism was to be expunged from postwar Germany, together with the demobilization and disarmament of the German armed forces, a demilitarization of the nation by neutralizing the Prussian influence, the release of all political prisoners, and the surrender to the Allies or other United Nations authorities of anybody who might be accused of war crimes. These measures were to be accompanied by fundamental political reforms to turn Germany into a true democracy in which individual liberties were protected by an appropriate bill of rights and a constitution. The defeated Germany would be occupied by U.S., Soviet, and British troops, although a formal partition of Germany was not envisaged.

The matter of partition was interesting, and it had already attracted considerable debate. On the one hand, a partitioned Germany might not be able to threaten European peace for a third time (France would no doubt say a fourth time, with the Franco-German war of 1870–71 in mind). However, enforced partition could subsequently provide a rallying call for a war of reunification, as well as making much easier a process of progressive Soviet domination of a number of disparate German states. Moreover, in October 1943, Washington neither sought nor envisaged a long-term postwar U.S. military commitment in Europe—this was a task that, Roosevelt believed, should be borne primarily by Britain and the Soviet Union—and any solution for Germany that had the potential to destabilize central Europe would almost certainly involve just such a U.S. commitment.[2] Consequently, no clear decision on partition was taken, although the desire finally to deal with Prussian militarism was met by an agreement to uncouple Prussia from Germany, with the state of East Prussia going to Poland, and thus falling into what would become the Soviet area of control. Indeed, while the fate of Germany and Austria—which latter country would be liberated, freed from the 1938 political linkage with Germany, and become independent—were resolved harmoniously, the ministers' discussion of territorial matters proved somewhat more difficult, especially that concerning the ever-present and always difficult issue of Russia's western neighbor, Poland.

Indeed, Polish issues proved so hard to resolve that the foreign ministers finally decided that these questions were better left unanswered, and the record of their discussions simply indicates that "An exchange of views took place." Quite apart from the emotive fact that Britain had gone to war over the German invasion of Poland, Russia had long held the view that its neighbor was a lesser state, with undeserved pretensions to much greater international status, and, moreover, a state that also formed the strategic buffer between Russia and the West and between Russia and Germany in particular. The Soviet Union's postwar border requirements and its territorial claims on Poland were central to every discussion of this issue. The situation was made more complex by the presence in London of a Polish government-in-exile that was hostile to Moscow and looked forward to the day, once Germany had been defeated, when Poland resumed its place as an independent sovereign state. Meanwhile, a pro-Moscow puppet organization, the Union of Polish Patriots, existed in the Soviet Union. Moscow accepted the principle of Polish independence, although what this meant in practice was the resumption of a superficial form of national identity, with domination of Poland by the Soviet Union. The latter had long regarded Poland as no more than one of its provinces, and in 1939 Soviet forces had seized eastern Poland and killed hundreds of military officers, landowners, priests, and teachers who might oppose Moscow's rule. Thousands more Poles were interned as prisoners of war. This initial repression was followed by the programed deportation of some two million Poles to Stalin's camps of the infamous Russian gulag. Then, in April 1943, had come the disclosure by the Germans of the murder by the Russians during the spring of 1940 of almost four and a half thousand Polish officers and others in the Katyn forest, a charge that was emphatically denied by Moscow not only at the time but for many years thereafter. A request from the Polish government-in-exile for the alleged Soviet part in this massacre to be independently investigated quickly followed. This somewhat precipitate (although not unreasonable) request further worsened Soviet-Polish relations, and at the same time it placed Roosevelt and Churchill in the position of having to downplay the German allegation in order to placate Stalin in the interests of harmony.[3] Thus, as the foreign ministers embarked upon their discussion of Polish issues, the existing level of animosity and suspicion between the Soviet Union and Poland—and, by extension, of London's involvement, as that was where the Polish government-in-exile was based—was very considerable. It was little wonder, then, that Eden, Hull, and Molotov adopted a pragmatic approach, settling for no more than "an exchange of views" on that especially difficult subject and leaving many of the Polish questions unresolved.

The future of Czechoslovakia was more easily dealt with, although it involved a significant measure of compromise by Eden in particular. The way was opened for Molotov and the Czech leader, President Eduard Benes, to conclude a bilateral treaty that, in due course, established a significant level of Czech-Soviet cooperation and planning for the postwar era. The contrast between the Czech and Polish approach to what President Benes had already clearly identified as the future domination of eastern Europe by the Soviet Union could not have been more marked, albeit that Czechoslovakia had been ill-served by both Britain and France at Munich in 1938 and so its people were more receptive to a postwar security solution that did not depend on the Western allies.[4]

Meanwhile, the future of German-occupied Greece was also discussed by the three foreign ministers. By the late summer of 1943 Greece was in turmoil, as the two main counter-German resistance groups, the republican anticommunists of EDES and the communists of the EAM-ELAS (the stronger of the two groups), had embarked upon a rapidly escalating campaign against each other, in order to secure their political and military position in anticipation of the power vacuum that would follow a German defeat. Both groups were unfavorably disposed toward the Greek government-in-exile (based in London and, later, Cairo) headed by King George II, and indicated that the king should not return to Greece unless and until the people had demonstrated that they wished the monarchy restored after the war. They had also stipulated key government posts that were to be filled by resistance fighters. King George was not prepared to accept such terms, and had stated that the will of the Greek people concerning the future of their monarchy should only be sought after he had returned to Greece. Churchill and Roosevelt had already decided to support the king, and the former had ordered plans to be prepared for British troops to follow rapidly upon a German collapse or withdrawal from Greece in order to combat the communist resistance fighters of ELAS and restore King George to his throne. Already, during the same month that the foreign ministers conducted their meeting in Moscow, Britain had suspended its airdropped arms supplies to ELAS. Had Stalin chosen to balk the Anglo-U.S. intentions for Greece and support the ELAS fighters, an already difficult situation would have been greatly exacerbated, and the harmony of the Alliance threatened. However, Moscow accepted that Greece lay beyond the sphere of interest Stalin envisaged would be that of the postwar Soviet Union, and so, despite the impending clash of arms between British forces and communist freedom fighters in Greece, Molotov expressed no Soviet censure of the plans then being laid by the British, while Hull acquiesced in supporting the policy briefed by Eden.[5] With hindsight, this Soviet disinterest in Britain's plans for Greece could be explained fairly simply by the fact that, while British troops were engaged in dealing with the ELAS forces in Greece, they could not interfere with Stalin's immediate postwar plans for the subjugation of eastern Europe, and specifically with his plans for neighbouring Bulgaria, Albania, and, especially, Yugoslavia. While Moscow was content to see Greece fall into the Western camp, it had always intended that Yugoslavia and the Balkans would lie firmly within postwar communist Europe.

Rather as Stalin had dismissed Greece, so Churchill had accepted that Yugoslavia would eventually fall outside the Western area of influence. Moreover, Washington and London were both very wary of involvement in the political and security miasma that had been the Balkans since time immemorial: had not the spark which ignited World War I just three decades earlier originated in the Bosnian town of Sarajevo?[6] Just as had happened in Greece, two groups had emerged as the most effective resistance fighters in Yugoslavia, the communists led by Josip Broz Tito and the nationalists (known as the Chetniks) commanded by Gen. Draja Mihailovich. Again, the groups saw each other as rivals rather than as allies against the German occupiers. Yet again, in Yugoslavia it was the communists who proved that they were the more effective resistance group against the Germans, although the British had attempted to bring both factions together in common cause, as well as attempting to pave the way for a postwar return to power of King Peter II, whose government-in-exile was, again, based in London (and in Cairo by fall 1943). However, irrespective of the increasing dominance of Tito's forces and the consequent risk of a communist takeover of Yugoslavia by default, the damage that Tito was doing to the Germans—including his keeping up to thirty Wehrmacht divisions deployed in Yugoslavia on counterguerrilla operations—was undeniable. Pragmatically, therefore, Churchill was content to let Allied support for the nationalists wane and that for Tito increase, while all the time avoiding a postwar commitment of U.S. or British forces to resolve a Yugoslav civil war. The Western allies knew that Yugoslavia could best serve them as a possible strategic stepping stone toward Austria and southern Germany, and as an existing major problem for the German high command. With that in mind, neither Roosevelt nor Churchill chose to concern themselves over-much with the postwar political nature of Yugoslavia, and that view was faithfully represented to Molotov in Moscow by Eden, with Hull's support, when the three foreign ministers limited their discussions on Yugoslavia to ways that both resistance groups might harmonize and maximize the effectiveness of their operations against the Germans.

In parallel with the political debate in Moscow, the ministerial conference also addressed a number of military issues. Churchill had anticipated that Stalin would attempt to introduce the second-front question into this preliminary meeting, and so he had directed Gen. Sir Hastings Ismay to accompany Eden at Moscow in order to provide authoritative military advice as necessary. Gen. John R. Deane, head of the U.S. military mission in Moscow, fulfilled this function for secretary of state Hull. Sure enough, at the outset of the meeting Molotov presented Eden and Hull with a set of Soviet proposals for shortening the war in Europe, first and foremost amongst which was an Anglo-U.S. invasion of northern France. Understandably, the U.S. and British foreign ministers stated that they would need to consult Washington and London before responding to the Soviet proposals; understandably also, the replies they received mirrored all that had been said before, notably at the "Quadrant" meeting.

In essence, Washington stated unequivocally that the "Quadrant" declaration of an intention to mount the cross-Channel invasion on May 1, 1944, remained extant. However, while by no means reneging on that which had been agreed and confirmed at the conference in Quebec, the British qualified their reply by restating the operational prerequisites for this invasion to take place—although Generals Deane and Ismay concluded in their joint presentation to Molotov on October 20 that they were fairly confident that these necessary preconditions would be achieved. By the end of the presentation both generals believed that they had done all they could to indicate Anglo-U.S. concurrence with the Soviet proposals.

Despite this, just eight days later Molotov once again raised the issue, based this time on Soviet unease over the British stated requirement for there to be no more than twelve German mobile divisions in northern France in order for the invasion to take place. What if there were a few more than twelve divisions in France on May 1, 1944? asked Marshal Voroshilov at the ministers' meeting on October 28. General Ismay dealt with the matter by explaining the rationale for the figure of twelve divisions—the correlation between workable landing ports and Anglo-U.S. force development vis-à-vis that of the Germans—while also reiterating his belief that German forces in such numbers would not be available, and that this should not therefore become a critical factor affecting the viability of the invasion. Ismay and Deane could do no more, and it was left to Eden to state yet again the continued validity of the "Quadrant" declarations on this issue, while nevertheless, and quite properly, indicating that the May 1, 1944, date would necessarily be subject to the strategic and operational circumstances of the time.

Molotov appeared to be satisfied, and to have accepted that he could ask for no more definitive Anglo-U.S. commitment than this. Nevertheless, having experienced at first hand the misunderstandings consequent upon his meetings in Washington and London in 1942, he insisted that a properly and fully documented account be made of the U.S., British, and Soviet positions on this issue. With some reservations, Hull and Eden agreed, although they insisted, for the record, that the two generals who had briefed Molotov were merely describing that which had already been agreed, and the progress made, or in train, to implement those agreements. Both ministers were wary of being seen to have preempted at their level the discussions that they knew would soon take place among the three leaders at the Tehran summit. Nevertheless, in the evening of October 28, following the latest debate on the second-front issue, Eden briefed Stalin in person on the current operational situation in Italy, where matters were not proceeding as satisfactorily as Churchill had envisaged and urged, so that the Soviet leader would have an up-to-date overview of the theater that might yet have an adverse effect upon the timing of the cross-Channel invasion.

Interestingly, Stalin apparently appreciated the key import of Eden's briefing—that the British were entirely committed to Operation "Overlord," but that it would be illogical to conduct an invasion doomed to certain defeat simply in order to satisfy short-term political aspirations. At this private meeting, Stalin comprehended that, while there was no intention by the Western allies to delay matters, a delay might be unavoidable. At the same time, the Soviet leader applauded the Allies' intention to strike simultaneously at southern France with a view to forcing the Germans to dissipate their combat power. In many respects this bilateral meeting of Eden with Stalin in the margins of the main conference was of great significance, and demonstrated the degree of cooperation that such meetings, conducted out of the public eye, could achieve. It also indicated Eden's superlative abilities as a diplomat, together with the extent to which he and Churchill were in each other's minds, a closeness reflected in the amount of negotiating leeway that Churchill invariably gave Eden when the latter was acting as his representative.

When Eden related the details of his private session with Stalin to Hull, he also stated that Stalin had accepted the importance of supporting the campaign in Italy effectively, and that Stalin, remarkably, had even suggested that this campaign might constitute the second front. Although Stalin urged that the concept for "Overlord" should not be modified, and that it would be appropriate for the Italian campaign to halt north of Rome (so that all effort could then be directed toward the invasion of France), both Hull and Eden were able to report back to

Washington and London that, on this long-running and difficult issue, a considerable degree of harmony had apparently been achieved with the Soviets. There can be little doubt that Stalin's amenability to arguments and explanations put on a personal level was noted by Churchill and Roosevelt alike, and this boded well for the impending meeting of all three leaders at Tehran.

Two other military matters were addressed by the foreign ministers. First, in response to a proposal by Molotov, there was agreement that Turkey should again be actively persuaded to enter the war on the Allies' side by the end of the year, although Churchill's attempt to achieve this during his visit to Adana shortly after the Casablanca conference had been unsuccessful, and he now believed that gaining access to Turkish support facilities and territorial waters was probably a more realistic and useful objective for the Allies.

Next, the old question of Anglo-U.S. matériel support for the Soviet Union via the Arctic convoys, suspended through the summer months, was resolved successfully. The Western allies confirmed their intention to resume this aid and to dispatch one large convoy per month in the period November to February. Although this commitment attracted some difficulties due to the Soviets' suspicions, their paranoia, and a misinterpretation of the strength and nature of this statement of intent to resume the convoys,[7] Churchill, very ably assisted by Eden in Moscow, did not take offence at the Soviet reaction, and, yet again, a potentially divisive problem had been dealt with diplomatically and to the greater good of the Alliance. The first of these Arctic convoys was duly dispatched in November as planned.

Finally, at a grand closing dinner during the last night of the foreign ministers' conference on October 30, Stalin announced that, once the Allies had defeated Germany, the Soviet Union would join the Western allies to defeat Japan. This historic statement was greatly appreciated when it was reported back to Washington, although Stalin's motives were fairly transparent. This future commitment carried little military risk for the Soviet Union, while at the same time it strengthened considerably the Soviet-U.S. military link, and thus that of the Alliance as a whole. As such, it much enhanced Washington's view of Stalin's reasonableness and willingness to cooperate with his allies. Meanwhile, the seasoned European diplomats Churchill and Eden, while of course welcoming the Soviet Union's new commitment to enter the war against Japan, no doubt also noted the particular advantages that this might confer upon Stalin when negotiating with the two Western allies his future plans for the newly liberated nations of eastern Europe.

Both the imminent meeting of Churchill and Roosevelt in Cairo en route to Tehran and the summit itself were complemented by the preliminary meeting of the foreign ministers in Moscow from October 18 to 30. Indeed, over that twelve-day period, Eden, Molotov, and Hull effectively laid the foundations of the Tehran summit and at the same time established an harmonious and cooperative three-way working relationship involving the United States, Britain, and the Soviet Union that many in London and Washington had heretofore judged to be virtually unachievable; and the Soviets' future commitment to enter the war against Japan was particularly gratifying to Roosevelt. Thus, during October and November 1943, the "Big Three" strategic alliance matured and truly came of age, for which success much of the responsibility lay with the experienced guiding hand, judgment, and diplomacy exhibited by Eden in Moscow during the final two weeks of October that year.

However, unlike Hull, whose optimism and elation appeared almost boundless at the conference's close, and despite Eden's diplomatically warm praise of Molotov at the three ministers' final meeting, the British foreign minister and his prime minister in London had no illusions about the potential volatility and frailty of Western-Soviet relations in the future: there was the certain knowledge that the divergent aspects of their respective postwar agendas meant that many unavoidable difficulties still lay ahead for the great strategic alliance of East and West. Moreover, in Moscow, the U.S. diplomat at the head of the liaison mission, W. Averell Harriman, a man who knew the Russians all too well, expressed his personal view to Churchill that the failure of Eden and Hull to deal with the issue of the Soviet frontiers and their apparent acquiescence in the matter of the postwar future of Soviet-liberated eastern Europe had been taken by the Soviet leadership as firm Western approval of Stalin's intentions for that region. Nevertheless, despite such justifiable unease in some quarters, it was undeniable that the meeting of Hull, Molotov, and Eden in Moscow had made a vital contribution to the wider process of the Allies' war summits in general and to preparing the way for that shortly to take place in Tehran in particular.

The "Sextant" Conference:
The Meeting of Churchill and Roosevelt in Cairo

On November 12, Churchill, aboard the battlecruiser HMS *Renown*, left Plymouth bound for the Mediterranean. The intention was that the prime minister should disembark from the warship at Gibraltar and fly from there to Cairo. However, owing to bad weather it was decided that the *Renown* would continue to Malta instead, where the British party spent three days before completing their journey to Cairo. There, the Mena House Hotel and a number of villas had been temporarily requisitioned for the use of the British, U.S., Soviet and Chinese delegates. Soon afterward, Gen. Chiang Kai-shek and his wife (who also acted as interpreter for her husband, the Chinese nationalist leader) arrived by air. They were followed a day later by President Roosevelt, who had crossed the Atlantic onboard the battleship USS *Iowa*. The plan was for all of the delegates except for the Chinese to move directly from Cairo to Tehran—a six-hour flight—once the Cairo summit had been concluded.

Although it might be inferred that the decision that Stalin, Churchill, and Roosevelt would meet at Tehran had already been taken by the time of the foreign ministers' meeting in Moscow, this was not so. Certainly there had been agreement in principle to a "Big Three" meeting, but Roosevelt was most reluctant to travel as far as Tehran, and he had proposed to Stalin that the three leaders might meet in Basra instead. However, Stalin claimed that his role as the active commander-in-chief of the Soviet army meant that there was a need for him to remain in continuous touch with the operational situation on the eastern front, and that the immutable consequence of this was that he was unable to travel further than Tehran. It was undoubtedly true that the Soviet campaign against the Germans was developing rapidly (its situation was, indeed, changing almost daily), and the vertical nature of the Soviet political-military system of command and decision-making did require Stalin's constant attention.[8] However, the ever-present levels of paranoia and suspicion inherent in the Soviet state, and Stalin's personal perceptions and attitudes especially, no doubt provided another powerful reason for the Soviet leader not to move far beyond Soviet territory: to relinquish any degree of control in the Soviet Union was tantamount to relinquishing power, with the great and often irreversible personal risks that that implied. Nevertheless, there was no doubt that Stalin favored a "Big Three" summit, although some delay in achieving this would probably have been to his advantage, as it would allow the advancing Red Army to execute a *fait accompli* by occupying some of the liberated countries of eastern Europe, as well as placing a "Big Three" summit ever closer in time to the projected May 1, 1944, date that the Western allies had set for the cross-Channel invasion.

Roosevelt had tasked Cordell Hull with persuading Stalin to journey beyond Tehran for the summit, but Stalin was adamant that he could not do so, and Hull and Averell Harriman had begun to fear that this very necessary meeting was in danger of being postponed until the spring of 1944. At the same time, Churchill had been seeking another bilateral meeting with Roosevelt, in order that the Anglo-U.S. plans and intentions (those for "Overlord" especially) might be clarified and agreed before the two Western leaders together found themselves in the position of presenting and discussing them with Stalin. In parallel with this, Roosevelt was also actively seeking an opportunity to meet with the Chinese leader, Chiang Kai-shek.

After a flurry of activity during the last week of October, Roosevelt acquiesced in Stalin's wishes, and on November 8 agreed that he and Churchill would indeed meet the Soviet leader in Tehran. However, the president had already, on October 31, decided that he would meet Churchill at Cairo beforehand, on about November 20, and that Chiang Kai-shek should also meet with the two Western leaders at Cairo from November 25. These two meetings having been successfully arranged, an ideal foundation had been established upon which to base the subsequent Anglo-U.S. participation in a "Big Three" summit, and although Roosevelt had not finally given in to Stalin's wishes until the end of the first week of November, it was probably inconceivable that either Roosevelt or Churchill would have allowed the opportunity for this meeting to pass them by.

However, in his enthusiasm for the forthcoming meeting with Stalin, Roosevelt encountered resistance from Churchill to the U.S. intention that Soviet representatives should attend the Anglo-U.S.-Chinese meeting in Cairo in order to save time in Tehran by their having dealt with lesser matters beforehand. While welcoming the forthcoming meeting in Tehran, Churchill knew that the presence of Soviet delegates (including Molotov) in Cairo would inhibit the Anglo-U.S. talks, and the prime minister knew that it was vital for both Roosevelt and him to resolve a number of key issues before Tehran. Churchill was also concerned that the Chinese presence in Cairo almost from the outset would inhibit his discussions with Roosevelt, and indeed it proved to be China and the war against Japan that subsequently dominated the Cairo meeting. Although the president made light of Churchill's concerns—an indication, perhaps, of the Americans' continuing, somewhat naive view of their Soviet communist ally and the excessive worry on Roosevelt's part that Stalin might suspect his Anglo-U.S. partners of some deceit whenever they met bilaterally—there can be little doubt that these were well-founded and realistic British concerns.

However, in the event, and most fortuitously, Stalin decided that Molotov could not attend the Cairo meeting and so his deputy, Andrei Vishinsky, would attend briefly, merely as an observer, while en route to Algiers to fulfill another assignment. The reason given for this decision was, ostensibly, the pressure of work on Molotov, combined with Stalin's minor ill-health at that time; although it was just as likely that, once he knew that Chiang Kai-shek would also be in Cairo, Stalin decided that it would be politically unacceptable for the Soviet Union to be represented at a level which might be seen to confer a measure of "Big Three" status on a country that Moscow viewed as very much a lesser ally. It might be added that Churchill, just as much a pragmatist as Stalin, regarded the Chinese involvement at Cairo as a largely unwelcome distraction which diverted an unwarranted amount of discussion time to the consideration of a theater of operations that was of much less strategic importance than Europe. Nevertheless, with China, the United States, and Britain represented by their leaders, chiefs of staff, and advisors, and with the Soviet Union present only with observer status, the stage was set for the Cairo conference, the meeting that Churchill knew was an absolutely essential precursor to Tehran if the latter was to fulfill its true potential, and if the Anglo-U.S. allies were not to risk being caught off-balance by Stalin and Molotov.

Just as Churchill had feared, Roosevelt's preoccupation with the war against Japan in the Pacific led the president to engage in lengthy bilateral talks with Chiang Kai-shek as soon as all parties were present at Cairo. Certainly, the Chinese situation in late 1943 was by no means ideal, and it was appropriate for the Chinese leader to receive a degree of reassurance and support for his campaign against the Japanese. However, for Churchill there was a certain irony in the fact that Roosevelt's estimation of the postwar importance of China, and therefore of the importance of its war against the Japanese, threatened to affect the Western allies' plans for Operation "Overlord" in Europe just as Churchill's plans for North Africa and Italy had done at an earlier time. A further parallel with the eastern-western front situation in Europe was the fact that the vigorous Allied campaign within, and adjacent to, Burma that Chiang sought would provide a sort of second front in the Far East theater that could engage large numbers of Japanese troops on the mainland while MacArthur's forces conducted their "island-hopping" assaults against the Japanese Pacific garrisons.

Given the U.S. naval catastrophe at Pearl Harbor on December 7, 1941, and the understandable desire of the American people to close with, and destroy, the nation that had carried out that devastating attack, it would probably have been politically ill-advised for Roosevelt not to have devoted a considerable amount of time and effort to the Chinese ally, who, by October 1943, had already been locked in conflict for almost a decade with the enemy that had finally brought America into the war. However, despite Roosevelt's urgings and a promise of allied action in Burma, Churchill held firm to the view that a major escalation of the British commitment in Burma was not justified, and that the proposed deployment of additional amphibious resources to prosecute that campaign would be to the serious detriment of Allied plans for Operation "Overlord," and for the ongoing campaign in the Aegean and Italy. Consequently, by the time Churchill and Roosevelt left Cairo for Tehran, it was clear to the U.S. president and his military advisors that, the risk of Chinese disappointment and possible disaffection notwithstanding, any attempt to force upon the British the commitment to a major Allied amphibious offensive (Operation "Buccaneer") across the Bay of Bengal, against the Andaman Islands immediately to the south of Burma, posed the much greater risk of disharmony and division between the two Western allies at a critical point in the Alliance's development.

Despite this shortfall on Chinese hopes and aspirations at Cairo, Chiang's disappointment was to some extent ameliorated by the particular time and attention that Roosevelt and his delegation allocated to Sino-U.S. discussions, and by the statement of intent that was drafted primarily by Harry Hopkins in just twenty-four hours, following his initial meeting with Chiang Kai-shek on November 23. Roosevelt approved the draft declaration and Churchill made some minor amendments to it, although it was predominantly a U.S. initiative intended to placate the Chinese and set the broad parameters for the future political and strategic shape of the Far East and Pacific theater—with the neutralization of Japanese military power and the destruction of its ill-gotten empire as the primary objective. In essence, the declaration assured Chiang Kai-shek that all Chinese territories that Japan had seized would be restored to China. Indeed, the overall thrust of the declaration could be interpreted as an intention to supplant Japanese domination of the region by the positive transfer of its power and influence to China.[9] In addition to the restoration of Chinese territory such as Formosa, the Pescadores Islands and war-ravaged Manchuria, all the Pacific islands and other territories in the Far East region that had been occupied or seized by force of arms by Japan since 1914 would be removed from Japanese control. Finally, the declaration set the postwar goal of establishing a free and independent Korean state.[10] In deference to Stalin's known position with regard to China, it contained no specific mention of a Soviet perspective, although Molotov and the Soviet leader had certainly been apprised of the declaration's contents and had no comments to make upon it. Perhaps Stalin, ever the realist and with a good overview of events beyond Russia's southern and eastern borders, already anticipated that in the fullness of time a postwar China with its power and influence enhanced would in any case be controlled by the communists rather than by a Kuomintang (nationalist) government. He also had his own territorial ambitions in the Far East and would have gained nothing by exposing these at that stage.

Whereas the foreign ministers' meeting in Moscow had been notable for the harmonious note on which it had concluded, the apparent lack of enthusiasm of Churchill for dealing with Chinese and Far East issues at Cairo tended to confirm the view of some U.S. delegates that, rather than pursuing the albeit somewhat idealistic principles of national self-determination set out in the Atlantic Charter, the British prime minister was in fact seeking to divert attention from matters that might prejudice the restoration of Britain's imperial control over its Far Eastern territories once the war had ended. In fact, Churchill's frustration over the way in which the Cairo meeting had developed was undoubtedly prompted by the way in which Chinese and Far East issues had significantly deflected his purpose of ensuring that the Anglo-U.S. lines on Operation "Overlord" and other major European issues were absolutely clear prior to the Tehran meeting. Furthermore, although Churchill certainly envisaged a restoration of British sovereignty over its Japanese-occupied Far Eastern territories after the war, any lack of enthusiasm for an expansion of the Far East campaign on his part was prompted primarily by the adverse impact that such an action would have upon the Allies' declared priority of launching the second front into northern France by mid-1944. In Britain, the need for this operation had recently gained an even greater immediacy with the intelligence disclosure in October that the Germans had constructed a number of V-1 flying-bomb sites in northern France—in the Pas de Calais and on the Cherbourg peninsula—and, in addition to the threat they posed to London and other civilian targets in southern Britain, these pulsejet-powered weapons could presumably also be directed against the military assets that would be vital to the invasion.

Perhaps the most remarkable perception to emerge from the Cairo meeting was the increased emphasis that Roosevelt and the U.S. military chiefs were by then placing upon the war against Japan, even at the expense of meeting their own inviolable commitment to the May 1, 1944, invasion of France. Further evidence of this emerging change in the U.S. approach was borne out by a meeting of the Anglo-U.S. combined chiefs of staff on November 25, when the outcome of a discussion of "Overlord" vis-à-vis "Buccaneer" in the Far East was apparently an acceptance by the U.S. J.C.S. of a delay in the former operation to July 1 if necessary, in order that the latter might go ahead unimpeded. Such a noteworthy change of U.S. policy was indicative of the growing confidence of the Americans and their increasing role and influence in the Western alliance, together with the domestic need to inflict significant damage upon the Japanese. However, it also showed a unilateral and much less sensitive U.S. approach than heretofore to Stalin's possible reaction to any postponement of the cross-Channel invasion beyond the May 1 date.

As the Western leaders and their entourages decamped from Cairo and headed for Tehran and the "Big Three" summit conference that they had all sought and worked toward for so many months, Churchill must have realized that, despite its clear strategic and wider advantages, the impending meeting of Stalin with Roosevelt in Tehran, with the prospect of further such "Big Three" and possibly bilateral Soviet-U.S. summits and conferences thereafter, plus the fact that the war was now certainly proceeding toward an eventual Allied victory, would inevitably dilute the special relationship that had thus far existed between the British prime minister and the U.S. president. It was also becoming clear that the sheer scale of the resources, wealth, and military power of the United States would inevitably confer upon it preeminence in the postwar West, its occasional international naivety and inexperience notwithstanding. Accordingly, and irrespective of the validity or otherwise of perceptions in Washington concerning the nature of the postwar world and its abhorrence of colonialism and imperialism, the meeting of Roosevelt, Churchill, and Chiang Kai-shek at Cairo from November 22 to 26, 1943, was a prominent marker in the long decline of the British

Empire and the progress of the United States toward "superpower" status. Although the U.S. view—that of Roosevelt, specifically—would be modified in the future where this was necessary for the good of the Alliance, the ever-increasing size of the U.S. military contribution to the Alliance, plus the political pressures of the upcoming presidential election campaign in 1944, meant that the impact and influence of U.S. perceptions, needs, and concerns inevitably assumed an ever greater significance in the weeks and months ahead. The forthcoming meeting in Tehran was arguably the last occasion on which, due largely to the broader march of history and other matters generally beyond its control, Britain and its war leader were able to participate in the process of World War II summit meetings as a truly equal member of the Alliance.

12

The Power of Three

The Tehran Summit, November 1943

LTHOUGH OF ONLY A FEW DAYS' DURATION, the gathering of Churchill, Roosevelt, and Stalin in Tehran on November 27, 1943, was historic—a defining moment of World War II. It was the first time that Roosevelt and Stalin had met face to face. It was also the first occasion on which the full intellectual power of the "Big Three" leaders could be focused simultaneously upon the business of managing and directing the great enterprise in which they were then engaged.[1] Most appropriately perhaps, this first "Big Three" summit meeting in Tehran, which lasted from November 27 to December 1, 1943, was codenamed "Eureka."[2]

Significantly, the three leaders achieved as much in some four days as their chiefs of staff and representatives had done in weeks and sometimes months of negotiation, even allowing for the fact that the Moscow and Cairo meetings had, to varying degrees, prepared the way for that in Tehran. At the same time, Tehran presented the first opportunity for each leader to observe at first hand how the other two interacted with each other, just as all three were already looking toward the shape of the postwar world and the future roles of their nations within it. Finally, Tehran also exposed some of the more parochial national perceptions and personal foibles and weaknesses of the three leaders. Thus far, these had been sublimated entirely to the overwhelming need of the Allies to turn the tide of the war, but, with an Allied victory at last truly in sight (if still more than a year and a half away), they began to emerge during the program of informal discussions and bilateral, plenary, and social meetings and engagements that together comprised the "Eureka" conference—if always more evident amongst the military and political staffs and advisors than the three principals, who, by and large, managed to transcend the sometimes more limited vision displayed by their subor-dinates.[3] Nevertheless, such differences of perception were probably inevitable, given the very different personalities and national imperatives of Stalin, Churchill, and Roosevelt. Certainly the three-way dialog and process of negotiation introduced at Tehran proved much less straight-forward than had been so at the earlier bilateral meetings. Churchill had undoubtedly anticipated this, and, while welcoming the coming together of all three leaders and the wider benefits that would flow from this, he understood that this event would inevitably affect his ability to shape the Alliance's strategy in the future—and his ability to influence President Roosevelt in particular.

The agenda for the conference fell, or rather developed, into four broad areas. Understandably, first and foremost was the Allied campaign against Germany. Stalin's main concern was, as ever, the need for the cross-Channel invasion to take place, a concern given added impetus by a new German offensive southwest of Kiev, and by intelli-gence reports that as many as a dozen panzer and infantry divisions had recently been redeployed from France, Italy, and the Balkans to rein-force the German armies on the eastern front. Next, Roosevelt was deter-mined that the increasing tempo of the war against Japan should hence-forth be reflected by affording it a much higher profile in the Alliance's discussions and deliberations. Thirdly, at Tehran the "Big Three" set out to resolve a number of items of unfinished business from some of the earlier meetings. Finally, the three leaders returned to the ever more pressing need to establish the sort of international security organization that would be required to safeguard world peace once the Axis powers had been defeated.

Although the conference officially opened on November 27, it was not until the next day that the discussions began. Indeed, during the evening of the twenty-seventh all three leaders dined separately, and Churchill had in any case found the Cairo meeting particularly wearing and had virtually lost his voice. The next day, November 28, all three began to address the business at hand.

The day began with a move by Roosevelt and his staff from the U.S. legation to the Soviet legation compound. The U.S. facility was some distance from the other two and Roosevelt had earlier, on November 24, asked Stalin to advise where the president and his entourage should stay in Tehran. Stalin invited Roosevelt to accept the hospitality of the Soviet legation throughout his stay, and, although the rationale took account of such mundane matters as travel time, distance, and security considerations—Stalin's invitation indicated his concern that Axis sympathizers might cause "an unhappy incident" involving any of the leaders while driving between the legations in Tehran—it would be have been naive indeed of Stalin's secret police chief, Lavrenti Beria, not to have made the most of having the U.S. delegation living within the Soviet compound. Nevertheless, as an act of faith and goodwill, Roosevelt's decision to seek Stalin's advice and agree to the move was undoubtedly astute in diplomatic terms, while the president certainly had few illusions about the surveillance threat that this decision involved.[4] It also demonstrated the importance Roosevelt attributed to making up for his previous lack of direct contact with Stalin, and to balancing his well-established relationship with Churchill. One consequence of this relocation, which occupied the morning of November 28, was that Churchill was frustrated in his hope of having a preliminary bilateral meeting with Roosevelt; and the first meeting of the summit, that afternoon, was in fact a bilateral first meeting between the U.S. President and the Soviet leader, which lasted for one hour.

During this first meeting between Stalin and Roosevelt, the two leaders concentrated on matters affecting the eastern front, France, Indo-China, China, and—remarkably perhaps, given that Churchill was not present—India. Although of short duration, this first exchange proved to be quite revealing of Roosevelt's developing views in particular, while confirming Stalin's existing position on various issues. In opening up the subject of China, Roosevelt was particularly positive about the way in which the talks with Chiang Kai-shek had gone in Cairo; Stalin maintained his view that China was of little consequence militarily or in terms of its future international impact, and should certainly not be regarded as a potential equal of the "Big Three" nations in the postwar world. Roosevelt continued by indicating the strong reservations that he harbored about de Gaulle and his suitability to lead postwar France. In a bid, perhaps, to gain or increase Stalin's trust, he also confided that Churchill favored de Gaulle to a much greater extent than he did. Certainly Roosevelt did not share Churchill's view that France would (or should?) soon regain its former great-power status in the postwar world. Diplomatically, Stalin remained noncommittal about this, and in any case his principal interest in France was then less about its long-term future than its impending role as the only battleground that could in his opinion induce the Germans to redeploy divisions away from the eastern front. Finally the discussion moved on to the Far East, when Roosevelt outlined his vision for Indo-China and India, where he envisaged these French and British possessions being allowed to determine their own postwar political future, a policy that Roosevelt hoped to see extended to other colonial territories in due course, even going so far as to praise aspects of the Soviet model. Once again, he confided that, not surprisingly, he and Churchill were at variance on this issue, especially where British India was concerned. Apart from observing that the sort of sea-change Roosevelt was postulating for postwar India could probably only be achieved through revolution, Stalin remained noncommittal on what was plainly a sensitive issue; but there can be little doubt that he registered the clear potential to exploit Anglo-U.S. discord over the future of Britain's colonial empire once the war had concluded and a new strategic game for global preeminence had come into play.[5]

Once Roosevelt's meeting with Stalin had ended, all three leaders gathered later that afternoon for the first of their plenary sessions at Tehran. The U.S. president chaired this session, at the start of which each leader in turn outlined his current view of the war and his principal concerns and preferred way ahead. Once all three positions had been stated and clarified as necessary, these views and proposals were explored, discussed, and debated.

Roosevelt launched at once into a lengthy statement of the U.S. view of the campaign in the Pacific and Far East, together with an explanation of Washington's strategy to defeat Japan. In the sure knowledge that Stalin's principal interest was Anglo-U.S. intentions concerning the invasion of France, he then projected the way in which the development of U.S. and British operations in the Mediterranean area would divert German capability from the eastern front and so assist the Soviets; however, this would almost certainly impose some delay on the cross-Channel invasion, Operation "Overlord." Stalin's response to the U.S. briefing was typically well-considered, and it showed the extent to which he was, by late 1943, both able and willing to play the game of diplomacy—especially in relation to the Americans—just as astutely as Churchill had done during the previous couple of years. Meanwhile, the Soviet leader never lost sight of his main aims.

Stalin immediately responded to Roosevelt's presentation by recognizing the increasing priority that Washington accorded to the Pacific conflict, while at the same time linking this directly to the war against Germany. He did this by reaffirming the Soviet Union's earlier commitment, made in Moscow on October 30, to join the fight against Japan once Nazi Germany had been defeated. That done, he was dismissive of the Anglo-U.S. preoccupation with Italy, and advanced the very valid argument that the Alpine region provided an important physical constraint on the campaign in Italy being developed into a full-scale attack into Germany from the south. But, having stated this view about Italy, Stalin raised the alternative possibilities of an Allied thrust launched into the Balkans—which, he believed, would find favor with Churchill, even though such an operation would not necessarily be conducive to Soviet longer-term plans—or, of more importance, of an Anglo-U.S. invasion of southern France. He knew that the latter option would appeal to the Americans, and that it could be linked directly to "Overlord," so ensuring that the cross-Channel invasion took place as planned. Finally, Stalin indicated his support for any action that might induce Turkey to join the Allies' cause, since Turkish forces could make a useful contribution to any operations in the Balkans. This line also accorded with Churchill's thinking on this matter, already evidenced by his abortive attempt to secure Turkish support at Adana the previous January.

At that stage, utilizing the opening provided by Stalin, Churchill developed his proposals for the Mediterranean theater. In addition to emphasizing his belief in the potential importance of Turkey's role, the prime minister pointed out that there was, in any case, a need to make good use of the forces available in the Mediterranean and Italy (he assumed that Rome would fall by January 1944) until the launch of Operation "Overlord." Churchill's unfailing enthusiasm for operations in the area led him to ask Stalin's views on expanding these at the possible expense of a significant delay of "Overlord," the timing of which Churchill, unlike Roosevelt, had always regarded as necessarily flexible. At this stage Roosevelt indicated a degree of support for the "possibility" of developing such operations in the eastern Mediterranean, the Adriatic, and thus into the Balkans to link up with Tito's partisans, followed by operations into Romania to join with the Soviet forces. Predictably, Churchill seized on this and immediately urged that this option should be studied and carried forward. In practice, Roosevelt's observation had probably been intended to be in part a diplomatic but fairly noncommittal demonstration of support for his British friend and ally, but in fact it meant that the "Big Three" now found themselves in the position of having to consider this proposal formally, together with the long-running issue of "Overlord" vis-à-vis other options in the Balkans and Mediterranean area. Although unanticipated, this was actually most timely, and the ensuing brief debate cut through much of the discussion of the previous year, to establish a firm policy and way ahead.

Stalin proved well-prepared to deal with Churchill on this issue. He argued that the further dispersion of Allied forces in the Mediterranean and into the Balkans could only be justified if Turkey entered the war on the Allied side, and he doubted that Turkey would do this. However, he supported strongly the concept of an invasion of southern France, which very conveniently complemented his unchanged position that Operation "Overlord" should be the principal focus of all Allied strategic action in 1944. The logic of Stalin's argument could not be denied; neither could the uncertainties and possible risks inherent in Churchill's proposals. By the end of the session, Roosevelt, as chairman, had stated that nothing should be permitted to delay Operation "Overlord", at the same time indicating that any expansion of Allied operations in the Mediterranean might have precisely that effect. However, he firmly supported the proposal to attack southern France, and suggested that a plan for this should be developed forthwith. Thus, by the end of the first full day of the Tehran conference, the views of the leaders of the two great superpowers in embryo were by and large in accord with each other, while those of the prime minister of the prewar superpower, Great Britain, had diverged and not stood up to the tests of argument and debate. The previously oft-stated principle of the inviolability of Operation "Overlord" had been endorsed by the "Big Three", as had the intention to launch a complementary invasion of southern France in 1944. Together, these firm commitments meant that any expansion of Allied operations into the Aegean was now a nonstarter, and that even the continuing hard-fought campaign in Italy would rapidly become of secondary importance to the preparation and execution of the Anglo-U.S. invasion of France.

That evening, the three leaders met informally at a dinner hosted by Roosevelt, and their conversation centered on the postwar political shape of Europe, and of Germany in particular. The principle of unconditional surrender that had been announced by Roosevelt at the end of his summit meeting with Churchill at Casablanca the previous January was raised again. This time it was Stalin who broached the subject, indicating that he viewed it as a unifying factor within Germany which could actually be to the detriment of the Allied cause. His observations were well-founded. Certainly, the uncompromising nature of the "total war" that Nazi Germany had waged against bolshevism—epitomized in Hitler's eyes by the Soviet Union—had had the effect of uniting all but a few national and ethnic groups within Russia against the German invaders: Stalin's totalitarian regime was by no means regarded as benevolent or popular by much of the Russian population, but it was the lesser of two great evils, and in any case the people really had little choice in the matter. In several respects, his direct experience of events in Russia and Europe during the first four decades of the twentieth century had given Stalin a much deeper understanding of the many-faceted nature of Germany than was possessed by Roosevelt. More recently, these historic events had included the "Great War" and the

Russian revolution between 1914 and 1917, and a civil war that continued to 1922, the Soviet-German friendship treaty of 1922, the neutrality and nonaggression treaty of 1926, and the Soviet-German pact of 1939— which was followed just a couple of years later by the surprise German invasion that had already led to two and a half years of ferocious warfare on the eastern front.

Indeed, after 1918, trade, military exchanges and cooperation, and diplomatic relations between Germany and the Soviet Union had for many years been close and extensive, despite the fundamental ideological differences between the two countries. Matters had only become strained as the 1930s drew on, with the durability of the infamous 1939 pact probably deluding neither Hitler nor Stalin: the latter regarded it as a necessary expedient to stave off the inevitable conflict, while Hitler used it to avoid the risk of a military confrontation in the east while his panzer divisions completed the defeat of France in the west. Of course, from June 1941, Soviet rhetoric and propaganda unremittingly despised, dehumanized and belittled the Germans. Nevertheless, Stalin's comment at dinner that evening in Tehran that, even in the wake of a comprehensive defeat, Germany could rise again within a couple of decades and again threaten the peace of the world clearly indicated his understanding of the national resolve and determination inherent in the nature of the German people. It also underlined his wish to see the defeated Germany effectively disarmed, dismembered, and placed under the direct control of the victorious Allies. Stalin's understandable desire to secure this definitive neutralization of Germany, and that country's inability to attack his for a third time, was also linked inextricably to a satisfactory resolution of the Soviet Union's postwar frontiers, and therefore, by extension, to the future of Poland, the postwar western frontier of which Stalin was adamant should be set on the River Oder. Stalin's points made both at Tehran and during many of the other war summits demonstrated the thinking on which so many of the Soviet leadership's policies for Europe would subsequently be based during the forty-five years of the "Cold War" from 1945.

By the end of dinner, the combined stress of the travel to Tehran and the long hours of discussion had told on Roosevelt—who was, by late

1943, a man with less than eighteen months to live—and the U.S. president retired early to bed, leaving Stalin and Churchill to continue their conversation. This focused on the emotive issue of Poland. In principle, Churchill was amenable to losses to the Soviet Union of Polish territory in the east being offset by the addition to Poland of territory taken from eastern Germany in the west. However, the close relationship between Great Britain and the Polish government-in-exile in London meant that Churchill envisaged a much greater degree of Polish involvement in decisions on the country's future than did Stalin. From his noncommittal reaction to Churchill's views on Poland, it may be deduced that the Soviet leader was quite clearly of the opinion that the principal role for that nation in the future was to be as a physical bulwark against future German aggression toward the Soviet Union, and no consideration of political niceties, sensitivity, or historical precedent would be allowed to affect that. Thus the fate and future sovereignty of Poland were just as uncertain in late 1943 as they had been in September 1939, when the German invasion of that country had finally forced Britain and France to declare war on Nazi Germany, igniting the conflagration which swiftly became World War II.

November 29, the third day of the Tehran summit, dawned. It would prove to be the least satisfactory day of the conference, for Churchill and the British delegation especially. Following his indisposition of the previous night, Roosevelt was pacing himself carefully and declined an invitation from Churchill to take lunch with him prior to the afternoon plenary session. However, the U.S. president had already agreed to a second bilateral meeting with Stalin that afternoon, before all three leaders came together for their joint discussions. Although very much a political realist, Churchill must have felt that both he and Great Britain were becoming increasingly isolated and relegated to a position of lesser importance now that the two great military power brokers, the United States and the Soviet Union, had come together and so speedily achieved a sound working relationship, albeit one that Churchill must have known was reliant in large measure upon Roosevelt's goodwill and desire to accommodate Stalin for the sake of the Alliance's unity. The British prime minister had little choice but to acquiesce in this, as the

Alliance's main aim—defeating the Axis powers—was inseparable from the British national interest at that juncture.

To a certain extent, Roosevelt's preplenary encounter with Stalin amplified and expanded aspects of their discussion the previous day. In a meeting that anticipated some of the historic Soviet-U.S. summit meetings of the "Cold War" era many years hence, Roosevelt and Stalin set themselves to considering the political shape and security of the world after the war. Whereas Roosevelt and Churchill had already addressed this weighty subject and crystallized their own thoughts on it, both the U.S. leader and Stalin had already recognized that it would be their two nations that would, by default, be in a position to shape the postwar world. Great Britain would, of course, have a major security role to play, specifically within the British Empire, but (in Roosevelt's view) the days of French international power and influence were at an end, and therefore only China was worthy of inclusion as a fourth member of the group of nations that would, in effect, rule and direct affairs after the war. However, Stalin maintained his position that China had neither the military power nor the international stature to warrant its involvement; certainly he did not believe that it would be acceptable for China to influence any decisions concerning Europe. He proposed that, rather than one global United Nations security organization, there should be two, one dealing with the Far East and the other with Europe. Only the latter of these two organizations would include the United States, but (presumably) the Soviet Union would be able to make a good geopolitical case for its own involvement with both. While potentially advantageous to Moscow—and in some respects similar to Churchill's own thinking on this, as Britain's global territories would have made its involvement in both organizations inevitable—this idea was flawed, as the United States clearly could not have been limited to deciding only those matters affecting Europe and the Americas. Indeed, while doubting the feasibility of Stalin's proposal, Roosevelt made it clear that he did not envisage U.S. ground forces countering a future threat to peace in Europe; rather, any such threats should be dealt with by Britain and the Soviet Union. He underlined the strength of U.S. feeling on direct American military commitment to Europe by stressing that, had Japan not attacked Pearl Harbor, it was unlikely that U.S. troops would have been deployed to Europe at all. For Stalin, this indication of Washington's desire not to become involved militarily in postwar Europe must have been particularly pleasing in the light of his own plans for that region. However, as the subsequent campaign in northwest Europe developed and the foundations of the "Cold War" were laid, Roosevelt's hope and that of the U.S. people that the latter might finally be able to disassociate themselves from European security issues once the war had been won proved to be both unrealistic and somewhat ephemeral. The discussion concluded with both leaders agreeing that the postwar security organization would need the strategic capability to achieve its purpose; but, while they agreed this in principle, it was doubtful that the means each anticipated of achieving it were the same.

Following Stalin's meeting with Roosevelt, both men joined Churchill for a brief ceremony at the British legation during which the Soviet leader (who was also a Marshal and commander-in-chief of the Soviet armed forces) was presented with the Sword of Stalingrad, a richly ornamented sword and scabbard that was a gift for the people of Stalingrad from King George VI, symbolizing the heroic struggle of the city's population and the decisive victory thereat of the defending Red Army against the German attackers. This ceremony was one of several interludes and overt displays of Alliance unity during the "Big Three" summit. Churchill's detective was present and described the occasion:

After the lunch I carried the case in which the sword had been transported from England into the Embassy, placing it on a table in the centre of the room. On one side stood twenty Russian privates with tommy guns [sub-machine guns] across their chests. On the other [side were] a similar number of Buffs [the Royal West Kent Regiment] with rifles and bayonets fixed. Between the two lines but slightly in front of our soldiers stood a British lieutenant with the sword between his feet. Mr. Churchill, wearing the uniform of an air commodore, arrived just as Marshal Stalin came through the door opposite. The President followed Stalin. The Prime Minister then stepped toward the Marshal. At the same time the British officer marched forward with the sword held in front of him. Mr.

Churchill then said: "Marshal Stalin, I have a command from His Majesty, King George VI, to present you, for transmission to the City of Stalingrad, this sword of honour, the design of which His Majesty himself approved. This blade bears the inscription 'To the steel-hearted citizens of Stalingrad, a gift from King George VI in token of homage of the British peoples.'" The national anthems of the two countries were then played and the Premier, taking the sword in his two hands, turned and with a very grave look on his face, handed it to Marshal Stalin's outstretched hands. The Marshal, smiling with pleasure, lifted the sword to his lips and in absolute silence kissed the scabbard. . . . The President expressed a wish to see the sword. When Stalin showed it to him he held it by the hilt and said aloud: "Truly a heart of steel. Yes, the word steel-hearted represents the people of Stalingrad."[6]

With the formalities of the presentation over, all three leaders embarked upon their second plenary session.

Churchill led the discussion by summarizing the vital importance of landing craft to the strategic debate. With near-concurrent amphibious landing operations being or having been proposed for the cross-Channel invasion (now with a probable complementary landing in southern France), for Italy and the Mediterranean, and for the Far East (in the Bay of Bengal), it was clear that there would not be sufficient assets to support all of these. Furthermore, of course, what was primarily an amphibious U.S. campaign in the Pacific required hundreds of landing craft to support it, although this fact was not included in the discussion. Much of the preparatory staff work for this session had been carried out by the military chiefs of staff and their advisors at a separate meeting on the morning of November 29, and so all three leaders were already briefed and well aware of the need to make the right decision on landing craft prioritization—a matter that affected the Anglo-U.S. allies very directly.

Thus far, having outlined the competing operational priorities, Churchill was reviewing familiar matters, albeit matters that needed resolution. However, having gained the floor, in an ill-judged move the prime minister then launched enthusiastically into a further exposition of his ideas for the involvement of Turkey and for expanding the Mediterranean campaign into the Aegean. Notwithstanding his political acumen, he appeared to have misread both the qualified support for this action from Roosevelt and the disfavor with which Stalin had earlier viewed it. Perhaps, if Churchill and Roosevelt had met for lunch that day, the British prime minister might have been persuaded not to pursue what had become a very personal cause. Indeed, his own military and political advisors were against what they regarded as an ill-conceived Aegean adventure. In any event, with Stalin already very aware of the possible effect of all these operations on his hopes for Operation "Overlord," it was not sensible of Churchill to advocate actions that, as he conceded, would quite probably have the effect of further prejudicing and delaying the Anglo-U.S. invasion of northern France in mid-1944. However, in practice, Churchill's proposals actually proved timely, as they forced the issue and led Roosevelt to state that he was in favor of maintaining the date of May 1, 1944, for the invasion, as had been decided at the "Trident" conference in Washington the previous May—although the pragmatic British had then, and continued now, to regard this date as flexible. But there was no escaping the wishes of the U.S. and Soviet leaders at this stage.

Stalin was content to see the invasion take place at any time during May, but in conceding this degree of flexibility he reiterated, and made quite clear his view, that the issues of the prosecution of the Italian campaign, the partisan groups in the Balkans, and the unlikely entry of Turkey into the war on the side of the Allies were minor matters compared with the launch of Operation "Overlord." Building perhaps on his fast-developing awareness of those areas where the U.S. and British views were not entirely in accord with each other, Stalin accused Churchill and the British of merely continuing the dialog about "Overlord" in order to placate the Russians—and so keep them in the Alliance—while really not believing in the concept of, and need for, a cross-Channel invasion at all. Churchill took considerable exception to such an accusation, and indicated this in suitably forthright terms. On this unsatisfactory note, the second plenary session ended, although all three leaders were due to meet later that night for dinner at the Soviet embassy. It promised to be a difficult evening, and so it turned out to be.

As host, Stalin continued to put pressure on Churchill, while making clear his general support for much of that which Roosevelt had discussed with him privately, earlier that afternoon, concerning postwar global security. No doubt Churchill felt somewhat discomfited and excluded, having had no opportunity for such talks with Roosevelt since their arrival in Tehran, and in the knowledge that Stalin and Roosevelt had already had two such bilateral meetings in the last forty-eight hours. The point at which Churchill could contain himself no longer occurred when Stalin stated that, as a matter of fact, it would be necessary to execute between fifty and one hundred thousand German officers and military experts in the course of winning the war and once it had been won. Remarkably, and revealingly, Roosevelt did not demur at this amazing statement, other than to suggest a compromise figure of forty-nine thousand! Furthermore, Stalin indicated that he would require four million German males to work indefinitely in Russia after the war in order to rebuild his country. With regard to these mass executions, Churchill took great exception and stated that, while true war criminals who had been tried and found guilty were one thing, it was unacceptable routinely and for political purposes to murder in cold blood soldiers who had fought for their country. In light of the turn that the conversation had taken, Churchill left the dining table and made to leave the embassy. However, having perhaps nudged the British prime minister a shade further than intended, Stalin immediately adopted an entirely different and nonconfrontational demeanor, persuaded Churchill to return to the table, and thus ensured that, although the evening (and, indeed, the day) had proved particularly testing, it at least ended on a note of cordiality. It had been an interesting evening: even though Stalin's suggestion may have been made lightly, it had revealed more of the views and principles held by the "Big Three" as individuals and of the way that they might interact in the future.

Accounts of the dinner—especially those by U.S. commentators—present Roosevelt's response to Stalin's statements on the measures he envisaged being taken against the German military and civilian population as "bantering" in tone.[7] However, the fact that the matter was raised at all says more about the contemporary views of the three leaders concerning Nazi Germany than any number of formal political or propaganda statements. It provides no real surprises in respect of the Soviet Union, given the horrors that had been visited upon that country by Germany since mid-1941: Stalin needed to demonize the German invader in order to motivate and subdue the nation that he ruled, and the numerous excesses of the Wehrmacht and Waffen-SS in Russia ably assisted him in this. But, where Churchill and Roosevelt were concerned, this matter represented a considerable revelation and should not be dismissed lightly. By late 1943 Britain had fought and won the Battle of Britain, its civilian population had been the subject of the devastating bombing blitz by the Luftwaffe, and its land forces had suffered a series of defeats at German hands in France, North Africa, and the Mediterranean before Alexander and Montgomery had turned the tide at El Alamein. Nevertheless, Churchill still viewed Germany and its people as a nation in human terms, while at the same time reserving his strongest rhetoric and condemnation for the Nazi leadership, focusing on the political concepts of Nazism and fascism rather than upon the nation that had in recent times spawned these two evils. This showed his sense of history, vision, and pragmatism, for he well appreciated that, one day, Germany—albeit as a defeated state—would once more need to take its place amongst the community of nations, and this process, and the development of a suitable postwar security organization, could be fatally prejudiced by creating a general perception that the German responsibility and guilt for the war were due in equal measure to each and every German. This perception had already been implied in the principle of unconditional surrender announced by Roosevelt at Casablanca.

Indeed, although Roosevelt would not have wished to prejudice his relationship with Stalin by disputing the latter's pronouncement on this issue, it is still striking that the leader of a great Western democracy, its homeland—Hawaii apart—untouched by enemy action and its land forces only recently engaged against the Axis powers, should have apparently treated so lightly the matter of the summary execution of thousands and the enslavement of millions of Germans in the closing years of the war and the postwar period. The U.S. president's response to Stalin illustrated the extent to which Washington's propaganda machine had already created a dehumanized image of the German enemy. This, together with the U.S. pressure to call for the unconditional surrender of Germany, says much about the need for the U.S. administration to motivate for war a population whose armed forces were still predominantly European in origin, that perhaps found it much easier to go to war against an Asiatic nation that had committed unprovoked aggression against the United States than against the citizens of a nation with which many Americans could still identify directly. But if Roosevelt had not maintained this line, the overriding need to mount the cross-Channel invasion and to liberate Europe from German occupation might well have been relegated in favor of the very understandable argument in the United States that called for America's armed forces to deal with Japan as a matter of the highest priority.

Thus the verdict upon the controversy that arose on the night of November 29, during the informal dinner at the end of a long and tiring day, must be that Stalin had simply maintained his view of the future of Germany, which accorded absolutely with his vision of the postwar security needs of the Soviet Union. Meanwhile, although Roosevelt's reaction at first sight appears to be out of character and remarkably flippant, it none the less met his need to maintain harmonious relations with Stalin. It also accorded with the general propaganda line then being promoted in the United States concerning the nature of the German enemy that large numbers of American troops were scheduled to fight in northwest Europe from mid-1944. The implied criminality of large numbers of German military personnel and officials also strengthened the argument about the need to liberate the oppressed countries of Europe as a matter of priority, and so reinforced the case for the cross-Channel invasion to take place as soon as practicable. In the United States, it was well understood at the highest levels that the effective management of the population's perceptions was indivisible from the generation and committal of the armed forces necessary to prosecute the war to a successful conclusion.

THE POWER OF THREE

Churchill's reaction to Stalin's pronouncement had undoubtedly been instinctive and genuine, and it had characterized the personal views of a European statesman with considerable former experience of war against Imperial Germany, with a clear understanding of the flaws in the punitive Treaty of Versailles of 1920, and with an awareness of the once close ties that had long existed between Germany and Britain. However, the incident also showed yet again that such matters could no longer be dealt with exclusively on a personal level between the three leaders: any issues raised by the "Big Three" and their responses to them now had invariably to take account of far wider agendas and target audiences in the nations that they led as well as within the Axis states. Lastly, the incident highlighted once again the way in which Roosevelt and Stalin had apparently drawn ever closer, while Churchill and his views on the postwar world had further diverged from those of his two coleaders. But if November 29 marked a less than successful day for the Tehran summit, the next day did much to set it back on course—and, by a happy coincidence, the substantive progress made was balanced by the fact that November 30 was also the British prime minister's birthday. So it was that Winston Spencer Churchill was due to celebrate his sixty-ninth year at a formal dinner party for thirty-four guests, with Roosevelt and Stalin, in the British legation that evening. However, before the birthday celebrations could take place there was a full day's work to be done. Fortunately, it proved a much more productive day than that which had preceded it.

In the morning of November 30 Churchill had a bilateral meeting with Stalin for one hour. Although this did not produce any significant changes of policy, it certainly allowed both to clear the air after the disagreement of the previous evening, as well as enabling Churchill to counterbalance and to some extent redress the perceived impact of Roosevelt's several bilateral discussions with the Soviet leader. In many respects this meeting followed an entirely predictable agenda, but it none the less permitted Churchill to reemphasize and explain quite clearly his particular concerns and priorities to Stalin. The options for future amphibious operations predominated, with Churchill making the point that the competing priorities for the allocation of the limited quantity of landing craft were not only between the Mediterranean and Operation "Overlord," but also between "Overlord" and Operation "Buccaneer," the major landing in the Bay of Bengal so favored by the U.S. military leadership, and supported by Roosevelt in line with his desire to aid Chiang Kai-shek and the Chinese nationalists. It was quite proper for Churchill to make clear to Stalin that the United States had aspirations for the war against the Japanese in Burma that might affect the timing of "Overlord," and, in the knowledge that Stalin had little regard for the Chinese role in the war or its aftermath, Churchill, not unnaturally, took the opportunity to highlight indirectly a matter about which he knew Roosevelt and Stalin certainly did not agree. Having gained the Soviet leader's undivided attention—and fully aware that Stalin would be attracted to anything that offered the probability of reduced numbers of German divisions on the eastern front— Churchill then warmed to his familiar theme and outlined the possible wider advantages of the continued Allied operations in Italy. Significantly, such operations would include an amphibious landing on Italy's west coast within striking distance of Rome, although the primary goal here would be the destruction of the German forces rather than the largely symbolic capture of the Italian capital. Stalin acknowledged the points made, but restated the overriding importance of Operation "Overlord," the nonimplementation, delay, or dilution of which could threaten the future cohesion of the Alliance. Churchill was content to accept Stalin's already well-known position on the cross-Channel invasion, but in so doing he was able to use this as an opening to restate the principal British caveat concerning "Overlord"—that the invasion should only be launched when the number of German mobile divisions in northern France was such that it stood an acceptable chance of success. Although Stalin and Molotov might have felt constrained to criticize the British on the grounds of excessive caution, the logic of Churchill's point was inescapable: a failed Allied invasion of France would not benefit the Soviet Union strategically other than in the very short term, and at the same time it would at the very least provide a respite for Germany and prolong the war significantly. Despite no changes in their positions—and none had realistically been antici-

132

pated—a degree of understanding had been achieved during the hour the two leaders spent together, and this boded well for a successful plenary session later that day, and for an equally harmonious dinner that evening.

While Churchill and Stalin had been meeting, the combined chiefs of staff had also been in conference on the morning of the thirtieth. They had made important progress on virtually all of the matters outstanding, apart from the proposals for an expansion of operations in the Aegean that were so favored by Churchill. However, it must be said that even the British prime minister's own advisors were less than enthusiastic about his almost obsessive preoccupation with that area. By the time that the plenary session opened that afternoon, the chiefs of staff were able to present an operational package that all of the "Big Three" agreed and endorsed after just an hour of discussion. The date for Operation "Overlord" was set for May 1944, and a complementary landing would be carried out in southern France. This Allied invasion in southern France would be carried out on the largest scale practicable, but this would necessarily depend upon the quantity of landing craft then available. Meanwhile, the Anglo-U.S. campaign in Italy would continue up to the Rimini-Pisa line, with some sixty-eight landing craft being retained in the Mediterranean until January 15, 1944, in order to enable the amphibious landing to cut off the German forces and, ultimately, to facilitate the capture of Rome. During the follow-on discussion, Stalin promised that the Red Army would launch a large-scale new offensive in May 1944, timed to coincide with the cross-Channel assault. By doing this he was also further ensuring that his U.S. and British allies had no room for maneuver on the date of "Overlord." Finally, it had already been understood that the size of the U.S. contribution to the invasion of northern France meant that its overall commander would be an American, and Roosevelt indicated that he would appoint this supreme Allied commander within the next three or four days. Thus the strategic course of the war in 1944 was set on November 30, 1943, and the level of agreement and harmony achieved so far that day augured well for the memorable sixty-ninth-birthday celebration that followed soon after the plenary session had concluded.

After the formality and import of the business of the previous few days, Churchill's birthday provided all present with a welcome opportunity to relax in an atmosphere of relative informality. During the pre-dinner reception it was noted that Stalin made a point of talking "animatedly" with many of the guests, circulating with Pavlov, his interpreter, closely in tow. The Soviet leader spoke at length to Churchill's son, Maj. Randolph Churchill, who was among the guests, as was the prime minister's daughter, Sarah. When Churchill led the assembly into the dining room they found that the long table had been graced by a large birthday cake decorated with sixty-nine candles as its centerpiece. Surrounding the cake were presents from Roosevelt, Averell Harriman, and Sarah Churchill. The U.S. president's gift was a blue and white porcelain bowl, while Harriman's present was a hand-painted Kamember silk illustration dating from 1794; Sarah gave her father a silver coin, an "Alexandrine" or four-drachma piece which had been minted in about 300 B.C. Other birthday gifts received the next day included items of silverware, ivory, an astrakhan hat (from the press corps), and a Korassa meshed carpet from the Shah of Persia. Once all had taken their seats, Churchill began the proceedings by announcing that, during the evening, all toasts were to be drunk according to the Russian custom whereby the gentleman proposing the toast would first leave his seat, touch glasses with the person who was the subject of the toast, and then return to his seat. This set the scene for the rest of the evening, and Churchill's detective recalled that when the prime minister toasted Stalin he said: "I sometimes call you Joe, and you can call me Winston if you like, and I like to think of you as my very good friend." Warming to this fraternal theme, he went so far as to indicate that the British people were "turning politically pink," before concluding by toasting "Marshal Stalin—Stalin the Great." In his response, Stalin said: "We want to be friends with Great Britain and America, and if they wish to be friends with us they can show it by their actions." The British and Soviet leaders touched glasses, and Stalin announced: "To my fighting friend." Quite apart from the fact that Churchill was evidently enjoying the occasion, he had judged it appropriate to humor Stalin—although the Soviet chief's response implied his continued concern over the need for early Anglo-U.S. action against the Germans in occupied France, and, by implication, in subsequent times as well. In his toast to Roosevelt, Churchill paid due respect to the president's support and friendship, and expressed the hope that "friendship and mutual understanding between our two countries will continue through the ages." In the course of his reply, Roosevelt returned to, and broadened, Churchill's imagery for the changing political scene in Britain by likening the Alliance's overall political coloring to that of a rainbow. Even at an informal gathering such as that on November 30, the "Big Three" could not entirely escape the realities of their world, as Stalin continually sought to further his long-term plans for eastern Europe, while Roosevelt sought to establish a neutral political start point for the bilateral meeting he was due to have with Stalin the next day—one that would be followed by a final "Big Three" meeting to deal with significant political issues. In the meantime, Churchill's reference to the changing political loyalties in Britain provided a prophetic indication of the socialist landslide that would sweep him from power just over eighteen months later.[8] The birthday dinner ended at about midnight, and all three leaders retired in anticipation of a busy final day of the "Eureka" summit in prospect.

The final day's activities focused mainly on political rather than military matters, and comprised a third bilateral meeting between Stalin and Roosevelt and a final meeting of the "Big Three." This was followed by the signing of the Three Power Declaration, which underlined the undoubted success of the Tehran summit. Inevitably, the discussion was directed at the future of Germany, and by extension that of eastern Europe—which in turn resurrected the vexed question of Poland and its postwar frontiers.

During his meeting with Stalin on December 1, Roosevelt moved straight to the issue of Poland. He stated that he would like to see the postwar western frontier of that ravaged country moved further west, even as far as the Oder, and the eastern frontier—that with the Soviet Union—also moved further west. The potential implications of this were noteworthy, as these changes would both bring large numbers of what were currently German civilians into Poland while at the same time placing similarly large numbers of Poles under Soviet control. Not surprisingly, Roosevelt indicated that, with up to seven million American voters of Polish extraction among his countrymen, he could not make his views public during what was a U.S. election year. The president's positive acquiescence in what amounted to an expansion of Soviet territory and the strengthening of Poland as a bulwark state on the Soviet Union's western frontier certainly matched Stalin's aspirations. Roosevelt completed his amelioration of Stalin by obliquely confirming U.S. acceptance of the fact that the Red Army would in due course occupy the Baltic States, and that the United States would not impede that activity. In one short meeting, Roosevelt had more or less provided the Soviets with all that they had wished for, and in doing so he had all but sealed the fate of Poland.

The final "Big Three" meeting at Tehran took place at the end of the afternoon (during much of December 1, Churchill had been occupied with further events to mark his birthday of the day before). Once foregathered, President Roosevelt moved straight to the point on Poland, and followed his earlier and more discursive discussion of this issue with Stalin by suggesting a reallocation of part of the territory of East Prussia to the Soviets, an action that would place Tilsit and the strategically important ice-free port of Königsberg under their control. This met Stalin's aspirations, although a definitive "Big Three" solution on Poland's future frontiers—a matter further confused by the considerable uncertainty that emerged over the true position of the Curzon line that delineated the old Poland-Russia border—was not achieved.[9] The discussion moved on to the postwar shape of Germany, where Roosevelt and Stalin were generally in accord on the need to dismember Germany, in order to frustrate any possibility of a German military resurgence. One option involved the division of Germany into five autonomous parts, with the strategically important city of Hamburg and the Ruhr-Saar industrial region being placed under U.N. or other international control, in order to be used in the future for the benefit of the whole of Europe. This solution was proposed by Roosevelt and generally favored by Stalin. Churchill proposed an alternative dismemberment that would decouple Prussia—the perceived traditional source of German militarism—from Germany, with southern Germany splitting away to become part of a Danubian confederation. Although this was not the solution favored by either the U.S. or the Soviet leader, it did show once again Churchill's understanding of the nature of Germany and its history: Prussian isolation would at a stroke remove the historical mainspring or core of German unity and military strength, while southern Germany, and Bavaria in particular, had long maintained its separate identity and culture within the greater German state, and so might, with comparative ease, be decoupled from the northern states and induced to resume its historical links with an Austria and Hungary that had long ago relinquished their military capability of former times. Clearly, a definitive political solution regarding Germany was not going to be reached by the "Big Three" at Tehran, neither was there yet a need for it to be so. However, all were agreed on the absolute need to prevent forever any possibility of Germany again threatening the peace of Europe, and so, having established the necessary parameters, the three leaders passed the complex question over to the European Advisory Commission in London for further detailed study based initially upon the proposals made by the "Big Three" at Tehran. The commission's remit was nothing less than to produce in due course the new map of postwar Europe.

The formal output from the meeting of the "Big Three" at Tehran was a declaration, signed by the three leaders on the final day, December 1, 1943. This was a broadly political document that looked ahead to the Allies' aspirations for a democratic and peaceful postwar world and an international community of nations that would adhere to the fundamental principles espoused much earlier by Roosevelt and Churchill. However, the declaration was also designed to demonstrate the extent of agreement and unity that had been achieved by the three Allied powers on the projected and closely coordinated strategic actions that they would take in the coming year to bring about the total defeat of Germany, on land, across the oceans, and from the air. The text of the declaration was designed as much for Axis consumption as for the populations of the Allied and occupied countries of Europe, for, albeit using other words, it underlined the Allies' commitment to securing the unconditional surrender of their enemy. The declaration was published and issued one week later, on December 6. Meanwhile, Roosevelt and Churchill departed Tehran, traveling via Cairo, where they conducted follow-on meetings with their chiefs of staff, as well as meeting with Turkish President Inönü.

Nevertheless, the nature and content of the "paper output" from the Tehran summit were predictable, and the thrust of its primarily political message could have been largely foretold—barring some catastrophic falling out of the "Big Three." Therefore, it is necessary to look beyond the more obvious and tangible product of the Tehran summit in order to appreciate the true significance of this milestone conference.

On a personal level, had there been competition between the "Big Three" to dominate events at Tehran, it is an inescapable fact that Stalin had won it. Given his background of education and experience, which contrasted markedly with that of Churchill and Roosevelt, this was note-worthy, and indicated the Soviet leader's very well developed under-standing of the arts of international relations, politics, grand strategy, and diplomacy, closely underwritten by sheer native cunning—together with a self-confidence in dealing with Churchill and Roosevelt that flowed from the absolute power that Stalin enjoyed within the Soviet Union. He had also demonstrated time and again an unshakable ability to maintain his key objectives—based upon the Soviet national interest— whatever changes in strategic circumstances or priorities the two Western allies might have presented him with. Foremost amongst these was the need for the Anglo-U.S. cross-Channel invasion to take place at the earliest opportunity, and, Churchill's cautionary caveat apart, Tehran had certainly and irrevocably set the seal upon the Allies' firm commitment to carry out Operation "Overlord" in mid-1944.

Stalin and Molotov now believed that they had Roosevelt's unquali-fied support on the future of Poland and its postwar borders with the Soviet Union, albeit that the U.S. president could not "go public" on this just yet, owing to political sensitivities in the United States. It transpired much later that Roosevelt's support for Stalin's plans for Poland's fron-tiers had perhaps been somewhat more qualified than Stalin had under-stood or chosen to believe. Nevertheless, the subsequent betrayal of

Polish sovereignty that took place in order to create an effective geopolitical and strategic Soviet-controlled buffer zone between Germany and Russia was directly attributable to that crucial bilateral meeting between Roosevelt and Stalin at Tehran, and to the U.S. president's desire to accommodate his Soviet counterpart wherever possible. Although this issue had apparently been resolved at Tehran, the complex and invariably vexed question of Poland and its frontiers, together with the uncertain status and authority of its London-based government-in-exile, would yet again demand the attention of the "Big Three" and their political advisors in the months ahead.

Next, Stalin had resisted Roosevelt's wishes for any substantive Chinese involvement in the formation of the postwar world. In this he had Churchill's support and, shortly after the "Eureka" summit, the U.S. president ended the long-standing aspirations of the J.C.S. to mount Operation "Buccaneer," the amphibious landing in the Bay of Bengal directed against the Japanese in Burma. This important and politically courageous decision—given the continued pressure in the United States to expand U.S. involvement in the war against the Japanese—meant that an amphibious operation which would inevitably have had to compete with the Mediterranean theater and later with Operation "Overlord" for landing craft and other resources was removed from the equation. This policy decision also signaled the relegation of Allied support for Chiang Kai-shek to a much lower priority than the Americans had originally envisaged.[10] Thus both Stalin and Churchill achieved their separate aims over the issue of China and Allied amphibious landing priorities, while Roosevelt's decision also meant that the intended landing in Italy close to Rome could now be undertaken with a good chance of success.

A subject on which Churchill and Stalin had disagreed was the matter of Turkey. Stalin had expressed his reservations over the likelihood of President Inönü committing Turkey to enter the war with the Allies, and his judgment was once again proved to have been correct when Churchill and Roosevelt met the Turkish leader in Cairo straight after the Tehran summit, as they found that President Inönü's position was unchanged from that which he had stated to Churchill at Adana at the end of January.

Meanwhile, Churchill could probably be judged to have been the next member of the "Big Three" to have profited most from Tehran. Notably, he had secured the necessary amphibious capability to carry out what would be called Operation "Shingle" at Anzio, on the west coast of the Italian peninsula: the potential distraction of "Buccaneer" had been removed, and Roosevelt's subsequent agreement to a further delay of the redeployment of landing craft from the Mediterranean for "Overlord" would enable the landing at Anzio to take place. However, this success notwithstanding, Churchill's hopes for the Aegean and Balkans had not been realized, although the plans to maintain the momentum of the campaign in Italy largely compensated for this. Although he had achieved something on the strategic front, the meeting of the "Big Three" at Tehran had been something of a revelation for Churchill. From that first face-to-face meeting of Roosevelt and Stalin had come the realization for the British prime minister that, in the postwar world, real power would flow from Washington and Moscow, and that the price of bringing the United States and the Soviet Union together to defeat Germany would be a gradual but inevitable diminution of the global power of Great Britain and its empire. Directly linked to this was the reduced influence that Churchill enjoyed in his dealings with Roosevelt once Stalin had so successfully forged his new personal relationship with the U.S. president.

By default, therefore, it must be adjudged that Roosevelt had gained least from Tehran. However, this would be an oversimplistic assessment, as the overriding goal of establishing a sound working and personal relationship with Stalin had certainly been achieved. Moreover, the way ahead and the date for Operation "Overlord"—always the Americans' particular strategic priority—had been firmly set by the "Big Three." While Roosevelt had at times demonstrated an almost excessive desire not to offend Stalin at any cost, and gave ground on several issues in consequence, the implications of a fracturing of the Alliance at this first "Big Three" summit could have proved disastrous for the future conduct of the war. Looked at positively, however, this indicated both Roosevelt's flexibility and his vision of an internationally harmonious postwar world that, while perhaps naive, was broader than that of either Stalin or

Churchill, both of whom were to a greater extent prisoners of the history of the nations they led than perhaps was Roosevelt. At the end of the conference, and in the weeks that followed, Roosevelt could therefore reflect with considerable satisfaction upon the outcome of the summit.

While Stalin and, to a lesser extent, Churchill could probably have cried "eureka" with some justification, Roosevelt was already taking the long view, although his illness would deny him the chance to oversee or witness it beyond a further year and half. The U.S. president could afford to be magnanimous in his dealings with his two allies at Tehran, for, with every day, week, and month that passed, more and more U.S. personnel were completing their training, thousands more tons of war matériel of every type were rolling off U.S. production lines, and the bulk of this huge war machine was flowing inexorably along the sea lanes to the United Kingdom in preparation for the invasion of northern France the following summer. Consequently, the sheer scale of the U.S. war effort now meant that the balance of military involvement in the west had swung to such a degree that, although the British view would always be heard and taken fully into account, the overall command and control of the Allied invasion and the subsequent campaign in Europe would thereafter rest firmly in American hands. In accordance with his commitment made on November 30, before he finally left North Africa to return to the United States aboard the USS *Iowa* at the end of the first week of December, Roosevelt visited the Allied forces' headquarters in Tunis, where he informed Gen. Dwight D. Eisenhower of his new appointment as the supreme Allied commander of the expeditionary forces that would carry out the invasion of northern France in mid-1944—Operation "Overlord."

However, this summit at Tehran, more than any other, was not really about winners and losers within and among the three Allies: it was, in truth, the Alliance itself that had emerged triumphant from those few days of meetings and discussions. In the dark days of 1939 and 1940 Great Britain had stood alone. Then, in mid-1941, she had been joined in the fight by the Soviet Union, following the onset of Operation "Barbarossa," and almost six months later by the full commitment of the United States to the war, in the wake of the Japanese attack on Pearl

Harbor. It had taken four years to bring the "Big Three" leaders together at a single summit meeting; but, when the lesser issues and national agendas were set to one side, the most important message that emanated from Tehran for the world in general, and for the Axis leaders in particular, was that the "power of three" was now demonstrably irresistible. The resolve and strategic focus of Churchill, Stalin, and Roosevelt were as one, and the defeat of Nazi Germany and its ally, imperial Japan, was therefore absolutely inevitable—however long the "Big Three" might need in order to achieve their ultimate goal.

Part Three
SHAPING THE PEACE

13

The Fruits of their Labors

December 1943 to July 1944

I F THE ALLIANCE'S GRAND STRATEGY during 1942 and 1943 was characterized by diplomacy and negotiation, then 1944 was dominated by the major military actions that flowed from those historic meetings. Similarly, while the war summits of 1942 and 1943 had been focused mainly upon winning the war—and primarily that against Germany—those that followed in 1944 and 1945 were focused principally upon the business of managing the peace and the international scene in the postwar world, together with the matter of defeating Japan. This last would later introduce a whole new factor into the war summits agenda—the atomic bomb. Tehran had been in very many respects a watershed for the "Big Three," both personally and for the war summits process. The nature and priorities of these meetings would be much changed when they resumed from mid-1944; indeed, it would be fourteen months before all three leaders next met together at Yalta in the Crimea during February 1945. However, all that was for the future, and in the months that came between the meeting in Tehran and that of Churchill and Roosevelt in Quebec during September 1944, all three Allied leaders and their political and military staffs and advisors derived much satisfaction from seeing the discussions, negotiations, compromises, and subsequent planning over the previous two years at last translated into military action on the grand scale. Building upon the direction provided by the "Eureka" summit, the first six months of 1944 were dominated by several momentous events that had flowed directly from the decisions of the Tehran conference—a major amphibious landing on the west coast of Italy, a renewed Italian offensive, a major new Soviet offensive on the eastern front, an Allied invasion of southern France, and, foremost amongst all these events, Operation "Overlord," the Allied invasion of northern France in the midsummer of that year.

While the success of Tehran had been attributable primarily to the three principal participants and their advisors, the conference had also been most timely in light of the succession of military successes that the Allies had enjoyed during the closing months of 1943. These several achievements had further underlined the credibility of the Alliance, and had demonstrated its growing military strength and maturity, just as the "Big Three" had at last come together at Tehran.

On the high seas, the steady attrition of the German U-boat fleet had, in early August 1943, at last forced the Kriegsmarine to abandon the "wolf pack" operational concept that had proved so devastating against the Allied (mainly British) convoys, especially so in 1941 and 1942. Indeed, by July 31, 1943, new construction of Allied shipping had exceeded losses for the first time. From September, the remaining U-boats were, by and large, constrained to conduct their patrols independently. Between September 20 and 22, a daring attack by British midget submarines—"X craft"—had crippled the battleship *Tirpitz* while she lay in Altenfjord, Norway. Although this German raider that had long threatened Allied shipping in the North Atlantic was not finally destroyed until November 12, 1944, the September attack effectively neutralized the threat that she posed. Meanwhile, over Christmas Day and Boxing Day 1943, the Royal Navy cornered and engaged the battle-cruiser *Scharnhorst* during what became known as the Battle of the North Cape. The British cruisers that first intercepted the powerful German warship exchanged shellfire with her through much of December 26, until the arrival of the battleship HMS *Duke of York*, which, with the help of almost a dozen torpedoes fired by accompanying cruisers and destroyers, eventually sank the *Scharnhorst* with broadsides at the end of a duel that lasted for three hours. Finally, on the high seas, the fall of 1943 had witnessed the Italian fleet taken out of the conflict when it surrendered to the Royal Navy at Malta between September 9 and 11.

On land, the campaign in Italy had proceeded well, at first at any rate. The battle that followed the landings at Salerno on September 9 had been successfully concluded nine days later. Following the Allied landings, the Germans had withdrawn to the Gustav line by October 8, although by mid-October the U.S. advance had been halted, and by mid-November that of the British. The Allies did make some further gains during a new offensive from November 20 to December 27, but then the advance slowed and finally ground to a halt once more— although it was anticipated that the intended amphibious landing, Operation "Shingle," agreed at Tehran would resolve this unsatisfactory situation.[1] In the meantime, the island of Corsica was liberated during a short campaign that lasted from September 13 to October 3.

If the war had been proceeding satisfactorily for the Western allies in the Mediterranean and on the high seas, it was in Russia that the tide had truly turned against the Germans and their European allies. On July 5 the Germans launched what would prove to be their last major offensive on the eastern front. This developed into the Battle of Kursk, the greatest tank engagement of the war. From July 5 to 13, many hundreds of German and Soviet armored leviathans—predominantly the German Mark IV, Tiger, and Panther tanks and the Soviet T-34, together with a vast host of other armored vehicles and assault guns—contested the sweeping plains about Kursk within a salient that projected some one hundred and fifty kilometers into the German-held ground between Army Group Center and Army Group South. By the end of their offensive, the Germans had lost more than six hundred tanks, and on July 14 they were forced on to the defensive as the Soviets launched their own counterstroke. Thereafter, the Germans began to retreat in the face of a determined Red Army offensive that pressed forward without pause until August 23. Elsewhere, just as the Kursk counteroffensive was being concluded, the Soviets launched major attacks along a line from Smolensk to Rostov, and in the Caucasus. Meanwhile, to the south, in the Crimea the German Seventeenth Army was isolated and cut off. Then, on December 24, the Red Army launched a further offensive that would finally expel the Germans from the Ukraine. Casualties on both sides were enormous, but there was absolutely no doubt that, all along the eastern front, the Red Army had embarked upon the strategic offensive that would take it ever further westward, and eventually into the very heart of Germany. A telling indication of the worsening manpower situation in Germany came on December 2, 1943, when Hitler ordered the enlistment of German youth for operational service in the country's armed forces.

In the Far East and Pacific theater, the war against Japan was also gaining momentum. The landings by U.S. forces at Bougainville on November 1, and the clearance of Makin and Tarawa in the Marshall and Gilbert Islands by U.S. Marines from November 20, demonstrated that in this theater also the Allies were successfully turning the tide against the Axis powers. The accelerating pace of these U.S. amphibious operations against deeply entrenched and often fanatically defended Japanese positions benefited greatly from the steadily increasing scale and quality of Allied air power that supported the U.S. troops and ships in the region.

Despite these Alliance successes in the latter part of 1943, however, and that of the summit meetings that had underpinned them, the quickening pace of formulating, directing, and managing the grand strategy of the Alliance had taken its toll on those most involved with this process, notably Roosevelt and Churchill. The enormous determination and resilience of the two Western leaders notwithstanding, the health of both had suffered as a result of the huge workload required of them. At the time of the Tehran meeting, Roosevelt was almost sixty-two years of age. Two decades earlier he had been afflicted by the debilitating disease polio, an ailment all too common in those days, and one which affected him still, although his redoubtable spirit had thus far enabled him to overcome the worst effects of the disease during his working life. Achieving the U.S. presidency was clear testimony to this. However, the punishing schedule of meetings and travel through 1943 exacted its price, and from the beginning of 1944 the president's health deteriorated noticeably. An attack of influenza in January was followed by a slow recuperation and then by bronchitis in March. At that stage a full medical examination at the Bethesda U.S. Naval Hospital, Maryland, revealed that Roosevelt—a man in one of the most demanding and stressful positions of authority in the world, but one who also thoroughly enjoyed his food, cigarettes and alcohol—was suffering from heart disease, cardiac failure, and hypertension, and probably from the early stages of cancer as well.[2] Some enforced changes of his lifestyle were made in parallel with the appropriate program of medical treatment. These measures stabilized the situation and postponed what was, by early 1944, a real threat to the president's life, although the ground he had lost over 1942 and 1943 could not be regained. Consequently, throughout 1944 and until his death on April 12, 1945, Roosevelt's involvement in the war summits and the decision-making yet to come was always set against the background of his ever-declining health and the terminal nature of the illness that now afflicted him.

Although almost a decade older than his American colleague and ally, Churchill had generally fared better—an indication of the sort of life he had led thus far and of his determination, energy, remarkable physical robustness, and iron constitution. Churchill also enjoyed what were then considered to be the good things of life—food, drink and tobacco—sometimes in prodigious measure, but, however resilient he may have been, he was in his sixty-ninth year, and the awesome responsibilities that he had taken up since 1940 had borne heavily upon the British war leader; not least among which were the demands made by the war summits. While not suffering from any life-threatening disease, he had become more susceptible to minor ailments through the latter part of 1943. In parallel with this, an increasing awareness of Britain's reducing role in the Alliance from 1944, as the bond between Roosevelt and Stalin became ever stronger, must have been both a galling and a disappointing turn of events for a man who had for all his adult life been a leader and, in later years, a wielder of great power and influence. Churchill had been struck by pneumonia earlier in 1943, and the accelerating pace of events had never really allowed him sufficient time to recover from this illness before his departure for the "Eureka" summit in October. Although the imperatives of negotiation and decision-making in Cairo and Tehran fed and sustained his indomitable spirit through December 1, just over a week later the prime minister succumbed once again to pneumonia, the effects of which impacted upon the health of his heart. Convalescence followed, and he soon resumed his usual work schedule. However, these health problems, aggravated by straightforward exhaustion, had undoubtedly affected his physical resilience and his ability to resist further infections. This was evident through the first half of 1944, which culminated in a further bout of pneumonia in August that year. As a consequence, perhaps, of the prime minister's desire to restore what had become the lesser status of Britain within the Alliance after Tehran, Churchill became the most proactive "Big Three" leader over the next fourteen months. He traveled to meet Stalin in Moscow and Roosevelt both in Quebec and at his Hyde Park home in the United States, while the other two leaders remained in the Soviet Union and North America, respectively. While on the one hand Churchill thrived on the diplomacy and negotiating that these meetings involved, on the other this hectic program of travel compounded the problems of his already weakened health from the end of 1943, so that he, as Roosevelt, came to the subsequent "Big Three" war summits in somewhat less formidable form than had been the case in 1942 and 1943.

Meanwhile, as the two Western leaders suffered varying degrees of ill health through 1944, their Soviet ally, Joseph Stalin, nine years younger than Churchill but three years older than Roosevelt, apparently displayed few ailments apart from the outward physical signs of his age and of the unavoidable stresses and strains of the previous three years. Moreover, all the time Stalin was moving ever closer to achieving his long-term aspirations for his country and communism, as the star—the red star—of the Soviet Union climbed inexorably toward its strategic and geopolitical goals.

Tehran marked the zenith of the war summits, and had set the stage for the liberation of Europe and the defeat of Germany. The detailed ebb and flow of battle in the six months from January 1944 falls generally beyond this account of the meetings that shaped the war, notwithstanding that many of these campaigns and battles were, of course, a direct result of the decisions taken at those meetings. Nonetheless, a brief review of the progress of the war to July is appropriate, in order to place in context the war summits that resumed in the fall of 1944, together with certain events and decisions that took place beforehand. As ever, even though Operation "Overlord" was by now imminent, much of the focus of the Western allies through the first few months of 1944 continued to be on the Mediterranean area, specifically the campaign in Italy.

On January 22, 1944, a sizable Anglo-U.S. force landed virtually unopposed at Anzio, some fifty miles to the southeast of Rome. This force quickly established a secure beachhead and consolidated what was undoubtedly an operationally propitious situation. A speedy end to the campaign in Italy seemed in prospect, and Operation "Shingle" was initially acclaimed a success. However, the U.S. corps commander at Anzio, Lt. Gen. John P. Lucas, then failed to exploit the considerable advantage of surprise that he had gained. Instead of breaking out of the bridgehead, outflanking the German forces and opening the way to Rome, he continued to consolidate and strengthen his positions. This excessive caution on the part of the Allied commander allowed Kesselring's armored formations to redeploy in response to the new threat to the German rear, and within two or three days the Anglo-U.S. landing force was immobile, contained within the perimeter it had occupied since shortly after the initial landing. By January 25, Operation "Shingle" had assumed the oft-quoted characteristics of a "stranded whale" rather than the "wild cat" that Churchill had intended it to be.[3] The operational concept of cutting the German lines of communication, outflanking the Gustav line and neutralizing the bulk of Kesselring's forces in Italy had been sound enough in theory, but, with hindsight, it may be argued that "Shingle" was in practice both misdirected and underresourced, although its fate was finally sealed by indecisive leadership at its highest level of command.[4] The subsequent stalemate at Anzio lasted until May 23, when the Allies' success in breaking through the German line at Monte Cassino, following the capture of the hilltop monastery on May 18, enabled the forces at Anzio to break out, link up with the Allied units driving north, and finally take Rome on June 4. There was a certain grim irony in the reversal of roles by which the breakthrough at Cassino permitted the breakout from Anzio. However, even the capture of Rome attracted criticism that U.S. Gen. Mark Clark's personal preoccupation with the largely symbolic liberation of the Italian capital had undoubtedly been at the expense of the operationally more laudable goal of interdicting and destroying the retreating German Fourteenth Army when it was at its most vulnerable. Therefore, while the fact of the agreement achieved over "Shingle" by the "Big Three" at

Tehran was a strategic negotiating success in its own right, its subsequent implementation and all that transpired at Anzio from January to May 1944 was an almost unmitigated disappointment, as well as a significant waste of human and matériel resources, despite the fact that the operation tied down the German forces needed to contain the bridgehead from January to May 1944.[5]

During the war summit discussions of 1942 and 1943, Italy and the Mediterranean had always, to varying degrees, been something of a distraction for the Allies, and the campaign of attrition that had taken place on the Italian mainland ever since the late fall of 1943 had frequently threatened the development of their plans for the invasion of France. However, so long as the Allies maintained a substantial military presence in the Mediterranean, this had allowed Churchill to continue to advocate an Allied attack on what he viewed as the "soft underbelly" of Axis Europe. This was a plan he had long favored, and one that, if carried through, might also forestall the communist tide that was now flowing toward eastern Europe and the Balkans.

With this in mind, it was perhaps predictable that the fall of Rome sparked a new debate between Churchill and Roosevelt over the subsequent use of the Allied forces in Italy. Arguably, the use of the ten divisions involved should not have been in doubt at this stage, as it had been clearly agreed at the "Quadrant" summit in Quebec the previous August that, with their principal task in Italy completed, these formations would be redeployed to take part in Operation "Anvil" (now renamed "Dragoon") against southern France. This redeployment reflected the need to concentrate all available Allied strength for the forthcoming invasion of mainland Europe through France. Nevertheless, with the fall of Rome, and with the remaining German formations in Italy in retreat, Churchill saw an opportunity to maintain the momentum that had been achieved in that theater, albeit belatedly. He proposed that the divisions earmarked for "Anvil" should remain in Italy, with a view to their continued advance north and east into Yugoslavia and through Slovenia, linking up with Tito's forces en route, liberating the Balkans, and then striking onward into Austria and Germany itself. Appropriately, if somewhat optimistically, this proposed plan attracted the title the "Vienna Alternative."

With the capture of Rome on June 4 and the invasion of northern France accomplished two days later, a capability surplus had occurred in Italy just as the success of "Overlord" was no longer in doubt. Accordingly, Churchill judged that the importance of Operation "Dragoon" in complementing "Overlord" should now be a lesser priority than exploiting the success of the Allies in the Mediterranean theater. He seized the opportunity to put this proposal to Roosevelt with great enthusiasm, and in so doing resurrected issues that had better been left dormant at that stage. This was especially so at a time in the development of the Alliance when British influence in Washington was considerably less than that of even a year before, and which would now not be regained during the remaining year of the conflict.[6]

Much of the detail of the flurry of communications between Churchill and Roosevelt in June and July 1944 concerning the "Vienna Alternative" is superfluous to the central theme of the great meetings of the war. However, a general awareness of what passed between the two leaders is useful both to inform any assessment of Anglo-U.S. relations post-Tehran and, more importantly, as a scene-setter for the summit meetings that resumed from August that year. Churchill's views on the Balkan region and his desire to expand operations in the Mediterranean were already very well known in Washington, and, even though it might be argued that the situation had changed by mid-1944, there is no doubt that Roosevelt identified this as a bid by the British prime minister to achieve a course of action which had already been exhaustively debated and rejected. Furthermore, Roosevelt saw that an operation launched across the Adriatic and into the Balkans could all too easily prejudice his newly established relationship with Stalin. Finally, in arguing his case, Churchill could not avoid opposing the already agreed plan for Operation "Dragoon," a plan positively favored by both Roosevelt and Stalin. With hindsight, therefore, the outcome of what threatened to create a potentially damaging split between Roosevelt and Churchill was never really in doubt.

Irrespective of the wider possibilities that might have followed the Allies' adoption of the "Vienna Alternative," it was unthinkable in mid-1944 that Roosevelt and the J.C.S. would have condoned anything that might well have resulted in the failure of the post-June 6 Anglo-U.S. campaign in northern France. Similarly, Stalin's reaction had he been informed of the proposal—though in fact the matter was resolved before this ever became necessary—would have been entirely predictable: he would have condemned the Western allies for failing to meet their commitment to place the weight of their effort in France and northwest Europe, thereby drawing away as many German divisions as far as possible from the eastern front. Indeed, just as Stalin had promised, the Red Army was already engaged in the major offensive timed to coincide with the campaign in northern France. Even more significantly, however, Stalin would, with some justification, have identified the potentially detrimental effect of Churchill's proposal on his longer term geopolitical plans for Soviet domination of eastern Europe and the Balkans.

Whatever the perceived military advantages of Churchill's proposal, these were far outweighed by the potential risks—strategic and political—it then posed to the Alliance, and Roosevelt was entirely correct when, at the end of June, he advised Churchill that, if he persisted with his proposal, it would be necessary to consult with Stalin about it. This set the seal on the matter. Having established that Roosevelt's decision against a new campaign from Italy into the Balkans rather than into southern France was irrevocable, Churchill was at last forced to accept that the "Vienna Alternative" was finally a dead issue. He also had to accept that his ability to influence Roosevelt, already much diminished, had been further reduced by this unnecessary controversy.

On August 15, a force that included, as planned, the divisions of the U.S. Fifth Army sent from Italy carried out Operation "Dragoon". The Allied invaders landed successfully on the French Riviera and pushed on into southern France. Lyons fell on September 3, and just over a week later the advancing troops linked up with those who had landed in Normandy on or since June 6. By mid-September the great Anglo-U.S. enterprise which had been the principal focus of virtually every war summit thus far was already almost three months old.

Despite the preeminent position of Operation "Overlord" in the history of World War II, and in the planning agendas of the meetings involving the chiefs of staff and those of the "Big Three" through 1942 and 1943, a detailed description of the events of June 6, 1944, and of the days and weeks that followed is largely unnecessary to this account, although a general awareness of that which transpired is necessary as a scene-setter before dealing with the strategic meetings which followed a couple of months later. So it was, shortly before dawn on that historic day, that the greatest invasion fleet in the history of modern warfare arrived off the coast of Normandy.

The seaborne invasion—Operation "Neptune"—was preceded by a large-scale airborne assault into the inland areas beyond, and on the flanks of, the intended landing beaches. This attack from the air was carried out by the Allied paratroops and gliderborne infantry of the U.S. 82nd and 101st Airborne Divisions and the British 6th Airborne Division. As the gliderborne British troops of Maj. John Howard's D Company, the Oxfordshire and Buckinghamshire Light Infantry, landed precisely on their strategically vital objective—the Caen Canal bridge near the village of Ranville—at sixteen minutes past midnight on June 6 (and were the first Allied invasion troops to engage the enemy as a unit that day),[7] the commitment made by Roosevelt and Churchill at the "Trident" summit in Washington in May 1943 was well and truly fulfilled.[8] By last light on D-Day, from Varreville in the west to Ouistreham in the east, the U.S. First Army and British Second Army, which together comprised General Montgomery's 1st Army Group, had gained a foothold at the five landing beaches codenamed "Utah," "Omaha," "Gold," "Juno," and "Sword"—albeit a foothold that was, for the first twenty-four hours, somewhat tenuous in the case of the U.S. landing at "Omaha."[9] Five U.S., British, and Canadian divisions, together with various independent brigades, Free French and other Allied and specialist units, were safely ashore and set about consolidating and exploiting their bridgeheads on the coast of Normandy. In the meantime, a combination of uncertainty and delay on the part of the German high command—and that of Hitler specifically, who clung to the belief that the attack in Normandy was merely a diversion to cover the main Allied assault across the Pas de Calais[10]— meant that, by dawn on June 7, the critical moment that divided possible success from certain failure had passed by the German defenders. The impact on the German defenders' response of their high command's incorrect assessment of the situation was exacerbated by the resolute action of the British and Canadian divisions to secure the Allied left flank against a counterattack by the German armored reserves, and by the exploitation and expansion of their bridgehead by U.S. troops from "Utah" beach on the right flank.

D-Day marked the culmination of so much that had been discussed, negotiated, decided, and planned by the Allied leaders and their military and political staffs and advisors over the previous two years. The Allies were at last in mainland Europe in strength, and the greatest single aspiration of the war summits and the three leaders had finally been realized. As the huge fleet of cargo- and troop-carrying vessels plied incessantly back and forth between the ports in England and the newly established beaches and artificial harbors in Normandy, that Allied strength would increase with each week and month that passed. It would soon become irresistible.[11]

Through June and July the Anglo-U.S. forces fought a series of hard battles to consolidate and expand their bridgeheads. This combat took place amidst the *bocage* countryside of Normandy, an area of small villages, thickly wooded copses, and a myriad patchwork of small fields, each surrounded by high earth banks topped with dense hedgerows. The many tracks and few made-up roads were usually set in deep gullies between the fields. This terrain favored the defender and the infantry, and was hardly conducive to the rapid movement of armored forces of either side. Nevertheless, the ultimate success of the D-Day landings depended upon the Allies' achieving a breakout from the coastal region as soon as possible. During the final week of June, an early attempt (Operation "Epsom") by the Allies to capture Caen failed in the face of fierce resistance, and this was followed by a determined German counterattack which lasted from June 29 to July 1. However, the Americans on the west flank of the beachheads experienced less resistance, and by June 27 they had cleared the Cotentin peninsula. Then, between July 17 and 21, Operation "Goodwood" at last resulted in the capture of Caen by British and Canadian troops, and this in turn facilitated the breakout from the eastern bridgeheads and prepared the way for the Anglo-Canadian advance toward the Netherlands. Finally, between July 25 and 30, the Americans struck out from the St-Lô area in Operation "Cobra," the success of which was followed by a general reorientation of the U.S. divisions toward the east and southeast in preparation for their rapid advance into central France. By the beginning of August 1944, the long-awaited Allied liberation of German-occupied northwest Europe was well and truly under way.

Meanwhile, although less visible than the dramatic events then taking place in Europe, the progress that the Allies were also making against the Japanese in the Pacific and Far East theaters was no less significant; and just as important strategically was the ailing campaign of Chiang Kai-shek's nationalist forces in China, which was giving rise to increasing concern in Washington. Once again, although a detailed account of the combat in these regions is superfluous to the central story of the war summits, certain aspects of it bore directly upon Roosevelt's decision-making in the first half of 1944. Moreover, the various fortunes of the Allied forces operating against the Japanese through much of that year inevitably gave rise to matters that had to be taken fully into account once the process of war summits resumed in September. Indeed, rather as many of the "Big Three" decisions already taken over eastern Europe paved the way for the post-1945 "Cold War," so some of the strategic decisions taken in 1944 contributed directly to the emergence of the communists as the dominant force in postwar China—which in turn affected very directly the course and outcome of the post-World War II conflicts in Korea and Indo-China.

In the Pacific, the U.S. Marines and soldiers were progressively regaining Japanese-held territory by means of their "island-hopping" campaign. These amphibious assaults were usually supported by over-whelming firepower from naval guns and carrier-based aircraft, and each island captured then became a base from which to support an attack on the next one. From the beginning of 1944 through to August, fighting took place in Dutch New Guinea, the Solomon Islands, Kwajelein, and Saipan. From July 20 to August 10, Tinian and Guam were cleared. While the U.S. ground forces battled for the islands, at sea the U.S. Navy inflicted severe attrition on the Japanese navy and its bases, culminating in the defeat of the Japanese fleet and the destruction of virtually all of its remaining aircraft carriers between June 19 and 20 during the Battle of the Philippine Sea.

In the meantime, far to the north, the once-victorious imperial Japanese army was also under pressure in Burma, where between March 8 and June 22 British and Indian troops decisively halted the Japanese advance toward northeast India. The Allied victory at Kohima was the turning point of the war in Burma; thereafter the Japanese were forced on to the defensive. From June 23, the Allies enjoyed complete air supremacy in the skies above Burma. At the same time, Gen. Orde Wingate's Chindits—British troops operating as a guerrilla force in all but name—continued to savage the Japanese lines of communication, bases, and units deep in the enemy's rear area, far behind the front line.[12] In northern Burma, the remarkable success of these long-range offensive operations by the Chindits also relieved Japanese pressure on the U.S. and nationalist Chinese forces, and thereby paved the way for their capture of Moguang and Myitkyina on June 26 and August 4, respectively. Despite this, the overall situation of the nationalists in China was much less certain than that enjoyed by the Allies elsewhere, and a major Japanese offensive begun on April 18 achieved considerable success before it eventually drew to a halt late in the year.

The success of this particular offensive, and the inability of the Chinese forces to resist it effectively, had a particular resonance for Roosevelt. He had already advocated an important international role for nationalist China alongside that of the United States, the Soviet Union, and Great Britain in the postwar world; he had declared his firm support for Chiang Kai-shek at the earlier war summits (most recently at Tehran), contrary to the judgment and advice of Stalin and Churchill on this particular matter. In mid-1944 the inadequacy, ineptness, and corruption of Chiang Kai-shek's regime were becoming ever more evident, as was the fact that the communist Chinese were rapidly assuming the mantle of a viable power-in-waiting in China. Despite this, however, Washington clearly could not renege on a policy of supporting a nation which ensured that a million Japanese soldiers could not be redeployed to Burma or the Pacific theater. Nevertheless, just as Roosevelt had already come to understand that the Soviet Union rather than Great Britain would be the major international power to rank alongside the United States in the postwar world, so he now came to accept that the Soviet Union rather than China would be the ally upon whom he should henceforth rely to assure the defeat of Japan.

Linked directly to his modified view of the probable longer-term international status of China was another significant strategic issue raised to Roosevelt by the J.C.S. and his principal commanders in the Pacific in mid-1944. This issue involved a review and confirmation of U.S. strategy for the ongoing war against Japan. In summary, the U.S. ground forces commander Gen. Douglas A. MacArthur—the principal advocate and architect of the "island-hopping" campaign—demanded that the Philippines should be invaded and liberated, a potentially time-consuming operation that would certainly result in high casualties to the U.S. forces and might even distract these forces from the need to attack Japan directly. However, MacArthur had very close personal affiliations to the Philippines, where he had been the principal U.S. officer when the Japanese forces swept into the islands in January to April 1942. The historic "I shall return" commitment made to the population which he had necessarily abandoned in 1942 was now a matter of honor, quite apart from any operational advantages that might be involved in the U.S. liberation of the Philippines. However, a contrary proposal for the future conduct of the Pacific war was advanced by the U.S. Navy commander, Adm. Chester W. Nimitz. He proposed that the Philippines should be bypassed, with Formosa—closer both to China and to the Japanese homeland—being the primary objective of the U.S. campaign. This of course reflected Roosevelt's long-held position on the need to support China, a position that had at first also found favor with the J.C.S.—not surprisingly, perhaps, in view of the potential for U.S. air power based in Formosa to strike into China and Japan itself. In any event, the outcome of this strategic debate was finally resolved in July, when Roosevelt called MacArthur and Nimitz to meet with him at Pearl Harbor. There, the president decided in favor of liberating the Philippines, and so set the seal upon the way in which the future U.S. campaign in the Pacific would progress. The extent to which the war in the Pacific had evolved as a discrete U.S. conflict—akin in many ways to the equally discrete campaign waged by the Soviet Union on the eastern front—was underlined by this decision of the U.S. president.

Had the fighting by the nationalist Chinese been more successful in 1944, and had the integrity of Chiang Kai-shek's regime been less suspect, Roosevelt might yet have decided to support the strategy proposed by Admiral Nimitz. However, quite apart from the Chinese factor and the wider strategic arguments, it should be added that MacArthur had indicated to Roosevelt that if he failed to sanction the invasion of the Philippines he would ensure that this matter became a political issue within the United States—and this was the year in which Roosevelt was seeking reelection.[13] Thus, as the fate of many thousands of Filipinos suffering under an oppressive Japanese occupation hung in the balance, one of the factors affecting whether their liberation would be sooner or much later was a political assessment by Roosevelt and his Democrat party political advisors concerning the president's domestic reelection prospects.[14]

With the U.S. policy and future strategy for the Pacific campaign decided, together with that in China and the Far East, and for concluding the war against Japan, Roosevelt would soon find himself once more engaged with the familiar European and global issues, when the process of war summits that had by and large lain dormant throughout the eight months since Tehran resumed in September. In advance of this new round of meetings, there had already been a considerable amount of diplomatic activity during the late spring of 1944, much of which had revolved around the need to determine the fate and future of a number of European states. Some of these had been occupied by the Germans and so were now approaching the time of their liberation (notably France, Italy, Greece and Yugoslavia), while three others—Romania, Bulgaria and Hungary—were still active allies of Germany within the Axis. Overlaid upon all these considerations were the pressures exerted by governments-in-exile intriguing and competing with in-place resistance groups for postwar power, the growing awareness and concern in London especially over Stalin's plans for eastern Europe and the Balkans, and, finally, the inevitable personality issues that arose wherever Churchill or Roosevelt had reservations or had simply taken a disliking to the prospective candidate leader of one of these states. The "Big Three" had what amounted to a power of veto over such appointments, and thus over the political future of Europe. In an historical context, the power of these three men to decide the fate of nations in 1944 and 1945 was awesome, as was the responsibility which that power attracted.

Indeed, as early as May 4, Churchill had written to Eden highlighting the issues then emerging between the British perception of postwar Europe—notably those affecting Romania, Bulgaria, Greece and Italy—and the Soviet view of this matter. There followed a confused flurry of messages between Churchill and Roosevelt which failed signally to resolve Churchill's concerns, but did force Washington to clarify and state its overall policy on central and eastern Europe. For this reason alone, the debate over future control of the liberated countries was important. In essence, Churchill and Stalin were content for Britain to deal with Greece while the Soviet Union did the same in Romania (and would have done so irrespective of whether or not the two Western allies had formally signed up to this).[15] This proposal was put to Washington, but secretary of state Cordell Hull was firmly set against such an accommodation. Far from accepting the response from Roosevelt, Churchill pointed out pragmatically that the Red Army was already in a position to influence directly the future of Romania, and also that of Bulgaria. Consequently, he advocated that Moscow should have the leading role in both countries while Britain should assume this role in Greece and in Yugoslavia. Hull noted this new approach and urged Roosevelt to reject it. However, on one of the several occasions on which Roosevelt was seen to be trying to placate or satisfy the wishes of his old ally Churchill in the post-Tehran period, the president took advantage of his secretary of state's temporary absence on June 12 to agree to the proposal on a trial basis for three months, on the clear understanding that it would not allow spheres of postwar influence to be established. But then, inexplicably (apart possibly from the stresses and strains imposed by his deteriorating health in mid-1944), shortly after June 17 Roosevelt, urged by Hull, reversed his earlier decision. At that stage Moscow also became directly involved in the debate, and in mid-July

Washington produced a compromise solution which underlined its concerns over the possible division of the Balkans into spheres of influence, while at the same time agreeing the original three-month trial as a useful adjunct to the Allied strategy though without implying any degree of permanence. In practice, the issue was left unresolved, and the U.S. response was sufficiently noncommittal to send the signal to Stalin that Roosevelt was not prepared to lay down firm measures for the future control of Europe. This in turn provided a useful if unfortunate indication of the fundamentals on which U.S. policy toward Europe would be based when the war summits resumed in September, and indeed those that took place during the rest of the war. In many respects, this policy was representative of a return to the isolationism that had attended U.S. foreign policy after the 1914–18 war.

First, Washington was firmly against the creation of any specific spheres of influence. This mirrored its views on colonialism and imperialism, but demonstrated—or chose to demonstrate—a certain naivety concerning the nature of Europe, communism, and the aspirations of the Soviet Union. This naivety and its wider views on international relations carried through to its desire for any disputes or agreements to be resolved by discussion, negotiation, and agreement in line with the broad principles for the conduct of such matters that had already been formulated by Roosevelt and Churchill and (as they believed) accepted by Stalin. In turn, this meant that the narrow national interests of countries should be supplanted by a very much wider collective security organization—the subject that Roosevelt and Churchill had first discussed at some length at Placentia Bay in August 1941 and which formed the basis of the Atlantic Charter. Thus Washington's naivety was matched in almost equal measure by its laudable but misplaced idealism in a world that was already much changed since 1941. Finally, Washington made it clear that it wished to be involved neither in any decisions about postwar frontiers in Europe nor about the internal arrangements of these countries. Roosevelt's response at Tehran to Stalin's proposals over Poland and East Prussia had already demonstrated this. Taken as a whole, these policy fundamentals indicated America's desire to decouple itself from Europe and its problems as soon as the war against Germany was won. At the same time, it showed that, as at mid-1944, U.S. forces would certainly not be permitted to become involved in any political moves to forestall Soviet aspirations in eastern Europe in the future: the risk of prejudicing the cohesion of the Alliance by souring U.S.-Soviet relations was assessed to be infinitely greater than any need to calm British fears of an impending communist domination of eastern Europe. With hindsight, it is ironic how far removed from these policy goals U.S. policy in Europe, and indeed worldwide, actually turned out to be in the post-1945 era.

However, to return to the period from spring to early fall of 1944, it is instructive to review some of the decisions and events that took place concerning, and within, a number of European countries, and which preceded, affected, and so set the stage for the resumption of the war summits of late-1944 and early 1945.

Romania

The question of Romania had been raised in March 1944, by which time the Red Army was poised on the banks of the Prut river, ready to invade the country if Stalin had been minded to order this. Despite the fact that Romania had been an active participant in Hitler's attack on Russia in June 1941 and remained an Axis ally, the country's war leader, Marshal Ion Antonescu, now found that Romania's position was fast becoming untenable. With an excess of hope, based upon the fact that Romania's forces had been almost exclusively engaged against the Soviets ever since the start of Operation "Barbarossa," he sounded out the Western allies as to whether they would protect his country against the twin disasters that now loomed before him—Nazi retribution if Romania surrendered and was not immediately occupied by the Allies, and Soviet occupation and communist domination if they did. The Allies' response was, predictably, perfunctory. A selective surrender to the Western allies alone was unacceptable, and Romania's subsequent treatment by the Allies would depend mainly upon the extent to which she contributed actively to the defeat of Germany. In the midst of these secret approaches, the Soviets were forthcoming with their own intentions for Romania. In essence, these involved no major change in the country's form of government, the loss of some Romanian territory (albeit offset by the cession of compensating territory from Hungary), and a requirement for the Romanian armed forces either to surrender to the Red Army or to change sides and fight alongside the Russians against Germany. Finally, rather than occupying Romania, the Soviets required free movement through the country for the Allied forces. All in all, these terms to end Romania's involvement in the war were remarkably generous—arguably too generous, and therefore suspect—and Washington and London agreed to these Soviet proposals with little debate. However, with a greater suspicion of Stalin's deviousness than that shown by his Western allies, and in the hope that they might yet obtain even better terms from the Western allies alone, the Romanian government emissaries failed to adopt the Allied terms. At the same time, the Bucharest government possibly misread the temporary respite occasioned by the Red Army concentrating its main effort further to the north (in order to support and complement the impending invasion of northern France). Consequently, as the summer drew on, the Romanian forces continued to fight the Red Army on its borders and in the Crimea. In the meantime, King Michael sought various ways by which the Antonescu regime might be overthrown as a means to achieve the surrender. In late August, King Michael and a group of army officers and moderate politicians at last accomplished this, and the armistice was signed. However, although it was generally based upon the terms set out in the spring, the passage of time had weakened Bucharest's position, together with the ability of Britain and the United States to preserve the original arrangements in practice. Consequently, from August 23, 1944, Soviet domination of Romania became inevitable, although the most significant aspects of this for the future of Europe were the territorial changes enshrined in the armistice document. These implemented border changes involving Romania, Hungary, and the Soviet Union which further advanced Stalin's long-standing plans for the postwar Soviet empire, and its establishment of secure western borders as a bulwark against German and other Western aggression and influences in the future. This revised border was therefore agreed, and all but in place, before the next of the war summits between Churchill and Roosevelt in September.

Bulgaria

Bulgaria was a nation that had not, thus far, fought against the Red Army, but one that was also in danger of being overrun and occupied by the communist forces in due course. As Stalin's armies were still too far from the Bulgarian border in the spring of 1944 to be able to exploit a Bulgarian armistice, Moscow discouraged such moves by the Sofia government and implied that it would be to their greater advantage to seek an armistice once the Soviet forces had closed up to Bulgarian territory. Consequently, Bulgaria continued to fight alongside the Germans until the late summer. On September 8 it severed its support for Germany, however, and sought an armistice from the Soviet Union. Thousands of Soviet troops moved into Bulgaria on September 8 and 9, the Sofia government was displaced by an administration that was largely, although not exclusively, communist or pro-communist, and the days of Bulgaria's inclusion as a part of Soviet-controlled eastern Europe had begun.[16] In due course, Churchill secured Stalin's agreement to the withdrawal of all Bulgarian troops from Greece and Yugoslavia, but at the same time the Soviet leader exacted from Churchill the latter's agreement that Moscow would henceforth have the primary influence over Bulgarian affairs. Thus, just as had happened in Romania, the postwar spheres of influence so disliked by those in Washington were gradually emerging by default, and the seeds of the future "Cold War" conflict were being sown in the geostrategic furrows ploughed across Europe by the chaos of World War II.

Hungary

In the spring of 1944, the situation with regard to Hungary, the third eastern European country that had allied itself with Nazi Germany, was similar to that of Romania, a country that was by then already seeking a suitable armistice with the Allies and which stood to gain territory at its neighbor's expense. The twin threats of reprisals by the German forces that had occupied Hungary since March 1944 if Hungary signed an armistice, and of Soviet domination as and when the Red Army dealt with the German occupiers, concentrated the minds of the Hungarian government through the summer; all the more so following the Romanian armistice that had been achieved in August. The Hungarian administration was headed by Nicolas V. Horthy de Nagybanya. The secret negotiations conducted by Horthy's representatives with the Allies followed much the same pattern as that pursued earlier by Romania, but Hungary had left it almost too late, and by September its leaders could hope only to ameliorate, rather than benefit from, an armistice. Soviet forces entered Hungary in Transylvania during the night of September 22–23, and by the end of the first week of October, Red Army formations and Romanian units were striking toward Budapest from the southeast and from the Carpathian region in the north. As fighting continued, the armistice negotiations stalled while events on the battlefield overtook the diplomatic process. On October, 15 the news that Horthy had asked for an armistice was broadcast on the radio in Budapest, and German troops forced Horthy's abdication and installed a puppet Hungarian government. The Soviet divisions launched a concerted offensive from the south, while the German occupation forces consolidated their control of western Hungary. The Hungarian army divided, part fighting with its German allies and part fighting against the Germans alongside the Red Army. Thus, while the Allied leaders had returned to the business of the war summits and were already discussing the future shape and nature of Europe and the wider world, in Hungary the war was still being conducted at a level of intensity that precluded any resolution of that now divided country's future. None could doubt that the Soviet Union would eventually dominate Hungary. However, for the present the continued fighting—and the consequent turmoil throughout the country—meant that Hungary's path to peace would be much more fraught than had been the case for the other two eastern European allies of the German-led Axis, Romania and Bulgaria.

Yugoslavia

Bordering all three of the eastern European states that had supported Germany, and that former key member of the Axis, Italy, lay Yugoslavia. This Balkan country had long provided a focus for Churchill's aspirations in the Mediterranean and Adriatic, an irritating distraction for Roosevelt and the J.C.S. in Washington, and, until spring 1944, an area of concern for Stalin in the event that Churchill should ever have persuaded

Roosevelt to support the idea of an invasion of the Balkans by the Western allies prior to an attack toward Austria and thence into southern Germany. By April 1944, the Yugoslav resistance forces, led by the communist Josip Broz Tito, were probably the most effective of those then operating against the Germans in any of the countries of occupied Europe. Quite apart from their actual military successes against the occupying forces, Tito's partisans tied down a considerable number of German troops, including several of the elite Waffen-SS divisions. While Tito's communist partisans and Gen. D. Mihailovic's *Cetniks* conducted the war in-country, the Yugoslav government-in-exile, headed by King Peter II, resided in London and planned for the day when it would return to Belgrade—although it was progressively losing ground to Tito, who enjoyed considerable Allied support and, significantly, had a Soviet military mission embedded in his headquarters. As the government's influence waned and Soviet influence with the partisans increased, Churchill had urged King Peter to come to a suitable accommodation with Tito. By mid-May 1944, the king had made a number of changes to his government, including the removal of Mihailovic. Fortuitously perhaps, this coincided with a temporary setback for Tito consequent upon a new German offensive at the end of May. Forced to withdraw and then to escape from the German forces, Tito's partisans were supported by Anglo-U.S. air power, and then Tito himself was rescued from his Bosnian headquarters by the Allies. He was flown to Bari, and then conveyed by a British warship to the isle of Vis in the Adriatic, where he established his new headquarters. The key role played by the Allies who were then the hosts and supporters of the Yugoslav government-in-exile, together with King Peter's conciliatory moves, inclined Tito to cooperate with the distant but revamped Yugoslav government headed by Prime Minister Ivan Subasic. This also involved a number of Tito's supporters receiving important appointments in that administration. Despite deep divisions between the main partisan groups, Tito and Subasic communicated, and throughout the summer it appeared that a united approach and end state might be achieved in Yugoslavia. Soviet interest in the future of Yugoslavia continued to be apparent, although Britain, as its government's host, retained the lead in the Allied discussions on this.

However, Tito had his own nationalistic ambitions for Yugoslavia, and on September 21 he flew secretly to Moscow for talks with Stalin, the main aim of which was to secure Soviet assistance for the liberation of Yugoslavia's capital by Tito's men rather than an Allied force. This would then allow him to exert his authority over the whole of a united country as its liberator. In agreeing to assist Tito, Stalin urged upon him a degree of caution and the desirability of permitting a restoration of the monarchy, albeit temporarily. Ever the astute politician, Stalin judged that Tito's strength was such that Moscow would be better served by having a relatively independent, but still communist, Yugoslavia as a cooperative ally, rather than attempting to dominate it and so invite a clash that would certainly not be in the Soviet interest. In any case, with Romania, Bulgaria and Hungary under Soviet control, Moscow would have achieved an effective geopolitical bulwark in the Balkans without the need to include Yugoslavia as well. As the war summits resumed in the fall of 1944, Tito's own plans for the future of Yugoslavia moved ahead in direct proportion to what had become an increasingly successful coordinated offensive to eject the German occupation forces from his country.

Greece

On the question of the political future of Greece, Britain also took the lead. With Roosevelt's views on the U.S. approach to the internal affairs of the liberated nations in mind, Washington had no great difficulty with Churchill taking a particular interest in the postwar destiny of Greece, even though there was in that country a real possibility that the communist resistance forces could achieve power. This was clearly an eventuality that Churchill wished to preempt. While Stalin might perhaps have been expected actively to support the communists in Greece, the country was too far removed from what he viewed as the Soviet future area of interest, and so he restricted his disapproval of the Western allies' policies in Greece to the occasional word of criticism, but generally adopted a policy of Soviet passivity and noninvolvement. Greece was strategically important to the Allies' campaign in the Mediterranean, but Britain had long had close links with the country, and

Churchill was very aware of both the historical and the more immediate perspectives. Consequently, when the Greek communist resistance capitalized on the Italian surrender by seizing the majority of the Italian weapons and equipment, thereby gaining an instant military superiority over the other resistance groups, Churchill acted. He tried to persuade the Greek king, whose government-in-exile was based primarily, as were several others, in London, to establish a regency, ready to assume temporary power when the country was liberated, pending the restoration of a democratic and stable government in Athens. However, the king refused, and so opened the way, first, for the communists to set up a Committee of National Liberation, and, secondly, for the inevitable interfactional fighting that followed. Subsequently, Churchill managed to persuade the king to make substantial changes to the composition of the Greek government, while at the same time indicating that, although the monarchy should be restored initially, the final choice of the political system to govern Greece postwar would be a matter decided democratically by the Greek people. The internal squabbles eventually abated, and in September a more balanced Greek government was formed, although it was destined not to last long. However, by the time that the war summits resumed that September, Churchill was justified in believing that the Greek question had been resolved, at least for the present. Much more significantly in the wider scheme of things, however, he was convinced that it had been resolved principally because the process of negotiation and consultation between the Allies which had been advocated by Washington had been avoided, Britain alone suggesting, cajoling, and threatening the various factions and personalities into an acceptable solution. The resolution of the situation in Greece in 1944, albeit temporary, reinforced Churchill's pragmatic view that the creation of spheres of interest and influence by the Allies was both unavoidable and desirable. Then, once agreed and established by the "Big Three," the Allied power with responsibility for such an area should be permitted to proceed unfettered by the need to consult and debate its intended actions with the other two. It was with this very recent experience in mind that the British prime minister embarked upon the new cycle of war summits that fall.

Finland

If Stalin had been content to allow the future of Greece to be largely determined by one of his Western allies, this was not the case where Finland was concerned. This Baltic state had been engaged in a bitter winter war with the Red Army from November 1939 to March 1940, had lost territory to the Soviet Union at that time, and had then allied itself with Germany when Hitler launched Operation "Barbarossa" in June 1941. Because of the earlier winter war with the Soviets, its alignment with Germany against its former aggressor was virtually inevitable, and therefore its situation within the wider European conflict was always going to be difficult. Nevertheless, Finland's geostrategic position—including the closeness to its southern border of the strategically vital Soviet city of Leningrad—meant that its future would always be of critical importance to Moscow. This was something that Washington and London both understood, despite having some sympathy for the predicament in which this small Baltic state found itself as the decline of the Third Reich gathered pace.

In March 1944 the Soviet-Finnish front line lay less than twelve miles from Leningrad, and substantial numbers of German troops were still stationed in Finland and confronting the Soviet forces all along that front line. In the short term, this clear threat to the Soviet Union had to be dealt with, while in the longer term Stalin was adamant that Finland should become a buffer against aggression from the west through Scandinavia. He was prepared to accept Finland's independent status postwar, but the price of that would be a Finnish-Soviet border set by Moscow, together with the latter's ability to influence wherever necessary all but Finland's domestic affairs in the future. The Finnish government had considered the terms of an armistice offered by the Soviets in March, but had rejected these as it believed that they would entirely eliminate Finnish sovereignty. Moreover, Moscow had required the Finns to intern the German forces on their soil, an action that was, in practice, beyond their capability. A U.S. proposal that the three Allies would guarantee Finnish independence if they accepted the Soviet terms was judged impracticable by Molotov. Moscow was convinced that only military force would now produce a solution, and in June the Red Army launched a concerted attack against the Karelian peninsula. A Finnish approach on June 20 sought to resume talks with Moscow, but this was rebuffed. On June 30, as the Anglo-U.S. forces were poised to break out of their Normandy bridgeheads, Washington broke off its relations with Finland, which was therefore left to whatever fate the Soviets might inflict upon it. London's involvement with the conflict in Finland was generally conspicuous by its absence. The final outcome was inevitable, and, with the Red Army rolling rapidly across Finland toward the Baltic, crushing any German units that still stood in its way, a ceasefire was implemented on September 5, followed by an armistice on the nineteenth. By then, the German defenders had either withdrawn from Finland or had been overcome by the Soviets. These moves to settle an armistice had been preceded by the resignation of the Finnish foreign minister, who had earlier concluded the Finnish-German accord. In practice, the terms of the armistice were not as draconian as those originally proposed. However, some territory was lost, and the frontier was set on the line of March 12, 1940 (that established at the end of the Russo-Finnish War). Nevertheless, it was agreed that Soviet forces would not occupy Finland; Stalin was confident that the Soviet Union would be able to dominate the Finns quite effectively without the need to station Red Army units in a country that had already, in 1939 and 1940, proved itself well capable of mounting a guerrilla campaign and of inflicting heavy casualties on an unwelcome invading or occupying army. The events which led to the armistice in Finland were noteworthy primarily for the extent to which they had become an almost exclusively Soviet-Finnish affair—an indication of the extent to which, despite Roosevelt's dislike of the concept, there was already a pragmatic acceptance by the Western allies of the existence of a Soviet sphere of influence in the Baltic region.

Italy and France

To conclude the review of matters that directly affected, or would influence, the approach of the "Big Three" to the forthcoming summits, brief mention needs to be made of a difference of opinion that occurred between Roosevelt and Churchill over the makeup of the future governments of Italy and France—a matter that would also bear upon world events concerning France long after Roosevelt's death and well after Churchill had ceased to be prime minister. In Italy, in March 1944 Roosevelt had stated his preference for a politically broad-based administration, whereas Churchill favored a continuance of the predictable, and therefore controllable, government of Marshal Pietro Badoglio. The subsequent argument continued into the summer, and so paralleled Churchill's sometimes difficult relations with Roosevelt over the proposals for a new campaign into the Balkans, at the expense if necessary of the Operation "Dragoon" landings in southern France. Churchill's objections to the new Italian government culminated much later in the British vetoing one of the appointments to it—that of the liberal Count Carlo Sforza—following which Washington publicly disassociated itself from its ally's action. Eventually, the several Anglo-U.S. differences over Italy were resolved or set aside, but they had certainly contributed substantially to making the first half of 1944 the low point of the relationship between Roosevelt and Churchill.

There was also Roosevelt's almost obsessive dislike and mistrust of Gen. Charles de Gaulle, the general who was the leader of the Free French based in London, and who had announced, as soon as Operation "Overlord" was clearly a success, that his Committee of National Liberation was henceforth the provisional government of France. A committed and fervently patriotic French nationalist, he was determined that his country's future would be determined by the French (specifically, the Free French), and by them alone—without any British or, especially, U.S. influences involved. Under pressure from the U.S. state department and from Churchill (who had generally come to support de Gaulle), Roosevelt was finally obliged to recognize the Free French leader's status as the head of state in waiting, and de Gaulle was somewhat belatedly invited to visit the U.S. president in July. In any event, by October all three of the Allied governments had formally recognized de Gaulle's administration as the legitimate government of the liberated France; and with this recognition would in due course also come a seat on the Security Council of the future U.N. and entitlement to a separate French zone of occupation within postwar Germany. Although the matter of de Gaulle proved in practice to be more a source of future friction between the United States and France than a threat to the harmony of the Alliance, it nonetheless demonstrated that, whatever their vision of the postwar world and their undoubted ability to shape that vision into reality by the strategic actions of their armed forces, the "Big Three" were still subject to the human traits, foibles, and preferences exhibited from time to time by all men, irrespective of whether or not they might be world leaders.

A continuation of the virtually undiluted Anglo-U.S. harmony—that of Churchill and Roosevelt specifically—seen from 1941 to 1943 would undoubtedly have been the preferred way of things through 1944. However, the isolated but sometimes difficult exchanges that took place during 1944 highlighted not only their alternative views of certain matters as victory approached, but, much more importantly, the fact that, however insoluble these issues might have appeared, they were in every case resolved eventually. This was achieved by compromise and discussion, or simply as a consequence of the mutual respect and unshakable personal friendship that underlined the relationship between the U.S. president and the British prime minister, a relationship that would endure until the death of the president the following year, by which time the success of the joint venture they had begun in 1941 was in any case assured.

From the green jungles of Burma and the isles of the Pacific, to the hills of Italy and the blue of the Mediterranean, from the vast plains of the eastern front to the towns, villages and countryside of northern and southern France, Roosevelt, Stalin and Churchill were at last reaping the fruits of all that they had sown from 1941 to 1943. By 1944, the "Big Three" had all but concluded the cycle of war summits which had shaped the strategy for fighting and winning the war. Now a new cycle of meetings would not only conclude that process, it would also focus directly upon shaping the postwar world. And at its very core would be an even higher, but possibly unattainable goal—to create a new age of international harmony and security, and so to win the peace for which the world so longed after five long years of war.

14

Idealism and Realism

The Dumbarton Oaks Conference,
August 21 to October 9, 1944

EVER SINCE HIS UNSUCCESSFUL BID for the vice-presidency in 1920—when a cornerstone of the Democratic party's campaign had been support for the League of Nations—President Roosevelt had harbored a vision, a dream, of creating a new, much better international collective security organization. It would be an organization founded upon democracy and equality, one that would enable the states of the world to live in harmony, resolving disputes amicably, or by the imposition of solutions which reflected the will of the majority for the greater good of all mankind. In essence, this would be an organization that exhibited what Roosevelt identified as the very best principles of Western (specifically U.S.) democracy. Although the concept had long been in Roosevelt's mind, it had truly begun to assume a practical form when he had discussed with Churchill, during the "Arcadia" summit at Placentia Bay in August 1941, their joint aspirations for the new world order. These discussions had resulted in the signing of the Atlantic Charter, which had in turn provided a moral foundation upon which the Allies—more particularly, the United States and Great Britain—had tried to base their subsequent plans for the postwar world. Consequently, one of the tasks directed by the Tehran summit had been for a working group to develop the options, enabling measures, and modalities that would in due course allow Roosevelt's dream to become reality.

This work had continued ever since the end of 1943, but on August 21, 1944, the various groups and delegates came together at Dumbarton Oaks, Washington with a view to achieving nothing less than creating what would, in later times, become the United Nations (U.N.) organization. None of the "Big Three" was involved directly in the six weeks of negotiations conducted at Dumbarton Oaks, although they were of course regularly advised on their progress, providing direction as necessary. Necessarily, the work was conducted on a conceptual and largely theoretical level, and as such, without the inconvenience of real world problems to cause obstructions, the work proceeded apace. The absence of the "Big Three" from Dumbarton Oaks notwithstanding, this lengthy conference—or, more accurately, high-level political working group— certainly qualified as a meeting which shaped World War II, just as it shaped the postwar world, and thereby directly affected several major conflicts in the post-1945 era. It also highlighted the growing dilemma for Roosevelt, in particular, of needing to sustain Stalin's goodwill and commitment to fight the Japanese in the Pacific in due course, while at the same time the U.S. president was becoming increasingly aware of a divergence between the ideals of the Western leaders and those of their Soviet ally.[1] The latter awareness was all the more disconcerting as it bore out much of that which Churchill had long been predicting. While it was undoubtedly of considerable importance in the general run of the historic meetings of World War II, Dumbarton Oaks should also occupy a position of even greater significance in the story of a global conflict yet to come—the "Cold War" from 1945.

Ever aware of the priority status that Roosevelt had accorded the collective security project, and of its position at the very heart of the Alliance's war planning and the political justification for the conflict, U.S. secretary of state Cordell Hull was a strong advocate of the need for the three main members of the Alliance to present a united approach to the development of this international organization. He provided the U.S. lead, with a position based upon two broad principles which Roosevelt had preordained for the new organization: it was not to assume the characteristics or attributes of a state in its own right—it would have no permanently established military, police or other security forces; and it was to be fully representational of its members. Where the organization had to resort to force in order to prevent war or to resolve a dispute, the necessary personnel would be agreed and provided by the member states. Although undoubtedly well-intentioned in 1944, this constraint and concept subsequently ensured that the new U.N. organization would only once after 1945 be able to take decisive armed action to counter aggression against a member state.[2]

By and large, Dumbarton Oaks achieved a considerable level of agreement; indeed, it would have been difficult to gainsay the laudable principles which underwrote their discussions. However, three issues caused some difficulty, one of which in particular foreshadowed the more serious difficulties that would arise between East and West after the war. One of the revelations that emerged from the margins of Dumbarton Oaks was a growing awareness in Washington of Stalin's agenda for eastern Europe. As well as posing a potential threat to the harmony of the Alliance, this came in the fall of 1944—just as Roosevelt and Churchill were embarking upon the next of their bilateral summit meetings in Quebec, and at a time when Roosevelt was especially determined not to prejudice Stalin's promise of assistance against Japan once Germany had been defeated.

The first issue was that of membership of the General Assembly, and when the matter was raised by the Soviet ambassador in Washington, Andrei A. Gromyko, it provided an illuminating insight into Moscow's view of its Western allies. Gromyko proposed, and had expected, all sixteen of the Soviet republics to be included as individual members, rather than under the single umbrella of the Soviet Union, a solution which would of course have significantly increased Moscow's representational and voting base. However, quite apart from this, the Soviet rationale was based upon the belief that the dominions of the British Empire and the republics of the American continent were entirely equivalent to the Soviet Union's sub-states. It was incomprehensible to Moscow that nations with such close ties to Britain and the United States could nonetheless have the political freedom to decide and vote contrary to the policy of the mother country. British and U.S. concern over the proposal was duly registered, and Roosevelt ensured that Stalin was apprised of the potential harm that would result from the suggestion that U.S. and British control over their historically affiliated but politically independent nations was the same as the degree of control Moscow exerted over the Soviet republics. In the knowledge that there was still time in hand, the matter was not brought to a satisfactory conclusion by the attendees at Dumbarton Oaks.

The membership of the Security Council, wherein the ultimate decision-making authority would reside, also attracted some discussion over the Americans' insistence that China should be a permanent member; in the fall of 1944, of course, the China which Washington had in mind was that headed by the nationalist Chiang Kai-shek, not the communist Mao Tse-tung. However, it was agreed that the five permanent members should be the United States, the Soviet Union, Great Britain, France, and China, plus six other countries serving as temporary members of the Security Council. However, if membership of the Security Council was resolved satisfactorily, this issue gave rise to one that proved far more difficult—Council voting and the use of the veto.

Where two sides have fundamentally different perceptions, but with each assuming that the other both understands and has accepted the other's position, an impasse is almost inevitable. So it was over the question of voting procedures and the use of the veto by the members of the Security Council. The Soviets had assumed that voting unanimity was a fundamental principle applying to the Security Council, and that there would be no constraints or qualifying rules imposed upon how the members voted. This meant that a permanent member of the Council could always block any U.N. action by its single vote. The United States, on the other hand, envisaged the veto only being used for major issues, such as the proposed use of armed force to prevent or resolve a conflict. Similarly, Stalin clearly saw the veto as a key diplomatic weapon for dealing with matters affecting Soviet national interest, whereas Roosevelt believed that where a Security Council member was directly involved in a dispute, it should abstain from voting to affect its outcome. This ran directly contrary to the use Stalin already anticipated of his country's vote as a means of advancing his plans for expanding Soviet domination, and for ensuring that neither lesser nations nor the Western powers would have the means to frustrate his aspirations. Here again was a very clear indication of the still shadowy lines that were being drawn between the democratic West and the communist East—albeit lines that were gaining more substance by the month. It was abundantly clear that the matter of the veto would not be resolved at Dumbarton Oaks, and, rather than prejudice the good work which had been done, the delegates provided a form of words typical of the art of the civil servant or diplomat, in that the phraseology sounded good but meant very little. It was agreed that disputes involving the interests of the members of the Security Council could be settled without considering the votes of such interested parties, but that wherever the use of force might be involved the permanent members' veto would apply. Predictably, neither Churchill nor Roosevelt—who were by then together in Quebec— thought this a helpful solution; neither did it meet Soviet needs. Accordingly, the Security Council voting issue remained the single most significant matter unresolved at Dumbarton Oaks. Although this matter, together with the question of the size of Soviet representation in the organization, was more or less resolved at the next "Big Three" meeting in Yalta the following February, it was nonetheless an issue that would severely hamper the U.N. and also bedevil the foreign policy intentions of a succession of U.S. and British governments throughout the "Cold War" years from 1945 and into the 1980s. In September 1944, however, the priority for both Roosevelt and, to a lesser extent, Churchill was to guarantee Soviet military support against Japan in due course, and so their idealism was necessarily modified by pragmatism, in order to reflect the realities of the moment.[3]

The statement issued at the end of the Dumbarton Oaks meeting on October 9 belied the fact that further work remained to be done, and that some major areas of disagreement were as yet unresolved. Despite this, a great number of lesser issues, protocols, and organizational and procedural matters had been successfully resolved. Accordingly, the official news release provided to the U.S. and British media indicated that the arrangements for an international collective security organization for the postwar world had been successfully developed, and would ensure peace and security for all peoples in that not too distant future. This positive and heartening statement was greeted with universal approval and enthusiasm by the peoples of two Western nations who could at last believe that the end of the war was truly in sight, and by the populations of those countries still under German or Japanese occupation.

Above: An alliance in embryo: British prime minister Winston Churchill meets U.S. president F.D. Roosevelt aboard USS *Augusta* at Placentia Bay, August 1941. Roosevelt's son, Col. Elliot Roosevelt, is on the president's immediate left.

Below: Hitler's Operation "Barbarossa"—the invasion of Russia in June 1941—brought the Soviet Union into the war as an ally of Britain, and Stalin as the second member of what subsequently became the "Big Three."

Above: The "Day of Infamy" at Pearl Harb[or] December 7, 1941, bro[ught] the United States fully [into] the war, when Roosev[elt] became the third men[ber] of what was hencefort[h] the "Big Three."

Center left: The U.S. "island hopping" campaign in the Pacifi[c] theater constantly competed with the European theater for resources. Here, U.S. infantry and tanks bat[tle] the Japanese during th[e] bitter fighting on Kwa[jalein] Atoll, February 1944.

Left: Understandably, [U.S.] national interests mea[nt] that operations in the Pacific theater were always a high priorit[y] issue in Washington. [Here] Roosevelt is briefed i[n] Hawaii, 1944, on the developing Pacific campaign by General MacArthur (left) and Admiral Nimitz (stand[ing]). Seated on the right is Admiral Leahy.

Above: Despite Roosevelt's early support, nationalist China was increasingly sidelined by the Allies. Here, Chiang Kai-shek is shown (left) with Roosevelt, Churchill, and Madame Chiang Kai-shek at the Cairo summit, November 1943. Anthony Eden is shown standing immediately behind the seated Chinese leader.

Right: Gen. George Marshall, U.S. Army chief of staff, was the mastermind behind much of the U.S. and Allied strategic planning, although his ideas did not always find favor with Roosevelt and Churchill. Marshall is shown here with Henry Stimson, U.S. secretary of war.

Opposite page: D-Day. Allied troops landing on the Normandy beaches on June 6, 1944. For almost three years, the strategy, politics, and planning for the cross-Channel invasion dominated the war summits' process.

Right: General Eisenhower, the supreme Allied commander (center), with Patton (right) and Bradley: the principal U.S. Army commanders in northwest Europe from late 1944.

Right: Field Marshal Montgomery, seen here with U.S. General Ridgway during the British operation to restore the situation in the north of the Ardennes, January 1945.

Below: The unforeseen but fortuitous capture of the Rhine river bridge at Remagen in March, 1945, enabled the Allies to develop Eisenhower's controversial broad front strategy in northwest Europe.

Above: Yalta, February 1945, the last occasion which all of the origina members of the "Big Three" would conduct war summit.

Left: Unavoidably, Fren perspectives and aspirations impinged increasingly upon the summits from mid-194 although Roosevelt mistrusted the Free Fre leader, Gen. Charles d Gaulle (seen here with Truman in 1945).

bove and below: The victorious Allies: Churchill, Truman, and Stalin at Potsdam in July 045. Sadly, U.S. president Roosevelt had died just three months before this final war summit. y the end of the Potsdam meeting, the new British prime minister, Clement Attlee (seated, ft), had replaced Churchill as Britain's leader.

Above: Götter-
dämmerung: victor
Red Army troops
amidst the scene of
devastation at the
Reichstag, in the he
of Berlin, Germany
May 1945.

Left: Retribution a
final victory: the U.
atomic attack on
Nagasaki, Japan,
August 8, 1945.

Perhaps one of the most revealing aspects of the negotiations at Dumbarton Oaks was an assessment contained in a memorandum produced by the diplomat George F. Kennan, who was then stationed at the U.S. embassy in Moscow. Amongst the correspondence sent to Washington updating Cordell Hull on the embassy's interpretations of Soviet policy and future intentions was a note which included the statement, "An international organization for the preservation of peace and security cannot take the place of a well-conceived and realistic foreign policy . . . and we are being . . . negligent of the interests of our people if we allow plans for an international organization to be an excuse for failing to occupy ourselves seriously and minutely with the sheer power relationships of the European peoples."[4] Clearly, the gulf between idealism and realism was widening as Roosevelt pursued his dream of a collective security organization, and the critical need to maintain the goodwill and support of the Soviets for the war against Japan—despite the fact that the pursuit of these two overriding priorities would in due course create enormous difficulties for the peoples of postwar Europe. It was with these priorities firmly established in Roosevelt's mind that the first of the 1944 bilateral war summits between the president and Churchill took place in mid-September, a meeting which had coincided with, and had been overlapped by, the Dumbarton Oaks conference. This resumption of the core war summits process was once again conducted in Quebec, from September 12, and this next meeting between Roosevelt and Churchill was codenamed "Octagon."

15

Strategy, Economics, and "Tube Alloys"

The "Octagon" Conference, September 12–16, 1944, and the Hyde Park Meeting, September 19, 1944

AFTER JULY 1944, Churchill became increasingly concerned over Roosevelt's apparent unwillingness to deal conclusively with a growing number of European issues, or, indeed, to expose himself to any of Churchill's arguments or proposals on these particular matters. Of course, with the campaign in northwest Europe now well under way, Roosevelt was understandably looking more and more toward the Pacific theater, the war with Japan, and what he knew would in due course be a primarily U.S.-Soviet assault on the Japanese home islands and territories. At the same time, after almost four years of working closely with the British prime minister, Roosevelt knew all too well that most of the European key issues Churchill sought to raise with him had implications or consequences that would, to varying degrees, conflict with Stalin's aims and objectives in eastern Europe; and Roosevelt could not afford to prejudice the Soviet support needed to conclude what had become primarily "America's war" against the Japanese in the Pacific. Certainly, Roosevelt was not seeking a bilateral meeting with Churchill, and so he proposed that a "Big Three" meeting might be conducted in Scotland. However, Stalin was once again not prepared to leave the Soviet Union at a time when the Red Army was making significant progress on the eastern front and toward southeast Europe, as he once again claimed that he was required to provide overall policy direction for its operations on a daily basis. Nevertheless, Churchill, who was also very much aware of the Red Army's successes in southeast Europe, as well as of the early indications of difficulties emerging at Dumbarton Oaks with aspects of the postwar collective security organization, persisted in arguing the need for a bilateral summit with Roosevelt. At last, Roosevelt conceded that a full-scale bilateral summit would be useful, and agreed to meet Churchill and the British chiefs of staff and ministerial advisors in Quebec from September 12. The principal (but by no means exclusive) focus of this summit would be Asia and the Pacific, together with a number of matters affecting the Anglo-U.S. relationship specifically. "Octagon" would be the last of the series of full-scale bilateral summits between Churchill and Roosevelt and thus concluded a process which had begun with the Placentia Bay meeting in August 1941. Much later, it would emerge that a very private meeting had also taken place between Roosevelt and Churchill at the president's home at Hyde Park on the Hudson River on September 19, shortly after the "Octagon" conference—an historic meeting that would subsequently directly affect the course of the war in 1945, as well as the whole nature of warfare and international relations thereafter.

As he had done in 1943, Churchill once again traveled by sea to Halifax, Nova Scotia, and thence by rail to Quebec, where he arrived on September 11. Although Britain's strategic circumstances had improved immeasurably since the dark days of August 1941, the sea journey in September 1944 was less happy than had been the case when he had voyaged to Newfoundland on board the now long-gone HMS *Prince of Wales* bound for Placentia Bay. The prime minister was not now in such robust health as he had been three years before, and he found the humid Atlantic weather oppressive; he was at odds with his chiefs of staff over several key strategic issues, and he was away from London just as a new German weapon—the V-2 missile—had started landing in southern England. Nevertheless, "Octagon" would prove to be a timely and productive conference, and an historic war summit in its own right—one which took account of the truly global nature of the enter- prise in which the Allies were now engaged. The conference began with a review of each of the theaters of war, and a summary of these start- point briefings clearly illustrated the sheer scale of the conflict at that stage of the war (see table opposite).

This summary revealed several matters that would affect future Alliance strategy and would therefore influence the future war summits. Amongst these was the clear indication that Soviet forces in southeastern Europe were already well placed to continue their advance through

Hungary and into Austria, eventually to seize Vienna. This was the strategic-political situation which had concerned Churchill for many months already, but which Roosevelt had generally chosen thus far to defer as a topic of discussion. The ongoing crisis in China heralded a steady reduction of U.S. support for Chiang Kai-shek, notwithstanding the fact that the nationalists were still occupying about a million Japanese soldiers who might otherwise have been deployed in the Pacific or Burma. However, the steady demise of the Japanese virtually

"Octagon": Summary of the Strategic Situation, 12 September 1944		
Theater	Strategic Situation	Impact and Comments
Pacific	U.S. Navy had cut lines of communication between Japan and Central Pacific.	All oil imports into Japan ceased. Support to island garrisons ceased.
	Severe attrition of Japanese fleet.	Japanese maritime countermove no longer viable.
	Guam, Saipan, and Tinian captured.	Japanese home islands within USAAF bomber range.
	Way clear to attack the Philippines.	U.S. J.C.S. decided at "Octagon" to bypass southern Philippines and attack at Leyte (where Japanese fleet was finally destroyed during Battle of Leyte Gulf, October 23–26).
China	Chiang Kai-shek's nationalists at Chungking cut off from coast by Japanese offensive. U.S. airbases in China at risk of capture.	Overall situation for Allies in China deteriorating rapidly. Washington wanted U.S. General Stilwell (chief of staff to Chiang) to assume full command of all Chinese forces, and for nationalists to join with communist forces against Japanese. Chiang refused, resulting in reducing U.S. support for nationalists and, in longer term, removal of U.S. obligation to support Chiang against Chinese communists.
Burma	British successes at Kohima and Imphal, which finally shattered the myth of the Japanese soldier's jungle fighting ability. Second Chindit operation in progress. Slow but steady progress against Japanese, despite climate and operational environment.	Operations progressing, relieving pressure on Chinese and U.S. forces in China, but progress slow, and Japanese still achieving local successes.

"Octagon": Summary of the Strategic Situation, 12 September 1944 *continued*		
Theater	**Strategic Situation**	**Impact and Comments**
Eastern front	Red Army advancing steadily on 800-mile front from Finland to the Black Sea.	Assessed to be engaging about two million German and Axis troops.
	Finland had requested armistice; Romanian army destroyed; Bulgaria neutralized; Germans in Yugoslavia and Greece isolated.	See also amplifying summaries at Chapter 13.
	Red Army advancing into East Prussia and northern Poland.	German front broken north of the Pripet Marshes.
	Red Army formations poised on River Vistula, near Warsaw.	German forces in full retreat.
Europe	In north, Allied forces seeking to secure Channel and North Sea ports of France, Belgium, and Netherlands. Brussels, Antwerp, and Le Havre all in Allied hands. In centre, Allied forces driving toward Saar and Germany on broad front, having already breached Siegfried line. Luxembourg and Liège captured. In south, Allied forces at River Moselle and Nancy taken. Linkup achieved with forces in southern France (Operation "Anvil/Dragoon").	German forces withdrawing, along line from English Channel to Swiss border. Eisenhower envisaged the Allied advance cutting off and destroying German forces in the Ruhr and Saar, then driving for Berlin, utilizing broad-front strategy to exploit best opportunity as and when it presented itself.

everywhere else meant that the chances of any such redeployment were much less practicable. Nevertheless, the Japanese successes in China reinforced the probable future need for joint Allied (including Soviet) military action against Japan. Finally, Eisenhower's presentation of his broad-front strategy in Europe gave rise to much debate, as two of his most senior commanders, the British General Montgomery and the U.S. General Patton, were both convinced that a single concentrated thrust was the best way to strike for Berlin and end the war in short order. This debate between Montgomery's 21st Army Group in the north and Patton's U.S. Third Army in the south, and the competing priority for finite stocks of combat supplies and vital material resources, would later produce a number of difficulties for the Western allies, and for Eisenhower in particular. At the same time, the politically sensitive issue of who was destined to take the hugely symbolic prize of Berlin had now emerged almost in passing, although this would assume rapidly growing significance as the campaign in Europe, both west and east, progressed. While he was, of course, not present at this Anglo-U.S. bilateral summit, Stalin was already perfectly clear about which of the three allies had earned the inalienable and historic right to take the capital of Adolf Hitler's Third Reich.

The main business of the "Octagon" summit was conducted over a mere four days, during which an Anglo-U.S. consensus was achieved on the several strategic matters put before the conference. With regard to the war against Japan, it was estimated that a further eighteen months would be required before the Allies could achieve a final victory. Their future planning assumptions would therefore be based on a "best-case scenario" of the war ending in March 1946—a projection which would have other important political and economic consequences for the Anglo-U.S. relationship, as it meant that the current arrangements for U.S. aid to Britain (notably lend-lease) had at least another eighteen months to run, and the British government would plan accordingly. The eighteen-month assessment took account not only of Stalin's unhurried responses to Washington's attempts actively to involve the Soviet Union against Japan, but also of a strategy—approved by Roosevelt and Churchill at Quebec—that called for a full-scale invasion and subjuga-tion of Japan by Allied ground forces. Although the final assault on Japan would be U.S.-led and be by a predominantly U.S. force, it was agreed that a Royal Navy task group, together with RAF units, would take part in the operation under U.S. command.[1] Both Roosevelt and Churchill acknowledged that the defeat of Japan by bombardment alone might have eventually proved viable, but that the achievement of a total victory by this means would take an unacceptably long time. In the open forum of "Octagon," there was no mention of a certain highly secret device, the development of its technology already well advanced, which would in less than twelve months' time render totally redundant all of the Allies' discussion and planning for a conventional assault on the Japanese homeland.

In the meantime, it was confirmed that the U.S. campaign to complete the liberation of the Philippines should continue as planned, with landings on Formosa (Taiwan) and elsewhere on the Chinese littoral as opportunities to make them arose. While the U.S. forces under MacArthur and Nimitz carried forward their campaign in the Pacific, the British combat forces in Burma—which included significant numbers of Indian troops and which were now supported by substantial quantities of U.S. logistic resources and manpower—would continue their ongoing campaign until all Japanese troops in Burma had been overcome or withdrawn. With a view to striking a final decisive blow against the Japanese, the British commander in Burma, General Slim, was to launch Operation "Dracula," an amphibious landing and airborne assault to seize Rangoon, by March 1945.[2] To assist this goal, the combined chiefs of staff would increase the already high level of U.S. logistic and air transport support, although it was agreed as a general principle that U.S. combat units would not be deployed in Burma.[3] Finally, it was to be made clear to Chiang Kai-shek that those Chinese forces already fighting the Japanese in Burma were to continue to do so, and were not to be withdrawn to strengthen Chiang's deteriorating position in China, in particular the positions he was holding in a largely vain attempt to stem the influence of the Chinese communists.

In their wider consideration of the war against Japan, the chiefs of staff judged it prudent to maintain the current level of support from the Western allies to the Soviet Union, notwithstanding the very favorable situation which the Red Army now enjoyed on the eastern front. This decision was undoubtedly linked to the U.S. desire not to send any signals to Moscow that might be misinterpreted and later prejudice Soviet military support against Japan; it was also based on the pragmatic assumption that, as the level of aid for the eastern front diminished, this reduction would in any case be offset by an increased requirement for Western aid to be dispatched to the Soviet Far East forces.

With regard to the Allied campaign in western Europe, Eisenhower's report to the conference provided grounds for a justifiable degree of optimism. It was even suggested that the war against Germany might yet be over by the end of 1944. Certainly, the main issue here was that of where the point of main effort was to be set, if indeed there was to be such a concentration of resources. "Octagon" confirmed the first part of

Eisenhower's intentions—to trap and destroy the German forces in the Saar and Ruhr region—but it was then more ambivalent about his broad-front strategy. Certainly, the combined chiefs of staff advised, the advance into Germany should be conducted with axes both to the north and south of the Ruhr, but thereafter the main effort should be to the north rather than the south. However, there was no clear statement on whether or not Eisenhower's ultimate objective was to be Berlin, and, given Roosevelt's awareness of Stalin's sensitivities, it was never likely that such a statement would have been forthcoming.

Thus, although "Octagon" failed to address directly the single-main-axis concept advocated by Montgomery and Patton, the conference required Eisenhower to note that there were "advantages of the northern line of approach into Germany, as opposed to the southern," and "the necessity for the opening up of the northwest ports, particularly Antwerp and Rotterdam, before the bad weather sets in," and therefore the chiefs of staff nonetheless provided a suitably clear indication that the 21st Army Group's advance should be regarded as the main line of advance.[4] This direction was reflected in Eisenhower's subsequent orders to his commanders. However, in the north, Montgomery would increasingly interpret this direction as an endorsement of his axis of advance as (in all but name) the single main axis of the Western allies, while, in the south, Gen. George S. Patton, commanding the U.S. Third Army within Gen. Omar N. Bradley's 12th Army Group, was not prepared to accept the preeminence of the northern axis, nor would he forgo any opportunity—often supported by clear operational successes— to try to persuade Bradley and Eisenhower that the Allies' main axis should be that to the south, with the bulk of the available fuel and ammunition allocated accordingly. Consequently, although on the one hand "Octagon" provided the necessary direction for Eisenhower to prosecute the campaign in northwest Europe successfully, it quite understandably failed to take account of the personalities of the senior field commanders involved, and so opened the way for oft-quoted and ongoing (but frequently exaggerated) Anglo-U.S. friction at the operational level of command during the months that lay ahead, involving Montgomery, Patton, Bradley, and Eisenhower.

While the Allied divisions were to continue the advance toward Germany, in Italy it was agreed that no reduction of Allied force levels would be made until the successful conclusion of General Wilson's offensive, which was then in progress. At the same time, "Octagon" directed that the landing craft then in Italy would be retained there in anticipation of a possible landing on the Istrian peninsula in northwestern Yugoslavia. There would in due course be a need for amphibious landing equipment in the Far East, but, with "Overlord" and "Dragoon" completed, the debates on the allocation of these scarce resources that had dominated so many of the earlier war summits were truly a thing of the past. This agreement on Italy and the decision to retain the landing craft allowed Roosevelt to meet one of Churchill's long-standing aspirations without antagonizing Stalin, for a landing in Istria could enable the Western allies to advance against Germany's southern flank into Hungary or Austria and on to Vienna, thereby preempting Soviet ambitions in that area. At Quebec, Roosevelt knew full well that the Istrian offensive was unlikely ever to take place in practice, but, by providing this strategic decision backed up by the tangible military assets to carry it through, the U.S. president achieved a great deal by way of placating Churchill and restoring much of the ground that had been lost between the two during the many months since Tehran, thus cementing and reinforcing the wider unity of the great Alliance. The fact and timing of Roosevelt's decision on this matter was politically most astute, as this Istrian expedition would be an almost exclusively British venture, planned by General Wilson but commanded overall by General Alexander, an officer who had thus far consistently enjoyed the personal support and friendship of Churchill. It also proved to be a sound judgment call by Roosevelt, as no suitable opportunity for the British landing in Istria ever presented itself.

The long-term future of postwar Germany was addressed by the two leaders at "Octagon." A plan proposed by the U.S. secretary to the treasury, Henry Morgenthau, on September 12 to eliminate entirely Germany's military industrial capability in the Saar and Ruhr regions, with the country then being transformed into an almost exclusively agrarian economy, was actually approved by Roosevelt and Churchill.

Certainly, a postwar Germany that would be essentially pastoral in nature would provide a politically most attractive image for the populations of those nations which had now fought two global conflicts against what was perceived by many to be an insatiable German (or Prussian) militarism. Moreover, this neutralization of German industrial—and therefore commercial—competition could only benefit British trade. However, this proposal was plainly impractical in reality, and, alongside the Allies' unconditional surrender principle (which it tended to reinforce), it provided a further disincentive for Germany not to fight on. In any event, apart from being another insight into Washington's view of a key European issue, the flaws in the Morgenthau proposal were all too evident once it became public knowledge, and it was taken no further.

Of greater importance, perhaps, was one other decision Roosevelt made on postwar Germany. It had already been anticipated that the victorious Allies would occupy zones within the country, but, with the considerable reservations Roosevelt had already expressed about France in general and de Gaulle in particular, the U.S. president had previously stated that it would be unacceptable for the U.S. forces in their postwar occupation zone of Germany to have to rely upon lines of communication which ran through France. However, at "Octagon" he changed his position on this, and agreed that U.S. forces would occupy the southern zone of Germany; provided that they had unrestricted access to the major North Sea ports of Bremerhaven and Bremen. While the practical logic of this decision in September 1944 was clear—the vast majority of the U.S. ground forces were already operating on the right, or southern, flank of the Allied advance into Germany—it was nonetheless a decision that would shape not only the final months of World War II but one that would later have a fundamental impact upon the strategy of the "Cold War" that succeeded it from 1945.[5]

Although "Octagon" dealt, in the main, with strategic matters affecting the several ongoing campaigns against Germany and Japan, Churchill and Roosevelt also took the opportunity to review the existing and future bilateral arrangements between the United States and Britain for the provision of aid to the latter. The vital U.S. lend-lease assistance to Britain had been formally in place since March 1941, although as early as

September 1940 the United States had provided the Royal Navy with fifty obsolescent destroyers in exchange for base facilities in British overseas territories. In Quebec, the two leaders agreed that lend-lease—by then with more of a commercially and industrially regenerative emphasis than a military one—would continue to operate, certainly until the end of the war with Japan, which, based upon the current strategic estimate, would guarantee at least eighteen months more of this aid for a British economy already devastated by five years of war. The details of this "Stage II" aid agreement were finalized by Washington and London in November. Little did those involved know that the trigger which would terminate lend-lease, then precipitate an economic crisis and years of austerity in Britain, and eventually lead to the implementation of the Marshall Aid Plan for Europe, was no more than twelve months away.

With the "Octagon" conference concluded, Churchill joined Roosevelt at the president's family home and estate at Hyde Park, New York, for two days of almost exclusively one-to-one discussions between the two leaders. Although of short duration and conducted in almost total secrecy, this meeting in very many respects qualified as a summit in its own right, for the discussion and decisions of the two men on the apparently innocuous subject of "tube alloys" shaped directly both the end of World War II and the very nature of the "Cold War" that would follow it. As time would show, the Hyde Park summit of September 1944 was one of the world's truly historic meetings.

Hyde Park, New York, September 1944

Throughout the war, the race had been on in Germany, Great Britain, and the United States to "split the atom" and so harness the energy released in order to create an atomic weapon, the power of which would far exceed that of any manmade weapon invented. Research was also being carried out in the Soviet Union, although by late 1944 it was considerably more advanced in Germany and in the United States. Initially—as early as 1940—British-based scientists such as Otto Frisch, Rudolf Peierls, and, later, Niels Bohr[6] had secured and maintained Britain's leading position in this work, but not until about October 1941 was Roosevelt fully seized by the vital significance of atomic energy to the war effort. Then, from March 1942, as the United States was able to provide significantly greater resources and almost unlimited funding to take forward what became the "Manhattan project," the British expertise and research results already achieved were passed to the U.S. scientists and pooled with the less advanced progress that had been made by the latter. This was done on the understanding that the follow-on results of the project would also be pooled. However, the United States clearly assumed the lead in, and the practical control of, the West's atomic energy research and development program.

The actual extent of the subsequent pooling of information authorized by the U.S. administration—particularly after the succession of postwar spy scandals involving Burgess, Maclean, Philby, and others—and the advisability of Britain's relinquishing its original lead in this field and then needing to catch up postwar, in order to develop the hydrogen bomb and support a British independent nuclear deterrent capability, are part of a complex subject which is beyond the scope of this account of the war summits of World War II.[7] Suffice it to say, however, that in September 1944 the joint Anglo-U.S. approach to the development of what was codenamed "tube alloys" to defeat a common enemy as soon as possible, and to ensure that Germany did not gain this weapon before the Allies, was both pragmatic and logical; and it was on this basis that Roosevelt and Churchill came together at Hyde Park to discuss the awesome destructive power that their two nations were by then well advanced in the process of making a reality. As far as it can be ascertained, the two had first discussed this most secret of subjects face-to-face in mid-1942, also at Hyde Park, and then again in the margins of the "Quadrant" conference in August 1943, when the basic protocols for managing the "tube alloys" project by the United States, Great Britain, and Canada were formalized.[8]

Understandably, that which was discussed and agreed at this latest "tube alloys" meeting on September 19, 1944, was not publicized while the war was still in progress. Nevertheless, its import was thereafter in the forefront of the mind of the president and the prime minister during all of their subsequent decision-making. When a summary, or "aide-mémoire," of their conversation was finally released, it was remarkable for its simplicity, its clarity, and its implications.[9] First, both men agreed that the work on atomic power—still referred to as "tube alloys" throughout the document—should remain absolutely secret. Despite Roosevelt's views on international collective security and the embryo U.N. organization, he was quite clear that it would be imprudent to disclose this matter to wider scrutiny and international regulation. Furthermore, it was agreed that, when a viable atomic bomb existed, it might perhaps, "after mature consideration," be used against Japan; and, foreshadowing precisely the strategy that would be applied the following August, this atomic bombardment would be repeated until the Japanese surrendered. At a stroke, the two leaders had obviated the need to invade Japan, although the detailed planning for this major operation of course continued, just in case the atomic option might eventually prove nonviable, as well as to mask the real progress of the Manhattan project.

Next, and of considerable significance for the "Cold War" era yet to come, it was agreed that this Anglo-U.S. cooperation on the development of atomic energy for military and commercial applications should continue after the defeat of Japan, unless and until the agreement was terminated by both parties. History would later show that Churchill had placed excessive faith in the postwar U.S. government's continuing willingness to carry on this cooperation on an unconditional and unconstrained basis, especially once the personal relationship he had established with Roosevelt no longer existed following the president's death in 1945. Similarly, once the more immediate need of the Allies to win the war had been achieved, it was always unrealistic to expect that future U.S. administrations would be able to accept the constraints on American sovereignty imposed by the Anglo-U.S. veto over the use of their atomic weapons, as agreed by Churchill and Roosevelt in the margins of the "Quadrant" conference on August 19, 1943.

Finally, in dealing with the specifics of the work being carried out by the Manhattan project scientists, the need for absolute security was reiterated, including the telling phrase that there was to be "no leakage of information particularly to the Russians."[10] Nevertheless, as late as August and September 1944, Roosevelt had been actively considering Stalin's possible inclusion in "tube alloys," a course of action strongly advised by Niels Bohr and some of the other scientists involved with the project. Indeed, U.S. possession of the atom bomb could in any case well make the need for Soviet military action against Japan an irrelevance. Whatever the future need to guarantee Stalin's support against Japan, this illustrated quite clearly that Churchill's longstanding concerns over Soviet intentions were now shared by Roosevelt to a much greater extent than had perhaps been evident during some of the earlier war summits. Already Churchill and Roosevelt were looking ahead to the security issues that would dominate the postwar international environment they were shaping together, and to the as yet unquantifiable ramifications of the existence of the atomic bomb.

Understandably, Churchill was considerably buoyed up by the success of "Octagon," but more so by the two days at Hyde Park. Here, again, was at work the special Anglo-U.S. relationship that had served the Alliance so well through the war thus far; and here also was the mutual confidence that came from the sharing of a secret of momentous historic importance, and therefore of the power and influence that inclusion in that secret conferred.

With all that in mind, Churchill returned to London on September 26, where all agreed that the prime minister seemed both fitter and with much of his former resilience, enthusiasm and energy restored. Not even the costly failure of the British 1st Airborne Division's operation to seize the bridge over the River Rhine at Arnhem noticeably affected his reinvigorated demeanor. But he was still preoccupied by the growing issues associated with Soviet ambitions in Europe— those for Poland in particular, but also for Greece and the other eastern European countries—and he had already decided that it was time for him to visit Stalin in Moscow once again, with a view to ascertaining both Stalin's wider agenda for the expansion of Soviet communism beyond the Soviet Union and the true strength of his commitment to join the war against Japan. Clearly, the subject of "tube alloys" would not be on the agenda. Despite the closeness of their relationship at Hyde Park just days earlier, Roosevelt was less than pleased by the prospect of Churchill's proposed visit, especially where it might impinge upon Soviet involvement in the Pacific region, as this was patently an issue that was primarily of U.S. rather than British interest. However, he could hardly stop Churchill from conducting this bilateral meeting. Accordingly, U.S. involvement by Averell Harriman (but only as an observer) was reluctantly agreed by Roosevelt, although the president secured Churchill's particular agreement not to prejudice the U.S.-Soviet position with regard to the war against Japan by discussing with Stalin the still outstanding and sensitive matters (notably that of the veto) from the Dumbarton Oaks conference.

Although a successful outcome of the Manhattan project might yet make Soviet support against Japan less crucial, it would have been negligent to assume that this would be so, and, in any case, by maintaining the line that it would be needed, the two Western allies could deflect conjecture in Moscow about the progress of the project. With Roosevelt to some extent placated and the prime minister's agenda for the meeting with Stalin clearly set in his own mind, Churchill and Eden set off by air for Moscow on October 7. The party stopped at Naples and Cairo and arrived in Moscow on October 9 for a bilateral Anglo-Soviet summit conference which was most appropriately codenamed "Tolstoy," after the celebrated Russian author of the epic historical novel *War and Peace*.

16

The Bear and the Bulldog

The "Tolstoy" Conference, October 9–19, 1944

T HE NEXT MAJOR WAR SUMMIT to be attended by all members of the "Big Three" would be that which was code-named "Argonaut"[1] and would take place at Yalta in the Crimea early in 1945. However, prior to that major meeting of all three Alliance leaders, Churchill conducted two bilateral meetings, the first of which was with Stalin in Moscow in the late fall of 1944—the "Tolstoy" conference; the second was a brief meeting with Roosevelt in Malta immediately prior to the "Argonaut" summit. As had been the case in all the war summits so far, these lesser meetings were instigated by Churchill. Indeed, with some four years of this process already completed, it would be entirely fair to credit Churchill—well matching his war leader's media image as the tenacious British bulldog—with being the principal motivator in ensuring and maintaining its overall momentum, despite Britain's diminishing influence within the Alliance. Yalta would prove to be another milestone in the sequence of war summits, but, just as all of the previous meetings and conferences had to varying degrees dovetailed into those which succeeded them, Churchill's bilateral meetings with Stalin and Roosevelt would inevitably impact upon aspects of the "Argonaut" summit and upon the geostrategic backdrop against which it was eventually set. The first of these two meetings—that with Stalin in Moscow from October 9—was also the first occasion on which the anticipated extent of Soviet military involvement against Japan was addressed in some detail.

The "Tolstoy" Conference, Moscow, October 1944

During his ten-day visit to Moscow, Churchill was accompanied by Gen. Alan Brooke and Anthony Eden, as well as the British ambassador to

Moscow, Archibald Clark-Kerr. The U.S. representation for the visit included Averell Harriman and Gen. John R. Deane, the head of the U.S. military mission in Moscow. Both men later became much more involved in the meetings than Roosevelt had originally envisaged, once the discussions moved on to the subject of the war against Japan, when Churchill, quite properly, asked the U.S. delegates to take the lead. Indeed, Harriman's undoubted qualities as a diplomat and the fact that he enjoyed Churchill's absolute confidence were both very important contributory factors to the success of this bilateral Anglo-Soviet conference. Nevertheless, Roosevelt had already made it quite clear to Stalin that "Tolstoy" was, from the U.S. perspective, no more than a preliminary meeting to complement the work which would need to be done during the next "Big Three" meeting: any matters of substance could only be decided by all three of the Allied leaders. However, even with that constraint in place, much could still be achieved at the "Tolstoy" summit. Stalin's principal advisors at this conference were Molotov and Gen. Alexei E. Antonov.

The first meeting with Stalin commenced at ten o'clock in the evening of October 9 and lasted for about three hours. This reunion of the two leaders developed into a good-humored negotiating session that became increasingly surreal, for the outcome of these early talks produced nothing less than Anglo-Soviet agreement on a pragmatic division of postwar responsibilities for the control of the Balkans, Greece, and part of eastern Europe. Undoubtedly Churchill had set out that evening to establish a precedent of straight-talking for the discussions yet to come, while at the same time seeking to identify Stalin's true intentions for those particular countries where British and Soviet interests were perhaps greater than those of the United States. This was also an opportunity for Churchill to obtain an insight into those European issues which Roosevelt and Stalin might have discussed bilaterally at Tehran. In any event, having quantified the extent of the Allies' (but principally Britain's and the Soviet Union's) respective interests in these regions, Churchill drafted a note that summarized the proposed future of a large part of the population of Europe. The text on the half sheet of paper allocated Allied control responsibilities as follows:

195

Roumania *(sic)*

Russia	90%
The others	10%

Greece

Great Britain (in accord with U.S.A.)	90%
Russia	10%
Yugoslavia	50–50%
Hungary	50–50%

Bulgaria

Russia	75%
The others	25%

Churchill passed his jottings to Stalin, who considered them, then annotated a large blue pencil tick to the paper. Surprised, perhaps, by their resolution in short order of the future of Europe, Churchill then suggested to Stalin that it might be prudent to destroy the document, lest it might attract future criticism as a trivialization of a most serious matter, but Stalin merely suggested that Churchill should retain it, which he did.

The contents and means of origination of this "naughty document"—so-called by Churchill—subsequently attracted varying reactions, both at the time and during the years that followed, ranging from outright criticism to apathy. Stalin clearly attached little importance to it, and in many respects it simply summarized quite neatly a *de facto* geostrategic situation. However, the Soviet leader's blue tick on this summation was particularly useful to Churchill, for it confirmed Stalin's willingness to give Britain a virtually free hand in Greece, and implied that the Soviet Union would not intervene to support the increasingly active communist resistance movement in that country, despite the fact that Stalin would, in practice, gain much more from this accommodation than would Churchill. However, conspicuous by its absence from the "naughty document" was any mention of Poland, although this country was shortly destined, yet again, to occupy much of the "Tolstoy" conference time in Moscow.

The events of the night of October 9 were reported back to Roosevelt by Churchill entirely positively, with no mention of the fact that the prime minister and Stalin had, in effect, agreed Anglo-Soviet spheres of influence in parts of Europe and quantified these in percentage terms. In practice, Roosevelt was content with Churchill's account of that first meeting; the president was in any case at that time considerably more concerned with the U.S. election campaign than with the complexities and volatilities of certain European countries. For now, he agreed on October 11—by which date he had also received Harriman's initial report from Moscow—that his two Allied colleagues should continue their discussion of these matters "to insure against the Balkans getting into another international war in the future." As had now been so for some time, Roosevelt's principal priorities continued to be the war against Japan, the Pacific campaign especially, while in Europe his main focus was the future disposal and control of Germany. Roosevelt's agreeable responses to the updates passed to him by the British leader and Harriman from Moscow in turn enabled Churchill and Stalin to take forward their work on other matters, although some of Roosevelt's advisors in Washington remained uneasy at their leader's apparent willingness to disassociate himself, albeit temporarily, from direct involvement in the affairs of Europe other than those directly affecting Germany.[2]

Over the next few days Churchill, Stalin, Eden, and Molotov arrived at various compromises and solutions for Greece, Bulgaria, Rumania, Yugoslavia, and Hungary, based upon the broad divisions of responsibility or extents of influence noted by Churchill on October 9.[3] But then, on October 13, the time had come once again to address the always difficult subject of Poland, its political future, and its frontiers.

One of Churchill's particular aims for "Tolstoy" had been to achieve some sort of resolution of the vexed question of Poland—something that had eluded the delegates to successive conferences for so long. Churchill's position on Poland reflected his wish to ensure that the country would not fall under communist control after the war. There was also the prime minister's desire to recognize, by his support, the bravery of the Polish units in exile which had fought alongside the British in the Battle of Britain and then in Italy. Lastly, the place of Poland in the British national consciousness was still special, as it had been Germany's invasion of this country which had triggered Britain's entry into the war in 1939. Following its flight from Poland, the Polish government-in-exile had been based in London, where, since July 1943, it was headed by Prime Minister Stanislaw Mikolajczyk. Unfortunately, Churchill and Roosevelt had already found that the dash and decisiveness of Poland's airmen and soldiers was not matched by many of these Polish political exiles. While this administration continued to claim its right to represent and govern the nation again once it had been liberated, there was now in Lublin a Soviet-backed Committee of National Liberation, which also claimed these rights. The gulf between these two organizations was manifestly unbridgeable, and their intransigence had increasingly tested the patience of all "Big Three" leaders, none more so than Churchill. Nevertheless, Churchill had successfully applied sufficient political pressure upon Mikolajczyk and had persuaded him to journey to Moscow with a view to reaching a solution to the Polish issues. The Polish prime minister arrived on October 12 and joined the meeting with Stalin, Churchill, and others the following day.

The detailed substance of that which followed does not add significantly to this account, not least because, at its end, remarkably little had been achieved. However, certain matters were noteworthy inasmuch as they indicated or confirmed Stalin's views on Poland—views that would be repeated in the later "Big Three" summits—as well as demonstrating all too clearly the extent to which the Polish government-in-exile had, over almost five years of war, lost touch with the people it sought to represent and failed to understand the unpleasant but inescapable realities of Poland's new international circumstances. In essence, Stalin's longstanding position was unchanged. First and foremost, he wanted Poland as a buffer state between the Soviet Union and Germany, with secure and well-defined frontiers; to that end, he wanted the eastern frontier of Poland set on the 1920 Curzon line. Secondly, with the pro-Soviet Committee of National Liberation already established in part of Poland as a communist government-in-waiting, Stalin wished its members to have a controlling majority in the postwar Polish government. In stating the Soviet position to Mikolajczyk, Molotov drew additional strength from knowing that Roosevelt had generally agreed the postwar Polish frontiers with Stalin during the two leaders' discussion at the start of the Tehran conference. Significantly, Churchill had neither attended that particular presummit bilateral meeting nor was he aware of Roosevelt's apparently unreserved endorsement of Stalin's solution of the Polish problem, apart from the need to keep secret the president's acquiescence until after the U.S. election. Predictably, Mikolajczyk rejected Stalin's solution absolutely. Churchill attempted various compromises, but he found that Stalin, no doubt recalling his meeting with Roosevelt the previous November, was unwilling to modify his stance. At the end of the session, Mikolajczyk had agreed to nothing, while Churchill and Stalin were becoming impatient with the Polish intransigence. Ever the realist, Churchill had always believed that a Polish frontier set on the former Curzon line, but slightly amended so that Lvov fell inside Polish territory, would have to be accepted by the Poles eventually, especially since this compromise would be offset by Poland's gaining former German territory.

That evening, Stalin and Churchill met with the leaders of the Committee of National Liberation, headed by Boleslaw Bierut, the chairman of the Polish National Council. Predictably, these representatives of the Lublin-based provisional government of Poland presented a viewpoint diametrically opposed to that of the London-based Poles, while supporting unreservedly the Soviet position on the issue of frontiers. Although Churchill, still most keen to achieve a solution (even one that was less than ideal) was inclined to join with Stalin in his support for the Lublin Poles, Bierut's team then overplayed their hand by cataloguing an endless number of often unsubstantiated criticisms of their London-based countrymen. The British prime minister was unimpressed by this and therefore continued his mission with both groups and with Stalin to reach a compromise. This went on into the next day, October 14, and, with Mikolajczyk as uncompromising as ever, in the margins of the rest of the conference until October 18. On that day, Churchill's last in Moscow, he met Mikolajczyk once again, when the Polish prime minister quite unexpectedly softened his position and undertook to try and persuade the London Poles to accept the Curzon line frontier. Further, he stated his readiness to establish a Polish government that would be friendly to Moscow. This apparent change of heart by Mikolajczyk had probably been prompted by Churchill, who, when once again losing patience with the always voluble but politically unrealistic Poles, had indicated some days earlier that Mikolajczyk's continued unwillingness to compromise might well result in the withdrawal of British support for his government-in-exile. However, Stalin would not agree to any Polish government in which the Lublin Poles did not enjoy majority representation, and so a compromise appeared to be as far removed as ever. Therefore, despite the glimmer of hope which had emerged on October 18, Churchill failed to achieve one of his principal goals for the "Tolstoy" summit and the problems of Poland remained unresolved. In fact, Mikolajczyk resigned as Polish prime minister just a month later, and the failure of his London-based administration to recognize the invidious reality of Poland's situation in October 1944 effectively consigned the country to Western disinterest, and Soviet domination, for the next half century. Truly, the "Tolstoy" conference was a milestone in the troubled history of Poland.

Poland had always been scheduled as a major issue for the Moscow summit, and that country, together with other predominantly political issues, occupied much of the first few days of the conference, but from October 14 the emphasis of the conference moved to strategic matters, and therefore focused upon the work of the senior military delegates. As the bilateral summit in Moscow had been initiated by the British, Gen. Alan Brooke led these strategic briefings and the subsequent discussion on the current Allied operations and future strategy in Europe, although it later proved to be the U.S.-led session on the war against Japan which would give the "Tolstoy" conference its particular significance in the war summits process.

In a review of the situation in western Europe presented on October 14, the Anglo-U.S. briefing team indicated that their force levels were adequate to win their victory, but that the speed with which that could be achieved was largely dependent upon the scale and uninterrupted flow of logistic support and matériel, and the strength of the German opposition deployed against them. The strategy for the advance to the Rhine and on into Germany which had been agreed at the "Octagon" summit was explained to Stalin. Here Churchill interjected to say that success was also dependent upon no German reinforcements being deployed from the eastern front to oppose the Anglo-U.S. armies. Stalin confirmed that he would not allow this to happen. The Allied plans for the ongoing campaign in Italy were briefed with a fair degree of optimism, although, in the event, only a matter of days after the end of "Tolstoy" the German resistance in central Italy strengthened, and the Anglo-U.S. advance ground to a halt. Finally, the plans for Churchill's much-favored Istrian expedition were briefed, together with the Allies' follow-on intention to strike through Yugoslavia, across the Alps, and seize Vienna. Here, surely, Churchill might expect to receive from Stalin a measure of criticism at least, and possibly outright objections to an Anglo-U.S. impingement upon the edge of the Soviet sphere of influence?

However, Churchill had already broached this particular matter with Stalin during dinner in the evening of October 11; and had already ascertained that the Soviet leader's position on such an expedition was much changed since the Tehran summit a year before. Now, Stalin positively encouraged the idea, even suggesting that its viability might be improved if the Allied campaign in Italy were halted and forces redeployed for these landings. Perhaps, on the other hand, Stalin's change of opinion was not so remarkable, given the time that had passed and events that had taken place since Tehran. First of all, he was well aware of Roosevelt's views on Churchill's sometimes obsessive desire to extend Allied operations in the Adriatic and Balkans, and might quite reasonably have assumed that the U.S. president would never allow a suitable opportunity for this to exist in practice. Indeed, given the speed of the Red Army's recent advance into southeast Europe, such an operation made little or no strategic sense at this stage of the war in any case. Next, if such an Anglo-U.S., or exclusively British, landing had taken place, there was every chance that it would have come into direct conflict with Josip Tito's forces in Yugoslavia, and Stalin had already wisely decided that the Red Army would not attempt to liberate or impose itself upon Yugoslavia. However, in the most unlikely event that the Istrian operation did take place and actually succeeded in passing through Yugoslavia, far from adversely affecting Stalin's plans for the region it could at the very least assist these by ensuring that no German troops from the south would be moved to threaten the Red Army's own plans for Hungary and Austria. Finally, of course, Stalin's apparent change of

heart postdated Operation "Overlord." So long as the Anglo-U.S. invasion of northern France had still not taken place, Stalin was always much
concerned by anything which might prejudice the operation or diminish
its success, as this would, in turn, allow even more German divisions to
engage the Red Army on the eastern front. However, with D-Day in June
now a matter of history, he could afford to be magnanimous in his dealings with Churchill, as well as conforming to the terms of the "naughty
document" that Churchill had penned during the course of the two
leaders' first evening together. Certainly, as the briefing and discussion
moved on to Greece—where British airborne forces were already
heavily engaged and would shortly underwrite the newly established
Papandreou government in Athens at the direct expense of the Greek
communist resistance forces—Stalin did not demur from the principle of
"90%" British responsibility for dealing with Greece to which he had
agreed late that night of October 9.[4]

In due course, all but the first of these observations concerning
Stalin's change of thinking on the possible intentions of the Western
allies in the Adriatic and the Balkans proved largely academic in the
light of a number of other factors. There was the slowdown of the
campaign in Italy and northwest Europe (the abortive airborne operation at Arnhem had taken place only a few weeks earlier). Then there
was the continued distinct lack of enthusiasm for the operation in Washington, in parallel with Tito's own increasing hostility to the British.
Finally, but most tellingly, the conclusion of the combined chiefs of staff,
based on General Wilson's plan produced after the "Quadrant" summit
was that no such landing could be carried out before February 1945. All
of these factors taken together resulted, by the end of December 1944,
in the cancellation of the much-discussed but always improbable plan to
land on the Istrian peninsula.

After the Anglo-U.S. presentations on, and subsequent discussions of,
the situation in western Europe, General Antonov provided a detailed
briefing on operations on the eastern front—something that had been
addressed only in summary form by the "Octagon" summit, owing to
Stalin's not having attended it. In summary, on all fronts the Red Army
was enjoying success. In Finland and the Baltic, some thirty German divi-

sions were cut off and gradually being destroyed, their only means of withdrawal now being by sea. The Red Army's point of main effort was currently against the German forces in Hungary, where it was seeking to encircle some twenty-three German divisions, prior to advancing into Austria, to Vienna, and then on into Germany following an axis first to the west of Czechoslovakia and then toward the River Oder at Breslau. In support of the major operations in the Baltic and Hungary, holding operations would be conducted from Lithuania to the Carpathians, while the Red Army's planned assault into East Prussia and to seize Warsaw would depend upon the progress made with its two main offensives in the north and south. Finally, once these two actions were concluded, the Soviet forces would decide how they would carry out the invasion of Germany. All this was duly noted by the Anglo-U.S. delegates, and General Deane provided a summary of the Soviet intentions to Roosevelt and a more comprehensive version of their plans to the J.C.S. in Washington. Clearly, there was nothing there with which either the American or the British delegates or their leaders could take issue. However, with the benefit of hindsight, the lack of any mention of Soviet intentions with regard to Berlin is conspicuous by its absence. Linked to that, it would be disingenuous to suggest that by late 1944 Stalin had not already determined that the Red Army's main thrust into Germany would be launched through East Prussia, and then along the shortest possible route to the capital of Hitler's Third Reich, to ensure that the ultimate prize fell to the Soviet forces, not to those of either of his two Western allies.

Indeed, despite its obvious importance, little enough time was spent at "Tolstoy" on the subject of Germany. Churchill once again advanced his proposal for the country to be divided into three parts, with a confederation comprising Hungary, Poland, and Czechoslovakia, but Stalin and Molotov could not agree to this, and so the conference had moved on to other matters. In any case, a definitive new plan for postwar Germany certainly could not have been agreed without Roosevelt having had an opportunity to discuss it with both of his "Big Three" colleagues.

On October 14, the strategic briefings and discussion had included an update by Gen. Alan Brooke and Churchill on the situation in Burma, China, and Southeast Asia, together with the Western allies' plans and intentions in those operational theaters. Not surprisingly, this résumé more or less reiterated the "Octagon" briefing and statements of intent. Following this, Churchill indicated that General Deane and Averell Harriman should assume the lead to deal with the Pacific campaign and the business of carrying the war to Japan itself. It was, perhaps, fortuitous that the conference discussions had reached the point where the Americans could take the lead, as the next day, the fifteenth, Churchill was found to be suffering from a fever with a temperature of 101 degrees. Consequently he spent the rest of that day confined to his bed. This was hardly surprising given the energy he had already expended on "Tolstoy," often continuing his evening meetings with Stalin into the early morning hours. However, although he heard General Deane's initial briefing on October 14, this did mean that Churchill missed the briefing by the Soviets the following day on their intended action against Japan after the defeat of Germany—the first substantive statement of Soviet intent on this vitally important matter.[5] He also missed Stalin's thinly disguised remark to the effect that he would expect to be assured of any Soviet claims—territorial or otherwise—in the region before he would finally commit to the war against Japan. Eden represented Churchill at the October 15 meeting and duly reported back to the prime minister. However, neither Churchill, nor Harriman, nor Deane perhaps appreciated at the time the potential significance of Stalin's price for Soviet involvement; neither, indeed, did Roosevelt or the J.C.S. when they in turn were apprised of it. Perhaps the sheer scale of the projected Soviet offensive was not fully appreciated, or, possibly, with Roosevelt and Churchill having largely written off Chiang Kai-shek, Soviet ambitions in Asia and those concerning China were simply too far removed from matters affecting the future of Europe and Germany to be of any great consequence to Washington or London in late 1944. In any event, disputing what might well have been regarded by Eden and Harriman as no more than an aside by Stalin on October 15 would have risked prejudicing Soviet goodwill at a crucial moment, and Roosevelt had already established the precedent for not risking this—at almost any cost.

The U.S. team concluded its update on the war in the Pacific by indicating that contingency plans existed for the final assault against Japan by the Western allies (which meant, in effect, by U.S. forces) to be launched from east, south, and west, but that the success of these plans could only be maximized if they were also harmonized with an attack on Japan from the north in a major offensive mounted by the Soviets. Stalin acknowledged the point made and asked General Deane to indicate how, in Washington's view, the Soviet armed forces could best assist these plans. This opened the way for Deane to list the five tasks which the J.C.S. had identified as strategically critical and which needed to be carried out by the Soviets. The first and most important was the destruction of Japanese ground and air forces in Manchuria. Next, the lines of communication and supply on the Vladivostock peninsula and along the trans-Siberian railway had to be secured. Thirdly, it was envisaged that a Soviet offensive supported by U.S. air power would be launched against Japan from the maritime provinces and Kamchatka. Fourthly, the J.C.S. looked to the Soviets to cut all sea and air links between Japan and mainland Asia. Finally, Washington anticipated that the Soviets, operating with U.S. Navy forces, would secure the logistic lines of supply across the Pacific to the maritime provinces, for which task it would be necessary for Soviet forces to occupy southern Sakhalin. Whatever the specifics involved, Deane emphasized that the J.C.S. wished to see direct Soviet military action against Japan as soon as possible, in the maximum available strength, and urged that they should together begin preparing for these combined and joint operations as soon as practicable. Stalin, with Generals Antonov and Molotov, retired to consider their response to this strategic "shopping list."

Although events in August 1945 would, in practice, overtake significant Soviet involvement in the war against Japan, General Antonov's presentation of the Soviet response on October 15 is nevertheless important, as it indicates the full extent of the conventional military might that would have fallen upon Japan had not the Manhattan project been successfully concluded. Indeed, the destruction of life and property by the combined U.S. and Soviet onslaught might well, over time, have exceeded the devastating fate which would be visited upon Hiroshima and Nagasaki in August 1945. However, as of October 1944, it was reasonable to assume that Stalin expected that Soviet forces would indeed be committed against Japan—provided, of course, that this was to the benefit of the Soviet Union. Having briefed the conference on the five most likely axes of advance southward for the Red Army, General Antonov continued by expanding upon the actions Moscow anticipated were necessary to take forward the Soviet strategic offensive against Japan. Early in the briefing, Antonov made the important statement that it would be not until about three months after the defeat of Germany that the Soviet Union would be fully ready to move against Japan. Stalin interjected to amplify this estimate by saying that these three months would be required in order to redeploy the necessary forces and gather together sufficient war matériel to sustain these forces throughout a decisive campaign against Japan lasting up to two months. Harriman confirmed that the United States was ready to begin providing the necessary resources, provided that this did not adversely affect the supplies of matériel needed to conclude the war against Germany. With that principle well established, General Antonov continued with his briefing and the discussions on October 15. However, there was still much to be dealt with, and on October 17, Deane, Harriman, Stalin, and Antonov continued their more detailed consideration of the intended Soviet action against Japan. By then Churchill was also in attendance, although the U.S. team understandably retained the lead on these issues.

After almost three days of discussion about the Japanese perspective, the Soviet plans were judged by Harriman and Deane to be entirely in accord with the hopes and intentions of the J.C.S., and all this was enthusiastically communicated to Washington, where the activities necessary to provide the enormous amount of war material Stalin had requested were put in train.

Although the real significance of the "Tolstoy" conference in Moscow has been downplayed by some commentators—and it is true that it would in due course be shown to have delivered little in tangible terms—it was nevertheless another milestone in the process of the war summits, and as such it certainly complemented that wider process.

In the morning of Thursday, October 19, Churchill left Moscow convinced that his personal understanding of, and relationship with, Stalin had been much enhanced by the ten-day conference, and that this could only have benefited the great Alliance of which, together with

Roosevelt, they were the leaders. He arrived in London during the evening of October 22, having traveled via the Crimea, Cairo, and Naples. Churchill's optimistic assessment of "Tolstoy" was understandable, but, although it raised his personal profile within the "Big Three," it did not and could not change the fact that the United States and the Soviet Union were now the two preeminent powers within the Alliance in the process of shaping the postwar world.

The War against Japan: Summary of Discussions, October 15 and 17	
Operation, Activity or Issue	Remarks
Destroy Japanese forces (up to fifty divisions) in Manchuria. This assumed that Japanese forces from within China and from Japan would have reinforced those in Manchuria. U.S. airpower would be required to support this action, operating from Soviet airbases.	In fact, this was a gross overestimate of Japanese strength (less than twenty-five divisions) in Manchuria. However, a Japanese division was almost twice the size of its Red Army equivalent, and so Antonov's estimate was not entirely unfounded. Nevertheless, the "fifty divisions" estimate was used to justify an intention to double the size of the Soviet Far East ground forces to sixty divisions, primarily by moving forces from the west after the defeat of Germany
Need for additional air (bombing) support.	Harriman restated the U.S. offer to provide quantities of four-engine bombers to the Soviet air force and training support for the crews. Stalin confirmed that airbases would be made available to the Americans in the maritime provinces of Siberia and Kamchatka.
U.S. ground forces involvement.	Harriman confirmed that the J.C.S. did not envisage U.S. ground forces operating alongside the Red Army in Manchuria.
Wider strategy of Red Army offensive in Manchuria.	Stalin envisaged more extensive Soviet maneuvers beyond Manchuria, possibly even toward Peking. In essence, he endorsed the principle of Soviet forces dealing with the Japanese in China while U.S. forces completed the destruction of the Japanese garrisons on the southern islands. He also proposed Soviet occupation of the northern Korean ports.
U.S. matériel support for Soviet operations estimated at more than one million tons, in addition to aid already agreed.	This huge amount of war material would guarantee the viability of the Soviet offensive, even if access to Vladivostock were to be denied. Despite the scale, Roosevelt and the J.C.S. saw it as an acceptable price to pay for the defeat of Japan without the need to commit U.S. ground forces in China and Manchuria.

17

Matters of War and Peace

The "Argonaut" Conferences,

January 20 to February 11, 1945

D ESPITE THE MORE OBVIOUS military successes achieved by the Alliance in 1944, notably the invasion of France in the west and the great Red Army offensive in the east, the second half of the year had not been one of unqualified glory for the Allies. Within Germany, on July 20, the "July Plot" to assassinate Hitler, led by Gen. Ludwig Beck and Lt. Col. Claus Schenk, Graf von Stauffenberg, failed disastrously. The powerful time bomb which von Stauffenberg had placed under the conference table at the Führer's military headquarters at Rasten-burg, East Prussia, was inadvertently moved behind a substantial table support by another officer; consequently, although injured, Hitler escaped much of the force of the blast. The ruthless purge that followed this assas-sination attempt by Germans (predominantly military officers) who were opposed to Hitler engulfed guilty and innocent alike, and was both wide-ranging in its scale and savage in the several forms of its retribution. Then, just two months later, came the failure[1] of the British 1st Airborne Division to seize and hold until relieved what turned out to be a "bridge too far" across the River Rhine at Arnhem. The two U.S. airborne divisions also involved in Operation "Market Garden"—the 82nd and 101st—enjoyed more success with their separate operations at Nijmegen and Eindhoven. The lack of success at Arnhem meant that the much-needed Rhine crossing was not achieved in 1944, which in turn dashed the hopes of all but the most optimistic that the war against Germany might yet end by Christmas. However, if any such residue of optimism had persisted amongst the Allied troops, it was extinguished on December 16.

On that fateful day, out of the morning mists that swirled and eddied about the dark forests and deep valleys of the frozen and snow-covered Ardennes stormed twenty German divisions, seven of which were armored. A furious artillery bombardment preceded the assault. Nearly a quarter of a million men and almost a thousand tanks and self-propelled assault guns quickly overran and punched through the four divisions of Maj. Gen. Troy Middleton's U.S. 8th Corps and battled on toward their objective of the River Meuse and the port of Antwerp. At first, the onslaught spread panic amongst the U.S. formations and precipitated a generally chaotic withdrawal; but then, despite this initial success, the German offensive gradually lost its momentum and petered out after two weeks of high-tempo combat. Instrumental in bringing this about was the gallant defense of Bastogne by troops of the 101st Airborne Division, together with the British Field Marshal Montgomery's intervention to restore the situation in the north and U.S. General Patton's drive from the south—actions that first halted the German panzer and infantry divisions and then forced their withdrawal. By mid-January 1945 the inspired and audacious (but fatally flawed) bid by Hitler and Field Marshal Gerd von Rundstedt to advance to the Meuse and split the Western allies, thereby gaining time for Germany to generate new forces and to develop and produce in quantity its new weapons (such as the V-2 missile and jet aircraft), had failed.

Although the offensive—later known universally as the "Battle of the Bulge"—was unsuccessful, it was none the less an unwelcome wakeup call for the Western allied commanders, as well as for the U.S. president and British prime minister. It was also important in the wider context of the operational background against which the strategic war summits were necessarily conducted (and the next "Big Three" meeting was scheduled to take place only three weeks after the end of the "Battle of the Bulge"). This was so because it fuelled and demonstrated the increasing friction, petty rivalries, and differences amongst some of the senior Allied commanders at the higher levels of command of the Anglo-U.S. armies in Europe, as national politics, perceptions, and professional jealousies emerged in almost equal measure.

Unquestionably, the early days of the battle represented an almost unqualified debacle and a clear defeat for American arms—a setback that, potentially, compromised the integrity of the whole Allied front. For this near-disaster, Lt. Gen. Omar Bradley, commanding the U.S. 12th

Army Group, must bear most of the responsibility.[2] Certainly the U.S. paratroopers' stand at Bastogne and the spirited action of Patton's 3rd Army driving into the Ardennes from the south largely restored the reputation of the U.S. Army in the Ardennes, and enabled it to complete the defeat of von Rundstedt's offensive. However, without Montgomery's intervention to the north this U.S. action alone would not have been enough to deal with the German advance. The British part in saving the situation had been loudly trumpeted in the British press and even in the U.S. forces' newspaper *Stars and Stripes*.[3] With all that in mind, it was hardly surprising that the British field marshal's justified but nevertheless ill-timed and impolitic recounting of this truism to the media considerably offended American sensitivities in the United States and in Europe. Bradley—urged on by Patton—took particular exception to the fact that by the end of the "Battle of the Bulge" he had been largely marginalized, with Montgomery by then commanding some twenty-one U.S. divisions in addition to his original British forces and the only army group commander clearly in control of the overall situation. The sheer scale of the U.S. war effort in Europe, which now well exceeded that of the British forces, was therefore viewed both against the well reported fact of Montgomery having taken command of large numbers of U.S. troops to save the situation in "The Bulge" and the apparent failure of the U.S. generals and GIs at the outset of the battle.

Taken as a whole, in the United States these matters, not surprisingly, gave rise to a heady mixture of injured pride, political outrage, and national indignation, which, just as predictably, unleashed upon the British in general and Montgomery in particular the wrath of the American press, closely followed by American public opinion. Such thoroughly unwelcome discord magnified for General Eisenhower the already considerable practical problems of conducting the Alliance's high command while controlling his army commanders and dealing with their personal vanities. So it was that, although its armies had finally lost in the Ardennes, the German high command could at least console itself with the added disharmony that the offensive had caused amongst the commanders of the Anglo-U.S. forces that still opposed them across the Rhine. This thoroughly unfortunate situation affecting the Allied high command in Europe was therefore still ongoing at the beginning of February 1945, when Roosevelt—inaugurated on January 20 for a fourth term as U.S. president—and Churchill traveled via Malta to meet Stalin at Yalta, in the Crimea, for the second of their historic trilateral war summits.[4]

Planning for the summit had been attended by the familiar problems of identifying a suitable date and location. It was determined in November that a meeting before Roosevelt's inauguration was unacceptable, so February 1945 presented the first opportunity to conduct one. However, the choice of a location was less easily resolved. Of the "Big Three," only Churchill was prepared to travel virtually wherever necessary in order to maintain the war summits process. Roosevelt voiced concerns over a meeting proposed for the Soviet Black Sea coast on the dual grounds that it was an unhealthy area and that it was too far from Washington for him to maintain close contact with the J.C.S. The president favored Italy, Sicily, Cyprus, or Malta as suitable venues, and Churchill had at one stage even proposed that the "Big Three" should meet in Scotland. But Stalin had once again refused to leave Soviet territory; and a proposal by Churchill that Molotov might represent the Soviet leader at a meeting outside Russia was unacceptable to Roosevelt. The debate over the location had continued from July through December, at which point Roosevelt had decided that the importance of dealing with Stalin face to face outweighed his reservations over traveling to the Black Sea. Accordingly, Yalta was settled as the venue for the next conference, and, as a preliminary to the main summit, it was agreed that Anglo-U.S. staff talks and meetings at ministerial level would take place at Malta from January 20 to February 2, with a bilateral meeting between Roosevelt and Churchill on the latter date. To that end, a consolidated report would be prepared for the two leaders by the time of their arrival in Malta en route to Yalta, and this would form the basis of their joint position for the subsequent meetings with Stalin. Although Eden and Hopkins were involved throughout the staff conference at Malta, the output from this session was mainly military. Nevertheless, the ever-increasing overlap of Anglo-U.S. political agendas and military strategy was again evident.

Most of the detail of what was agreed in Malta understandably reappeared a few days later at Yalta. However, simply to dismiss this meeting as merely complementary to the major summit which followed it would be wrong. At Malta, certain themes and important statements of position emerged that would bear directly upon subsequent events. The most immediate of these was the ending of Churchill's aspiration to develop the campaign in the Mediterranean and into the Adriatic and the Balkans. The combined chiefs of staff, with the strong support of the British chiefs of staff, concluded that, in order to support the campaign against the Germans in northwest Europe effectively, the time had come at last to reduce Allied forces in the Mediterranean and redeploy them to Eisenhower's command. This decision involved the transfer of tactical air support and three British and Canadian divisions before March 15, 1945, plus two more divisions once the situation in Greece permitted this. In accepting the final demise of his longstanding hopes and intentions to attack Germany via Austria and to preempt a Soviet occupation of Austria and parts of southeastern Europe, Churchill knew that he was enabling Montgomery to launch a devastating assault into Germany in the north of Europe. But herein lay another unresolved issue, one that had been much exacerbated by the American debacle during the early part of the "Battle of the Bulge" and by Montgomery's politically insensitive handling later of the key role played by the British forces in restoring the situation in the Ardennes.

In dealing with the campaign in northwest Europe, the issue of a concerted blow in the north (favored by the British) vis-à-vis a balanced advance on a broader front (favored by the Americans) in order to ensure the destruction of all German forces west of the Rhine before striking into Germany was raised again. The military arguments had already been well-rehearsed, but with each week that passed the political imperatives and realities inevitably outweighed the straightforward military case. For all, the emphasis to be placed upon the Allies' northern axis would have meant a significant expansion of Montgomery's command, including the subordination of many additional U.S. divisions to British command. This would inevitably have rankled with, and been at the expense of, U.S. generals such as Bradley and

Patton; but, more significantly, it would have been unacceptable to U.S. public opinion and therefore to Roosevelt and Marshall in Washington. However, in practical terms, the overwhelming numerical superiority of U.S. ground forces within and flooding into Europe now meant that the combined chiefs of staff, and by extension Eisenhower, were bound either to give the American generals the leading roles in the campaign or to choose a path of compromise. Therefore, while acknowledging that the Allies' point of main effort would continue to be directed toward a Rhine crossing in the north after March 1, the combined chiefs of staff agreed to Eisenhower's plan to allow the southern axes to be actively developed by the U.S. armies, thereby more or less placating the British chiefs of staff while still keeping U.S. troops and generals engaged at the forefront of the campaign. What was therefore in all but name a "broad-front" strategy would also be most acceptable to Stalin, for it offered the best chance of preventing the redeployment of German forces from west to east and at the same time meant that there was little likelihood of Anglo-U.S. troops reaching Berlin ahead of the Russians— some of whose troops were by then little more than forty miles away from the capital.

Finally, the combined chiefs of staff produced an updated strategy for the Far East, Burma, and the Pacific war against Japan. It focused the U.S. emphasis upon China and the northern Pacific region, while leaving the British—or, at any rate, a nation other than the United States!—to deal with Malaya, Singapore, the East Indies, and Indo-China; with the future of northern China, Manchuria, and Korea to be dealt with by the Soviets and the Americans and thus left largely unresolved. Despite Roosevelt's abhorrence of spheres of influence, the forward strategy developed in Malta for the war against Japan in effect acknowledged these, and therefore inadvertently sowed many of the seeds that would in later times germinate to produce the French Indo-China War, the Korean War, the Vietnam War, the Malayan Emergency, and the Indonesian Confrontation, together with a host of lesser insurgencies and conflicts in the region.

Following their endorsement of the final report produced for them by the chiefs of staff on February 2, Churchill and Roosevelt dined together that evening before embarking for a night flight in their separate aircraft to Saki in the Crimea (Roosevelt had originally arrived at Malta by sea, aboard the USS *Quincy*). Most of their staff and advisors had flown ahead of them to the Crimea. At Saki, the two leaders were met by Molotov, and, after a six-hour road journey (which, although the distance was only about seventy miles, included a protracted halt en route for a substantial lunch hosted by Andrei Vishinsky), the party and accompanying entourage finally arrived at Yalta, ready to resume the "Big Three" war summits process. Although the facilities proved more comfortable than both Roosevelt and Churchill had anticipated, they were not luxurious, and this, together with a fairly punishing schedule,[5] made Yalta an arduous experience for the two Western leaders, who had both traveled far. It was particularly so for the U.S. president, who by then had but two more months to live. Indeed, little did the "Big Three" know that "Argonaut" would prove to be Roosevelt's last such meeting, or that, far from enhancing the wartime Alliance, the week's conference at Yalta from February 4 would further reinforce the fact that as the German threat diminished the divisions between the three allies became ever more apparent.

The Yalta Summit, February 4–11, 1945

The "Argonaut" meeting was significant for several reasons. The first of these was negative, in that it proved in many respects to be the least productive of the war summits. Next, it omitted, if with good reason, to take any account of the fact that the military head of the Manhattan project, Gen. Leslie R. Groves, had notified Roosevelt and Marshall on December 30 that the "tube alloys" project would be able to deliver the first atomic weapon in August 1945, a second weapon before the end of the year, and further weapons regularly thereafter. The first device was expected to have the equivalent explosive power of five hundred tons of TNT, while the second would have double that. However, despite the influence that this development would have upon the conduct of the rest of the war, in strict accordance with the secret agreement made by Roosevelt and Churchill at Hyde Park on September 19 the previous year the successful outcome of the Manhattan project was not exposed at Yalta. Consequently, all discussion of the war against Japan, and of the future Soviet contribution to this war, was conducted by the Western allies as if the atomic bomb did not exist.

Although the war summit at Yalta exposed several areas of friction between the Allies and was generally somewhat less productive than many of those that had preceded it, the "Argonaut" conference did nevertheless take forward a number of issues concerning the wider process of shaping the postwar world, including the resolution of some of the unfinished business from Dumbarton Oaks and revisiting— inevitably, perhaps—the seemingly interminable troubles of Poland.

The U.N. voting issues were reviewed once more and resolved, at least temporarily. Although the matter of whether or not the Security Council would be empowered to take action in a dispute where one of the permanent members was involved could not be decided entirely to Stalin's satisfaction, a compromise form of words was achieved. Then, on February 7, a solution to the voting question was finally agreed. The original Soviet bid for sixteen separate votes, with each of their republics treated individually, was reduced to three (Ukraine, Belorussia, and Lithuania),[6] which more or less matched the British dominion representation. The United States was allocated one vote, although in practice it would be supported by the votes of Central and South America in the U.N. for many years to come. Finally, on February 9, the "Big Three" addressed the question of U.N. trusteeship of other territories. This went to the heart of Roosevelt's cherished principle of national self-determination, and as such it was sure to provoke concern from Churchill over the future of British overseas territories. However, Roosevelt was not prepared to risk the collapse of all that had been achieved for the embryo U.N. organization thus far, and so he allowed secretary of state Edward R. Stettinius to present the U.S. proposals without suggesting that they threatened in any way the future status of the British (or indeed French) colonial empires. Once again, a suitable form of words and appropriate safeguards were produced that satisfied all parties and allowed the U.N. project to move forward once again on its uncertain way.

Early on at Yalta, the Soviets reiterated their request for Western allied action in Italy and northern Europe to prevent the move of German divisions to the eastern front. The Anglo-U.S. delegation made a similar request of the Soviets on the eastern front, and both sides agreed to coordinate their military actions accordingly. With hindsight, as the Red Army was almost within striking distance of Berlin, Stalin must have been particularly concerned that either a slackening of Anglo-U.S. action would permit the release of German forces from the west to protect the city, or that the Germans might try to effect a separate peace with the Western allies in order to save it from capture by the Russians. In any event, the updated arrangements for operational coordination in the future included direct liaison involving Eisenhower, Alexander (commanding in the Mediterranean), and the Soviet General Staff. The U.S. J.C.S. were especially enthusiastic about these arrangements, and Roosevelt urged Stalin to extend them to include Western allied liaison with Soviet field army commanders. However, the Soviet commander-in-chief did not agree to Alliance liaison at this relatively low level of command. One of the consequences of these much broadened chain-of-command and liaison arrangements would later attract Churchill's criticism. This occurred when Eisenhower had occasion to contact Stalin direct on an operational matter—a conduit of communication that should, in the prime minister's view, have remained exclusively within the control of the Allies' political leadership. Nevertheless, given that Stalin was head of his nation's armed forces and was actively engaged in the day-to-day conduct of the war on the eastern front, it is not difficult to understand why Eisenhower perceived him to be just as much a military commander as a head of state, and why he therefore felt justified in communicating directly with him when the need to do so arose.[7]

Although Yalta was remembered mainly for its discussion of the outstanding issues from Dumbarton Oaks, Poland, and the war against Japan, it also took further a number of important matters concerning Germany. Consideration by the "Big Three" of this subject also provoked a degree of discord when Churchill reversed his position on certain matters that had been agreed in principle in Tehran at the end of 1943, and at the "Octagon" summit in Quebec the previous September.

Not surprisingly, whatever the main business of the conference might have been, Germany had regularly provided a focus for political debate throughout the war summits, and Yalta proved to be no exception. At "Octagon," Roosevelt and Churchill had agreed the so-called Morgenthau plan,[8] which provided for the industrial (and therefore military) emasculation of Germany after its defeat. Viewed superficially—and irrespective of the impact of this upon the German people—the advantages of this plan would include the elimination of Germany's ability to wage war in the future, the removal of its ability to compete commercially with Great Britain in the postwar era, and the obviation of any need for U.S. troops to remain in Europe after hostilities had been concluded. Subjectively, however positively it may have been presented, the Morgenthau plan would be perceived by the general public in the Allied countries as the righteous punishment of Nazi Germany for the misery it had wreaked upon the world. However, the leaking of this plan to the U.S. media had exposed its significant economic weaknesses, as well as providing the Nazi propaganda machine with a weapon not dissimilar to those provided by the old principle of unconditional surrender and the requirement for Germany to surrender to all three Allies simultaneously. Then, however much Morgenthau's ideas might have appealed to Stalin in the short term as a means further to punish and humiliate Germany, the Soviet leader was determined to exact a huge weight of war reparations upon the country; and, quite apart from the practical problems of reversing the technological and industrial progress of centuries, what would have become a predominantly agricultural or pastoral economy could never have serviced the financial burdens Moscow intended to place upon its historic enemy. The flawed plan had therefore been shortlived, and Yalta provided another timely opportunity for the Allies' approach to postwar Germany and its capital to be considered yet again. Indeed, although they could not have known it in February, the final war summit would take place in July at a venue but a short distance from what would by then be the former capital of the Third Reich. The conference discussions about Germany led neatly into those concerning Poland.

At Yalta, Churchill expressed his new reservations over the plans which had been agreed in principle at Tehran for the dismemberment of Germany. He was in agreement about the need to neutralize Prussian power effectively. However, he favored a division of the country north to south, involving the creation of a new south German state based on Bavaria and Austria, with Vienna, possibly, as its capital. In so doing he demonstrated his awareness of the emerging European dimension and of the history of that continent; together with what was now the immediate need to consider practically, and with due care, the fate of some eighty million people. He also showed his residual and continuing preoccupation with the perceived importance and political significance of southern Europe.

However, the U.S. and Soviet positions were unchanged and somewhat more simplistic. Although he envisaged some form of dismemberment of Germany (producing probably up to seven smaller states), Roosevelt favored a policy of "wait and see," in the belief that a solution would probably present itself in the aftermath of the German defeat. While it would be very wrong to accuse the Americans of disinterest in this issue, Washington had consistently maintained its view that the future security of Europe should be a matter for the European powers, not for U.S. forces. It was at Yalta, when discussing the Soviet, British, and U.S. zones of occupation in Germany, that Roosevelt famously stated his beliefs that American troops would not stay in Europe for much more than two years and that the U.S. Congress would not support "the maintenance of an appreciable American force in Europe."[9] In concert with this belief, it was also during the discussion of this agenda item on February 5 that Roosevelt modified his earlier objections to France being allocated an occupation zone in Germany: he now supported Churchill's wish for such a zone.[10]

In the meantime, on the wider question of the future shape of Germany, Stalin was still quite clear that the country should be dismembered. This accorded with his firm belief that only with this could the future security of the Soviet Union be guaranteed. The issue of dismemberment was judged too important (or, perhaps, too difficult) to be dealt with at Yalta, and so a compromise statement was developed which called for the Allies to "take such steps including the complete disarmament, demilitarization and the dismemberment of Germany as they deem requisite for future peace and security."[11] However, the interpretation and therefore the form of this "dismemberment" were left unresolved. Instead, the complex matter was referred for negotiation and resolution to a tripartite committee, to be chaired by Eden. Indeed, much of the Yalta conference dissolved into compromise and procrastination by the "Big Three." Another such issue deferred was the need for the protocols to be agreed for the division and control of Berlin. The city was destined to lie well within the Soviet zone of occupation, and therefore the Anglo-U.S. military staff at Yalta highlighted the pressing need for the eventual arrangements for unrestricted access to Berlin to be clearly laid down. Predictably, the Soviet staff did not regard this as a matter of high priority, and so it was deferred by default.

If actual disharmony between the Allies was by and large avoided at Yalta through compromise and deferred decisions, one other matter raised by Britain was directly contrary to that of Moscow. This concerned the Soviet claim for war reparations. Moscow's declared position with regard to the reparations that should be exacted from Germany was that the total sum should be equivalent—in resources, industrial plant, transportation, and funds—to a massive twenty billion U.S. dollars, of which half would be due to the Soviet Union. The Soviets reasoned that, of all the Allies, Russia had suffered the greatest devastation at the hands of Nazi Germany and that this justified its compensation on that scale. However, Churchill and Eden pointed out that the sum involved was unrealistic, could not be collected, and would involve the United States and Great Britain subsidizing Germany in order that its population could survive and still pay the Soviet claim; in effect, they stated, other nations would be required to pay indirectly the German war reparations claimed by the Soviet Union. Prior to the final plenary session on February 10, the Soviet response to the British contentions was conducted by Molotov and Ivan Maisky, formerly a Soviet ambassador in London and now an assistant commissar for foreign affairs. However, Churchill and Eden were unshakable, and so on February 10 Stalin entered the fray. The Soviet leader stated his belief that the Germans would be well able to pay and still live as comfortably as the populations of countries to the east of them. More sinisterly, Stalin indicated that, irrespective of the Anglo-U.S. approach to reparations, Moscow would collect those due to it directly. More significantly for the

Alliance, he suggested that, in line with Churchill's views on the division or dismemberment of Germany, Britain actually wished to revive and support a strong Germany—by implication a threat to the Soviet Union and therefore to the future peace of Europe. Although the arguments advanced by the British delegates were entirely pragmatic, Churchill's growing unease over Soviet communist ambitions were also no doubt very much in his mind. Roosevelt found himself in the unenviable position of arbiter, with Stalin already suggesting that the twenty billion U.S. dollars figure, and half of that or any other figure that might subsequently be agreed, was the American-Soviet proposal.

Once again, compromise triumphed, although this was more in the interests of cooling the friction that had been generated between the Allies over this important issue rather than of producing a just and workable solution for Germany. Inevitably perhaps, the "Big Three" came up with an agreement in principle but then directed that this should be considered in detail and taken forward by the Allied reparation commission in Moscow. In another masterpiece of the art of diplomatic compromise that actually advanced the matter hardly at all, the protocol agreed by the "Big Three" at Yalta directed the commission to "take in its initial studies as a basis for discussion the suggestion of the Soviet Government that the total sum of the reparation . . . should be 20 billion dollars and that 50% of it should go to the Union of Soviet Socialist Republics" but that "The British delegation was of the opinion that pending consideration of the reparation question by the Moscow Reparation Commission no figure of reparation should be mentioned."[12] Right up to and including the final "Big Three" dinner during the night of February 10, Stalin tried to persuade Churchill to modify his position on this issue. In practice, the unresolved issue of war reparations paved the way for the Soviet Union's wholesale pillage of German industry and resources at the end of the war and, as an indirect consequence, for the U.S. program of aid—the Marshall Plan—for western Europe from 1947. Indeed, while agreement between the Allies was of course diplomatically desirable, there can be no doubt that the Soviets would always have exacted from eastern Germany whatever reparations they believed appropriate, both in amount and nature.

If Germany produced difficulties for the Allies at Yalta, these were potentially less controversial than those raised when they returned to considering Poland. Here, following the unsatisfactory outcome of Churchill's and Stalin's dealings with Prime Minister Stanislaw Mikolajczyk and the London-based Poles in Moscow the previous October, it was almost inevitable both that Poland would receive relatively short shrift at Yalta, and that Stalin would secure the agreement of his Western allies to matters that had lain at the heart of Soviet foreign policy since well before the formation of the great Alliance from 1941. The Soviet position on Poland's borders was already well known, but Stalin reiterated its principal features and rationale. Twice in three decades Poland had provided the route for Germany to attack Russia. While it was conceivable that the postwar Germany might lack the capability to repeat the exercise a third time, this was not a risk that Moscow was prepared to take. This in turn meant that Poland's eastern border had to be reestablished along the Curzon line, set by Lord Curzon and Premier Clemenceau many years earlier, and, contrary to Roosevelt's hopes, Stalin was adamant that Lvov should be Russian not Polish. From the Soviet perspective, rather than Poland being viewed as a separate or special case, Bulgaria, Romania, and Poland together formed a cohesive buffer of states that were of vital importance to the security of the Soviet Union. By the end of Yalta, Roosevelt and Churchill had agreed, apart from some "minor digressions," to the Curzon line border, and that Lvov should be under Soviet control. Stalin had therefore achieved all that he desired in the east.

Two other factors influenced Stalin's position on Poland, and these affected the "Argonaut" summit's negotiation of Poland's western boundary. Not long before the conference, *Pravda* had published a lengthy article under the auspices of the Polish National Committee. This proposed that the border should follow the River Oder to its junction with the lower or western River Niesse, and then follow the line of the Niesse to the Czech border at Gorlitz. In consequence, up to about nine million ethnic Germans then living to the east of this line and in Silesia and Pomerania would probably be forced to move to Germany when their homeland came under Polish (and therefore Soviet) control. The second factor had no doubt inspired the first, for it transpired many years later that, some six months prior to Yalta, Molotov had signed a memorandum of understanding with the Polish administration in Lublin. This agreement stated both parties' commitment to the Curzon line and Oder-Neisse line frontiers. In fact, Stalin and Molotov were not disappointed and gave little away at Yalta on other issues as offsets for their complete success over setting Poland's eastern border, together with a commitment to deal with the outstanding issue of the western border at the peace conference which, all now anticipated, would shortly follow the German defeat. Linked to this was an intention to seek in the meantime the views of a newly constituted Polish provisional government of national unity, which Roosevelt and Churchill intended to be a broadly based, democratic administration embracing balanced representation from Lublin and London. However, Stalin and Molotov interpreted it as the Lublin government with a small number of other representatives to support its presentation as "democratic." Here again, and irrespective of the final statement on Poland from Yalta, the Soviet view eventually prevailed in practice, and the week-long negotiations on Poland finally proved to have been time that might have been better spent resolving (for example) the complex issues about Germany and Berlin.

Mainly bilateral U.S.-Soviet negotiations about Poland and the composition of its government continued beyond Yalta, and an agreement brokered by the United States and also acceptable to London was finally achieved in mid-July. This followed some hard discussions between Washington (where Harry S. Truman was by then U.S. President) and Moscow. Harry Hopkins was the prime mover in this process and was the man mainly responsible for a generally acceptable Polish government being in place in time for the long-awaited peace conference which would finally decide the matter of Poland's western border.

At the end of the "Argonaut" summit, on February 11, the conference produced a Joint Declaration on Liberated Europe which illustrated the huge gap that had opened between the good intentions and idealism of Roosevelt and Churchill in 1941 and 1942 and the realities of the new world order that was developing so fast. The declaration built upon the Atlantic Charter and set out the standards by which the newly liberated states should live and conduct their affairs postwar. It called upon the three Allied powers to promote the principles of democracy, freedom, peace, and security, and to restore sovereign rights and respect the right to political self-determination and democratic government representation. However, with very many practical aspects of Europe's future at the very least still most uncertain, and with so many of the principles it espoused alien to the Soviet communist way of doing business and Stalin's intentions for eastern Europe, the declaration was of questionable value apart from its not insignificant function of conveying to the public an image of progress toward a better world, and of conference success with the continued unity of the great Alliance. But, even as he signed the document, Stalin must have known that most of its provisions ran directly contrary to his beliefs and to the longer-term aspirations for his country. There was therefore no chance that the document would be allowed to hinder his plans for expansion, or that the Soviet Union would even wish—or, realistically, be able—to follow its tenets in the future.[13]

The other major subject discussed at Yalta was, of course, the war with Japan. Deliberately, however, the U.S. success with the development of the atomic bomb was neither exposed nor taken into account during the meetings. Accordingly, the full-scale invasion of Japan remained the conference focus, and some time was spent briefing Stalin on those developments in the Allied plans that had occurred since they were last explained to the Soviet leader in October 1944. The situation of the Japanese briefed at Yalta was already dire, and it was deteriorating by the week. The Japanese air force no longer posed a threat to Allied bombing raids, the navy could no longer carry out a major engagement, and its merchant marine had been reduced from some seven million tons to just two million. The liberation of the Philippines was ongoing. Attacks on the Bonin Islands and Okinawa were scheduled to take place in or by early April, and their capture would provide air and naval bases within easy striking range of the Japanese home islands. The seizure of Kyushu would then follow. It was planned that some eighteen hundred Allied aircraft would routinely be deployed to carry out the air bombardment of Japan. The ground forces' primary objectives, following the invasion of Japan and a main axis of advance through the

Tokyo Plain, would be in the industrial centres of the country. The extent of Soviet support and the arrangements for it were unchanged, with the projected defeat of Japan set at eighteen months after the defeat of Germany. Roosevelt was of course well aware that the success of the Manhattan project could well curtail this timetable dramatically, as well as saving many thousands of Allied lives, and, although he maintained absolutely the secret of the atom bomb at Yalta, he did indicate in an aside to Stalin on February 8 his hope that "intensive bombing" would be able to destroy Japan and its army and thus save American lives.

Finally, in the margins of the "Argonaut" summit, Roosevelt and Stalin and their advisors produced a secret accord which was in effect the Soviet price for entering the war against Japan. Here was the formal statement of Stalin's demands, early warning of which Churchill had missed in Moscow on October 15 the previous year owing to his temporary illness on that day. Predictably, all that Moscow would gain was at China's expense, but Chiang Kai-shek had already alienated Washington, and, while less enthusiastic about Stalin's terms than Roosevelt, Churchill regarded China's future wellbeing as of little relevance, whereas the continued ability of Great Britain to influence Far Eastern affairs was sufficiently important to allow him to sign up to the Soviet-U.S. proposals. In summary, the Soviet Union undertook to take up arms against Japan two or three months after the defeat of Germany. This was on the understanding that the Kurile Islands would be given to the Soviet Union, all Japanese gains from the Russo-Japanese war of 1904 would be restored to the Soviet Union, and, lastly, Outer Mongolia should "maintain its status quo as an independent entity" or, in other words, should fulfill a role as a Soviet satellite state on Russia's southern border similar to that of Poland on its western frontier. All this was agreed by the Western allies, and all without any discussion with Chiang Kai-shek. Similarly, a bilateral discussion between Roosevelt and Stalin on February 8 about options for a future trusteeship of Korea took absolutely no account of the possible wishes of the Korean people—a revealing insight into Washington's current view of the region, given the principles that it had enshrined in the Yalta summit's Joint Declaration on Liberated Europe.

While the matter of Korea was, arguably, no more than a side issue, it exemplified the extent to which the great Alliance had moved away from many of its original aspirations and principles, and was now divided on a number of issues. The doubtful value of the "Argonaut" summit at Yalta demonstrated that these differences and separate agendas had permeated the summit process itself, as the political issues had become ever more complex, and had in many cases overtaken military matters in terms of their importance. This had always been predictable as the threat posed by Germany diminished, the cross-Channel invasion was successfully completed, and the military defeat of the Third Reich became inevitable. Nevertheless—and the detailed substance of the agreements that had been achieved notwithstanding—Yalta was undoubtedly a key element in the Alliance's campaign of perception management, as had been Tehran and the numerous bilateral war summits before it. Almost irrespective of the strategic and political output from Yalta and the extent to which the three leaders, their ministerial advisors, and their military staffs considered that the meeting had been a success, the simple fact that it had taken place at all was a success in its own right.

For the peoples of the United States, Great Britain and its dominions, the Soviet Union and its republics, the liberated countries of Europe, and those still under German occupation, Yalta showed that, despite its internal difficulties and shortcomings, the great Alliance was still intact and, apparently, thriving, as its leaders planned the final defeat of the remaining Axis powers and constructed a new and better world. Whether or not this conclusion was well-founded is of course debatable, but the continuing process of war summits and the perception of Allied unity that it underscored were a fundamental element in the process of reinforcing and maintaining the morale and fighting spirit of the nations who fought for the Allies. At the same time, the image of unity and purpose conveyed by the war summits was just as vital for the reverse effect it had upon the Nazi leadership in Berlin and the imperial Japanese government in Tokyo. In its simplest form, Yalta and all its predecessors demonstrated that, by February 1945, Germany and Japan were entirely isolated, and were opposed directly or indirectly by most of the nations of the rest of the world.

18
Götterdämmerung

The Final Defeat of Germany, March to May 1945

URING THE FIVE MONTHS that elapsed between the end of the conference at Yalta and what would prove to be the final such summit conference of the war at Potsdam in July (the aptly named "Terminal" meeting), events moved on apace. Churchill and Roosevelt both knew that much of that which had been agreed at Yalta had been a compromise, and their subsequent reports back to Parliament and Congress, respectively, indicated this, if not directly then by implication and by the emphasis both placed upon the strength and continued unity of the Alliance: despite the fact that this had been bought at the cost of Poland's independence and, ultimately, China in order to meet the price Stalin had set on his ongoing goodwill and the Soviet Union's eventual declaration of war against Japan. Over the weeks that followed, while Roosevelt journeyed to Warm Springs, Georgia, in the vain hope that he might restore his former energy and regain some of his rapidly failing health, the follow-on work on Poland by Molotov within the commission in Moscow provoked Churchill to return to this matter yet again.

The prime minister embarked upon an increasingly acrimonious correspondence with Stalin, in the course of which he largely abandoned the agreements made in the "naughty document" he had drawn up with Stalin during the "Tolstoy" conference in Moscow the previous October and all but exposed his twin fears that Yalta had in reality become less of a compromise and more of a failure; and in so doing he showed also his ill-concealed concerns over Soviet ambitions, exemplified by the Polish issue. Roosevelt, plainly, did not wish to become embroiled in this matter, and, while acknowledging that the Polish issue was less than satisfactory but could be taken no further at that stage, urged Churchill on April 11 to "minimize the general Soviet problem as much as possible." Quite apart from the fact that Roosevelt then had less than twenty-four hours to live, this was sound advice: the Western allies had, by their decisions at Yalta, determined that the Alliance's unity was paramount and, given the earlier intransigence of the London Poles, that the future of Poland was no longer worth the risk of a confrontation with Moscow or—of particular importance to Washington—a Soviet withdrawal from its commitment to join the war against Japan. However distasteful it might have been to Churchill, the line advocated by Roosevelt was both consistent with that followed at Yalta and appropriate to the needs of U.S. foreign policy. The long-running issue over the shape and composition of the postwar Polish government was concluded, for better or worse, in early July, when both the U.S. and the British governments at last recognized a new Warsaw-based administration, within which Mikolajczyk had been appointed deputy prime minister. This long-running matter had already threatened to prejudice the success of the postwar international security organization—the United Nations—when Washington and London had earlier indicated that it was unacceptable to them for the Warsaw-based Polish government to represent Poland at the inaugural meeting of the U.N. at San Francisco from April 25, to which Stalin had responded by refusing to send Molotov to the conference, although he later relented shortly before it was due to take place.[1]

In the meantime, less than a month after Churchill and Roosevelt had bade farewell to Stalin in the Crimea, and then, for what proved to be the very last time, to each other on February 15 as President Roosevelt boarded the USS *Quincy* at Alexandria for his sea journey home, the question of where the Anglo-U.S. point of main emphasis in Europe should be, or indeed how far eastward the Western allies should push their advance, was overtaken by events on the battlefield.

At the beginning of March 1945 the River Rhine, by then the western border of the Third Reich, and a significant obstacle with all its bridges destroyed (or so it was believed), had still not been crossed in any strength, although plans were already well advanced for the long-awaited major crossing (Operation "Plunder") in late March by Montgomery's forces to the north, with the intention of then striking toward the Ruhr and on into the heart of Germany. During the night of March 6, Company A of the 27th Armored Infantry Battalion, U.S. 9th Armored Division, was one of the leading units of Lieutenant General Hodges' First Army, which was then driving eastward toward the Rhine and the town of Bonn, on the left of General Bradley's 12th Army Group. General Patton's Third Army was to the south, advancing toward Koblenz, on an axis astride the River Moselle. Since the previous day, the infantrymen of Company A of the 27th Armored Infantry had been in the town of Stadt Meckenheim, where the company commander, Capt. Frederick F. Kriner, had been wounded and the command of Company A had passed in consequence to Lt. Karl H. Timmermann. At 6:00 in the morning of March 7, Timmermann was ordered to provide the advance guard for a task force that was to move to the town of Remagen, which lay some sixteen kilometers away on the west bank of the Rhine. His company would be supported by the Pershing tanks of Company A of the 14th Tank Battalion. By 11:00 Timmermann's force had reached Leimersdorf, about half way to Remagen, having met negligible resistance en route. Company A pushed on, through the deserted streets of the Rhineland villages, on roads and tracks through the dense pine forests, almost to the point at which the forest ended and the land fell away to the Rhine. Timmermann had paused at the Waldschlössen Gasthaus just within the woods to speak to Frau Allmang, the wife of the inn's owner, and 2nd Lt. Jim Burrow's armored halftrack had passed Timmermann's jeep to take the lead. In the midst of ascertaining from Frau Allmang that there were no enemy troops in the area, Timmermann suddenly noticed that the soldiers ahead of him had become agitated. He drove forward, around a bend and out of the woods. There, in the valley below, lay the River Rhine and the town of Remagen; but, much more significantly, there also an intact railway bridge still spanned the river, a steady stream of German troops and vehicles and refugees moving across it. While a quick attack plan was developed, news of the discovery flashed back up the chain of command. By 1:00 in the afternoon, the task force commander, Brig. Gen. William M. Hoge had arrived, and ordered the attack carried out forthwith. Events moved fast, and, despite several abortive attempts by the German defenders to blow up the Ludendorff bridge, the bulk of Lt. Timmermann's Company A crossed it successfully just before 4:00, completing its capture by 5:30. Despite its much-weakened state, during the night of March 7 eight Sherman tanks successfully crossed the bridge. Eisenhower was informed of the bridge's capture while at dinner in Reims and immediately ordered General Bradley to push as many of his troops as possible across the Rhine. Within twenty-four hours the U.S. bridgehead had achieved eight thousand men; and within a week twenty-five thousand U.S. combat troops had crossed the Rhine at Remagen. Although Montgomery's Operation "Plunder" still went ahead successfully on March 23, the whole balance of the Anglo-U.S. advance had been adjusted in order to exploit the good fortune which had attended Company A, 27th U.S. Armored Infantry, that historic morning of March 7, 1945.[2]

At a stroke, the lengthy war summit deliberations that had taken place concerning the point of main effort, and the related Anglo-U.S. politics of command and perceptions that this matter involved, became largely irrelevant as, much as Eisenhower had anticipated, the actuality of the operational situation overtook the theoretical strategic debate, as the Allies in the west pushed forward on what was in all but name a broad front strategy. Thereafter, the three armies of Montgomery's 21st Army Group struck into the industrial heartland and advanced into the northwest coastal regions of Germany, while General Bradley's 12th Army Group and, to its south, General Dever's 6th Army Group advanced east and northeast into Bavaria and southern Germany. Despite Churchill's desire for the Western allies to advance rapidly eastward and thus forestall the final extent of the Red Army's advance as much as possible—to include the capture of Berlin if the opportunity to do so arose—such action was certainly contrary to Washington's view and that of Eisenhower as the commander on the ground. If adopted, it would without doubt have prejudiced the cohesion of the Alliance. But all this was now academic, for the capture of the bridge at Remagen had set irrevocably the course of the final two months of the war in Europe.

As the Allies drove into the remaining territory of the Third Reich from west and east, the advancing troops began to uncover the true extent of the Nazis' "final solution" to the "Jewish Question" and the real nature and implications of a state totally in thrall to the Nazi ideology. On April 10, soldiers of the U.S. 80th Division in central Germany came upon a small wooded hill some eight miles from Weimar, surmounted by an extensive hutted encampment surrounded by wire fences and watch-towers. With rapidly mounting horror they discovered that they were the liberators of Buchenwald concentration camp: one of the three (with Dachau in the south and Sachsenhausen in the north) such major facil-ities of the comprehensive network of this type of camp that populated Nazi Germany and several of its occupied territories. Some fifteen thou-sand mainly Jewish inmates were freed at Buchenwald that day.

Meanwhile, in northern Germany, at Bergen-Belsen, about fifteen kilometers to the north of the picturesque town of Celle, British troops were made aware by the German army commander in Celle of the exis-tence of another of these camps. On April 15, troops of 63 Anti-Tank Regiment, Royal Artillery, plus an Intelligence Corps loudspeaker detachment, arrived at Belsen, which was set within a densely wooded pine forest on the undulating heathland typical of that region. The situ-ation of death, deprivation and disease with which these troops were faced far exceeded their capacity to deal with it, and on April 17 the first elements of what became an extensive British army medical organization arrived at Belsen and set about saving those of the camp's inmates who could still be restored to a semblance of health. Some forty thousand inmates were liberated from the camp in mid-April, although many died later. Indeed, in the month before its liberation, about seventeen thou-sand of its prisoners had died, and at least ten thousand unburied corpses still littered the ground when the leading elements of the British combat troops had passed by the camp shortly before April 15.[3]

In the meantime, on the eastern front, the Soviet forces were discov-ering the evidence of even greater horrors that had taken place behind the barbed-wire fences of the infamous extermination camps located in Poland and East Prussia, such as Treblinka, Auschwitz-Birkenau, Maid-enek, Stutthof, Sobibor, Belzec, and Chelmno. Although several of these death camps had already been demolished, so that the full extent of the inhumanity and genocide that the Nazis had visited upon their millions of victims remained unclear until some time after the war, the existence, or earlier existence, of many of these camps was nevertheless well known before the Allied leaders gathered at Potsdam for the last of their war summits.[4]

However, by then, one of the original members of what had developed into the "Big Three" was no more. Just after one o'clock in the afternoon of April 12, 1945, at Warm Springs, Georgia, President Franklin Delano Roosevelt was dealing with paperwork while a preliminary sketch was being made for a formal portrait. Suddenly, he said, "I have a terrific headache," and suffered a massive stroke from which he never regained consciousness. Shortly before four o'clock President Roosevelt was declared dead. He was succeeded by Vice-President Harry S. Truman.

The new president was then in his sixtieth year. He was a man who had been a sound appointee in terms of U.S. domestic politics, but one who had not ventured abroad since his service as an artillery officer in France in 1918, had not hitherto been briefed on the Manhattan project, and whose awareness of international affairs in general and of the ongoing difficulties over Germany and Poland in particular was at the very least somewhat limited. However, despite this, he tended toward the view held by many in Washington that European imperialism and colonialism were much greater evils than the spread of Soviet communism. This did not bode well for the future success of his relationship with Churchill at a time when the latter was suggesting that the previous agreement on the zones of occupation in Germany should now be set aside by the Western allies, with their forces retaining all of the territory they had conquered prior to Germany's surrender. Neither did the fact that Churchill had originally proposed both that the final war summit should take place in mid-June and that Truman should travel to it via Britain, in order to enable the two leaders to prepare a suitably robust Anglo-U.S. position with which subsequently to confront Stalin. Truman refused both of Churchill's proposals. Then, as well as continuing to take forward a number of key issues bilaterally with Moscow, including those concerned with Poland and China, he deliberately set the conference date for mid-July: by which date, Truman anticipated, the first full test of the "tube alloys" project would have taken place. It was against this background of Anglo-U.S. discord and growing mistrust that U.S. President Harry S. Truman would in due course join the British prime minister and the Soviet leader for what would be the last and the longest of the war summits—and the last chance for them to shape the peace of the postwar world.

On April 23, the battle for Berlin began in earnest, as the Red Army's Fifth Shock Army, Eighth Guards Army, and First Guards Tank Army spearheaded from the east and southeast an attack that would finally draw one and a half million Soviet troops into the onslaught against the German capital. From the north, the Forty-seventh Army, Third Shock Army and Second Guards Tank Army attacked into the suburbs, and from the south Third Guards Tank Army and Twenty-eighth Army worked their way into southwest Berlin. Twenty kilometers to the southwest, the Fourth Guards Tank Army struck northward toward the town of Potsdam. The city of Berlin was defended by just forty-five thousand Wehrmacht and Waffen-SS troops and sixty tanks, plus about forty thousand young, old, disabled, and infirm Volksturm soldiers. A further two thousand Waffen-SS troops of the SS-Leibstandarte regiment were also deployed, specifically to defend the Reich Chancellery and central government area.

Two days after the beginning of the Red Army's onslaught on central Berlin, on April 25 a patrol from the U.S. 69th Infantry Division, led by Lt. Albert Kotzebue, encountered a lone Soviet cavalryman near Stehla, a nondescript German village situated on the west bank of the Elbe, some twenty miles to the southeast of the town of Torgau. This incident marked the very first meeting of the Western and Soviet Allied ground forces, although the first officially recorded meeting of the Americans and the Russians took place on April 27, when other soldiers of the U.S. 69th Infantry Division linked up with their Soviet allies of the First Ukrainian Army at Torgau on the River Elbe.

On April 28, near to Lake Como, Italian partisans executed a number of Italian fascist leaders captured while attempting to escape to Switzerland. Amongst these unfortunates were Hitler's former Axis ally, the dictator Benito Mussolini, and his mistress, Clara Petacci, whose bodies were subsequently suspended on ropes in the main square of Milan. The news of details of Mussolini's demise shocked Hitler, deep in the Führerbunker adjacent to the Reich Chancellery and Brandenburg Gate in central Berlin. This came only days after Hitler had learned, on April 23, that Göring had betrayed him, followed by Himmler (who had tried to negotiate a separate surrender to the Western allies) shortly thereafter. He also heard that his retreat and home at the Obersalzberg in southern Bavaria had been all but obliterated in an Allied bombing raid. On April 29, with the Russians in the devastated city above almost at the gates of the Reichstag, Hitler married his mistress Eva Braun and then dictated his last will and political testament. The next afternoon, April 30, 1945, the man most responsible for World War II put a pistol to his head and committed suicide. Eva Braun —Frau Hitler—lay dead beside the body of her husband, having taken poison. Both bodies were doused with gasoline and burned by members of the Führerbunker staff in a shallow ditch adjacent to the main entrance to the bunker. Although fighting continued into and beyond the night of May 1, a special "Red Banner No. 5" had been prepared by headquarters Third Shock Army to be displayed on the Reichstag by May Day. Despite the fact that the building was not finally secured until 1:00 in the afternoon of May 2, at 10:50 in the evening of April 30 three Red Army sergeants, led by Sgt. Militon Kantaria, made their way to a balcony at the front of the Reichstag and there unfurled the blood red flag that signaled their victory. The remaining German troops in Berlin capitulated on May 2.

On May 2 also, the German forces in Italy surrendered unconditionally. Three days later, on May 5, the German armies in Denmark, the Netherlands, and north Germany surrendered. On May 7, Gen. Alfred Jodl signed the German unconditional surrender at Reims. Victory in Europe was declared on May 8, V-E Day, and this was followed the next day by the formal signing of the unconditional surrender documents in Berlin by Field Marshal Keitel with Soviet Marshal Georgii K. Zhukov. Almost six years of war against Germany had finally ended, and, although Japan still remained to be defeated, it was at last time for the

Allies to carry out the final act in the war summits process which, while sometimes imperfect, had nonetheless served them well during the long years of conflict. Most appropriately, the location chosen by the Russians for this final such conference of the war—the "Terminal" summit meeting—was but a short distance from the former capital of the vanquished Third Reich, at the town of Potsdam, some fifteen kilometers to the southwest.

In the meantime, as Götterdämmerung at last overtook the Third Reich, an even more devastating "twilight of the gods" was almost imminent for Japan. Ever since General Groves' cryptic message to Roosevelt and Marshall on December 30, indicating that the Manhattan project would be able to deliver an atomic weapon ready for use by August, work on the project at its Alamogordo, New Mexico, test site had proceeded apace. At last, at 5:30 in the morning of Monday, July 16, 1945, a blinding flash and a great pulse of heat and blast shattered the tranquility of the desert. A towering mushroom-shaped pillar of fire, smoke, and debris rose high above Alamogordo. The "tube alloys" project had been brought to a successful conclusion and the world had embarked upon the atomic age. The previous day, Churchill, Truman, and Stalin had arrived in Potsdam at the start of the last of the war summits.

The use of atomic weapons against Japan without warning, and as soon as practicable, had been recommended to Truman by Henry L. Stimson, the U.S. Secretary of War, on June 6. In accordance with the agreement of August 19, 1943, Churchill was advised of this on June 29, when he indicated to Field Marshal Sir Henry Maitland Wilson, the British member of the Combined Policy Committee in Washington, his concurrence with this U.S. intention. Initially, Stimson had advised the president that sharing the atomic secret with the Soviet Union should not take place before its use, and that this should then be conditional upon Moscow's involvement in its regulation and control after the war, or as a bargaining counter to influence and constrain its political intentions in eastern Europe. However, at the beginning of July, Stimson and the Anglo-U.S. Combined Policy Committee then dealing with the policy for all atomic energy matters advised Truman that it might be beneficial for the president to provide Stalin with an indication of U.S. progress with the project during the forthcoming meeting at Potsdam. Viewed in the context of the day, this was suitably pragmatic advice, as by July 1945 it would have been naive of Washington to believe that Stalin was entirely unaware of the Manhattan project, and the disclosures that emerged much later from the various spy scandals of the postwar era certainly confirmed that Moscow had in practice been well informed about it for some time. In any event, a broad-based indication to Stalin of U.S. progress with atomic energy could do little harm at that stage of the war, and, much more importantly, it would obviate the inevitable accusations of deceit and duplicity by Stalin that would have followed the weapon's use by the United States without any prior warning of this being given to the Soviet head of state by his Western ally. Furthermore, such an act of goodwill would reinforce U.S.-Soviet relations at a time when the atom bomb might not in fact produce the speedy surrender of Japan, and when it was still anticipated that Soviet intervention might well be needed to achieve this.

In mid-July the Potsdam summit had convened and on July 17, two days after the prime minister's arrival in Germany, Stimson informed Churchill of the successful test carried out the previous day. The prime minister declared himself strongly against informing Stalin of this development, although, when Truman made it quite clear to him the next day that he intended to follow Stimson's line and tell Stalin about the success of the project, he indicated that, while he continued to have reservations about it, he would not resist Truman's intended course of action. There are indications that Churchill, always the pragmatist, later modified his views somewhat, and in particular came to agree with Stimson's original line that the sharing of atomic knowledge with the Soviet Union might prove to be a useful negotiating tool.

On July 22, Truman and Churchill agreed the plan for the atomic attack on Japan, which was to be executed as soon as practicable after August 3; this "not before" date was driven by the U.S. president's wish to have concluded the Potsdam summit before the attack took place, mindful of the need to prepare for the political implications that would follow. The necessary directive was issued to USAAF Gen. Carl Spaatz on July 24, and in the margins of that day's summit meeting Truman mentioned to Stalin, in a manner that made it appear to be almost no more than an aside, the successful development in the United States of a "new weapon of unusual destructive force." The Soviet leader displayed neither surprise nor expressed any further curiosity about this matter; which probably tended to indicate that this was not the first he had heard of the subject, rather than that Truman had been excessively circumspect by intentionally omitting any reference to atomic energy.[5] So it was that an apparently chance remark by the new U.S. president to Marshal of the Soviet Union Joseph V. Stalin at the conference center in the Cecilienhof palace in Potsdam on July 24 provided closure on a policy matter that had much occupied Roosevelt and Churchill in earlier days during their secret talks at Hyde Park, and had later also concentrated the minds of the members of the Combined Policy Committee in Washington. With the Potsdam summit still in progress, a final ultimatum was subsequently issued to the Japanese government on July 26, and the lack of response to this was followed by the obliteration of Hiroshima on August 6 and of Nagasaki on August 9.[6]

19
Anatomy of a War Summit
The "Terminal" Conference, July 17 to August 2, 1945

Preparing the Conference

By the late spring of 1945, the intention to conduct the final war summit in Berlin was not in question, although this did mean that the U.S. and British delegations, despite their political equality with the Russians, would nevertheless be very much in their hands as far as the administrative arrangements for the summit meeting were concerned; and, no doubt, Truman was considerably more comfortable with this situation than was Churchill. In Berlin, overall responsibility for making the necessary arrangements for the conference fell to the Soviet Marshal Georgii Zhukov, whose 1st Belorussian Front had completed the capture of Berlin less than a couple of months earlier.

In early June, Marshal Zhukov had been visited by a number of officials from the Commissariat of Foreign Affairs. Their task was to provide the necessary administrative and policy guidance for the forthcoming conference to be conducted in Berlin itself. However, most of the city was still little more than a sea of rubble, and there were no facilities suitable for a meeting of the three Allied heads of government. Consequently, Zhukov proposed that the conference should take place in nearby Potsdam, which, although also badly damaged, did offer the intact former palace of Crown Prince Wilhelm of Prussia—the Schloss Cecilienhof—as a possible venue. The palace certainly had sufficient rooms to support such a meeting, and less than five kilometers away to the east lay the virtually undamaged residential area of Babelsberg, which could provide suitable accommodation for the three leaders, their foreign ministers, and other senior advisors. Before and during the war, the two-story villas of the pleasant, treelined suburb of Babelsberg had been occupied by many of the Nazi leaders and senior military and government officials. Zhukov's proposals were transmitted to the Western allies, who agreed with the choice of the Potsdam site. Immediately, units of Soviet military engineers and laborers set about preparing the area, the roadways, and the specified buildings for the forthcoming event. Directly responsible for overseeing the program of work was the chief of the quartermaster's division, Col. G. D. Kosoglyad, and under his direction the work was completed by July 10.

The palace itself required considerable preparation, with thirty-six rooms and a main conference room with three separate entrances all needing much work. The décor was refurbished and painted in colors that accorded with the specific wishes of Washington, Moscow, and London: the U.S. delegation chose blue, the Soviets white, and the British pink. Perhaps the British choice reflected the fact that in 1945 a great deal of the world map was still colored pink, conventionally the color used by cartographers to indicate Great Britain and its overseas territories. A large and specially manufactured round table of highly polished wood was made at the Lux furniture factory in Moscow and dispatched to Potsdam for use in the main conference room. Within the palace, the former writing room of the Crown Princess Cecilie was allocated to the Soviet delegation, the palace library was earmarked for the British delegation, and Crown Prince Wilhelm's former smoking room was set aside for the use of the U.S. delegation. Meanwhile, outside in the extensive grounds of the palace, hundreds of ornamental trees were planted, many new flower beds were dug and laid out, and some ten thousand shrubs and flowers were arrayed therein.

Not unexpectedly, the Soviet secret police, the NKVD, took a particular interest in the preparations made for Stalin himself, and on July 2 the head of the NKVD, Lavrenti Beria, reported to Stalin and Molotov on the progress that had been made at Potsdam. His report, which was in respect only of the arrangements made for Stalin and the Soviet delegation, conveyed some idea of the sheer scale of the preparations necessary to support this war summit:

> The NKVD of the USSR reports on the completion of the preparation of
> the measures for the preparation for the reception and accommodation of

the forthcoming conference. Sixty-two houses (10,000 square metres) have been prepared and a two-storey detached house for Comrade Stalin with fifteen rooms, an open veranda, and an attic (400 square metres). This house stands on its own and is fully equipped. There is a post and telegraph office. There are stocks of game, fowl, gastronomic goods and groceries as well as other produce and drinks. Establishments have been set up seven kilometres from Potsdam with cattle and chicken farms, and market gardens, as well as two bakeries. The whole staff [of the house and palace] is from Moscow. There are two special airports available. As guards there are seven regiments of NKVD troops and 1,500 ordinary troops available. The guard is organised in three rings. The chief of the bodyguard at the detached house [at Babelsberg, and presumably that to be used by Stalin] is Lieutenant-General Vlasik. The guard of the conference centre is under Kruglov [who was NKVD].

A special train has been prepared [to convey Stalin and the Soviet delegation to Potsdam]. The route is 1,923 [sic] kilometres long (1,095 through the USSR, 594 through Poland and 270 through Germany). The route has been secured by 17,000 NKVD troops and 1,515 ordinary troops. There are between six and fifteen men on guard for every kilometre of track. Eight NKVD armoured trains will form an escort.

A two-storey building has been prepared for Molotov (eleven rooms). There are fifty-five houses for the [Soviet] delegation, of which eight are fully detached.[1]

As well as the particular interest Beria had taken in the security of his own leader and that of the Soviet delegation, all of the road routes leading to and from the Schloss Cecilienhof, the Babelsberg accommodation area and villas, and the principal conference airfield[2] in the southwestern Berlin suburb of Kladow were heavily manned by Soviet troops. Movement along these secured routes was controlled by the use of special passes issued exclusively for the purpose by the Russian authorities.

The security measures put in place by the NKVD to protect Stalin were always intrusive and often overwhelming. On the occasion he visited Churchill and the British delegation, two trucks full of NKVD troops arrived to surround the villa and the British guard of honor provided by the Scots Guards, while senior Russian officers provided a human shield about the Soviet leader, which parted only briefly so that Churchill could greet him. Truman's security was somewhat less overstated, but was nevertheless very much in evidence, with a heavily armored civilian limousine and well-armed military police escort being used whenever he ventured away from the conference or Babelsberg sites. He also had a sizable personal protection team provided by the FBI, which was always present with the president. Such extensive measures, while undoubtedly reassuring for the Soviet and U.S. leaders, no doubt bemused the British delegation in general and Churchill in particular, accompanied as he had been throughout the war by a single permanent bodyguard, the redoubtable Detective Inspector Thompson.

Despite Col. G. D. Kosoglyad's best efforts, the British and U.S. teams who arrived in advance of the main delegations still found that there was much additional work to be done within and about the Babelsberg houses. The provision of reliable electric power and drinking water caused particular difficulties, as did the failure of a local sewerage system, which proved totally inadequate to deal with the additional demand now placed upon it. Finally, while the three delegations had been allocated an adequate amount of accommodation at Babelsberg, none had been earmarked for the non-Soviet military staff required to provide communications, clerical, and other routine administrative support to the British and American delegations on a day-to-day basis. Nevertheless, by the time that Stalin, Truman, and Churchill arrived at Potsdam on July 15, both the Schloss Cecilienhof and the facilities at Babelsberg were ready to accommodate and support the final historic summit conference of World War II.

The usual program of social events and entertainment that had attended the earlier (and much shorter) summits was greatly expanded at Potsdam, where the devastated city of Berlin provided a unique sightseeing opportunity for the three victors and the members of their respective entourages.[3] Moreover, since the fighting in Germany was now at an end, the summit was an ideal opportunity for the British and the Americans to stage formal victory parades in the capital of their erstwhile enemy.[4]

On Sunday, July 15, the three leaders arrived at Potsdam, the main conference being due to start on Tuesday the 17th. Although, quite bizarrely for the leader of a nation that was still at war, Churchill had spent much of the previous four months fighting what would later prove to have been for him and the British Conservative party an ill-fated general election campaign, he spent July 16 visiting the ruined Reichstag and the Reich Chancellery. Close to there, the prime minister and a few other members of his delegation ventured into the dark, dank depths of the wrecked Führerbunker, where they were shown the room in which Hitler and his wife had committed suicide, and the ditch in which the two bodies had been burned. That day he also took the opportunity to visit the famous Kurfürstendamm, where he opened a newly established club for the use of warrant officers and senior noncommissioned officers. On the 16th also, but separately from Churchill, Truman toured parts of the ruined city. Stalin declined to carry out any such visits, although both Beria and Molotov did venture out to view parts of the devastated German capital.

During the conference period, a number of national victory parades were staged for the Allied leaders and the chiefs of staff. On July 18 and 20, the soldiers, tanks, and other vehicles of the U.S. 2nd Armored Division were drawn up en masse for U.S. victory parades along much of the twenty kilometers of the "Avus" (Automobilverkhers und Übungsstrasse) autobahn and road racing track, which ran to the southwest out of Berlin.[5] Then, on July 21, the British 7th Armoured Division provided the men, armored vehicles and equipment for a similar British victory parade staged on the Charlottenburger Chaussee, close to the Brandenburg Gate. The Soviet forces had already held their national victory parade in Moscow on June 24, and so did not stage a further such event in Berlin during the Potsdam conference.

The program of entertainment was lavish and unashamedly competitive, as each of the three victorious Allies sought to outdo the other two. Although the conference was necessarily conducted within the Russian zone, President Truman had been appointed as its chairman at the outset; consequently, the U.S. delegation was responsible for laying on the first of these formal dinners in the Babelsberg villas. Truman, the host, provided violin and piano accompaniment during and after the meal for the enjoyment of his Russian and British guests.[6] Predictably, when Stalin staged the next of these events, the number of musicians providing the entertainment had doubled, he having brought several notable concert musicians from Moscow for the occasion. Then it was the British turn, and at this third summit dinner at Potsdam Churchill well and truly trumped his two colleagues by engaging the services of the Central Band of the Royal Air Force!

Such were the peripheral matters that attended the "Terminal" war summit, but, as its name so aptly indicated, this was the very last opportunity for the leaders of United States, the Soviet Union, and Great Britain to resolve those matters which remained outstanding from their earlier meetings and to set the world—and Europe in particular—on course for a more peaceful future than had been its lot since 1939 (and arguably since the rise of Nazism from 1933). It was, sadly, a somewhat vain hope, as future events would all too quickly prove.

Conducting the Conference

The organization and program of what was certainly the longest and arguably the most complex of the major war summits conducted during World War II involved a multiplicity of trilateral,[7] bilateral, staff, ministerial, and head of state meetings, including some thirteen separate plenary sessions. Indeed, the "Terminal" summit was notable for the extent to which the three leaders at Potsdam delegated much of the negotiation and discussion to their foreign ministers, which in turn contributed to a lack of meaningful decision-making. This resulted in the first week being taken up mainly with staff discussions rather than making substantive progress. Then, as the summit moved into its second week, the vital need for it to be presented as a success at its conclusion led to the development of a number of speedily conceived compromises. This process culminated on July 31 and August 1 in the three leaders finding themselves obliged to approve or agree in short order a number of important resolutions and protocols that had undoubtedly merited a much more considered approach. Many of these staff meetings necessarily took place in parallel with the plenary sessions and overlapped each other. Consequently, for clarity, it is appropriate to review the business that was conducted at Potsdam discretely by subject, rather than by following through the full spectrum of concurrent negotiations and discussions sequentially day by day.

Indeed, whereas the influence of the original "Big Three" had to varying degrees dominated all of the previous war summits—whether bilateral or trilateral—the conference at Potsdam was unique for the extent of this delegation by the U.S. (and later the British) leader, quite apart from the singularity of the summit's length and complexity. President Truman had succeeded Roosevelt for the one and only World War II summit the former would attend, and in practice the U.S. delegation was therefore in large measure guided and led by the new U.S. secretary of state, James F. Byrnes, a most competent diplomat, and one with an excellent grasp both of U.S. and of wider foreign policy issues. Byrnes had quite correctly perceived that only by dealing with the issues affecting Germany and Poland together rather than discretely could suitable compromises be achieved and progress made at the summit. Indeed, the eventual success of the Potsdam summit was due in large part to Byrnes's astute and pragmatic negotiating skills. Interestingly, Georgii Zhukov observed in 1974 that the early stages of the conference were difficult, and that "probably due to his then limited diplomatic experience, Truman seldom entered into sharp political discussion, giving priority to Churchill."[8]

Indeed, various descriptions of the demeanor and negotiating approaches of the three leaders at Potsdam indicated the much-changed circumstances in which the war summits were by then being conducted, with the conflict now all but won. Stalin would shortly be the only politically surviving member of the original "Big Three," and, although he maintained outwardly cordial relations with his two Western allies, his distrust of the United States and Great Britain had much increased since the days of Tehran and even Yalta. At Potsdam, as ever, he singlemindedly pursued objectives that were first and foremost in the Soviet national interest. The wider betterment of the way of life and security of the international community were of little interest or concern to him, other than where such matters might impinge upon Soviet national priorities.

Although Stalin was, as usual, an attentive and generous host at the Soviet delegation's formal dinner, and clearly enjoyed those hosted by the British and U.S. delegations, the almost conspiratorial rapport and comradeship which had characterized much of Stalin's relationship with

Roosevelt and Churchill in earlier times had greatly diminished by the time of the Potsdam summit; and the Soviet leader's relationship with those who succeeded them would decline even more rapidly in the years ahead. Although he unquestionably respected Churchill as an individual, as a former soldier, and as a war leader, by the time that the two men met for the last war summit at Potsdam, Stalin perceived that Britain's position as a world power was already much reduced, and that the importance and influence of its prime minister had reduced in consequence. Stalin knew also that the democratic idealism of the U.S. president, and the views of so many military and political advisors in Washington, would ensure that in the future Britain and its residual empire would never regain the power and influence it had enjoyed prior to and during the early years of World War II.

In the meantime, Churchill was all too aware of Soviet ambitions, which had become ever clearer with the end of the war in Europe. However, at the same time he failed to establish an effective relationship with Truman such as he had enjoyed with Roosevelt in 1941 and 1942. As was the case with so many Americans, Truman was anticolonial and antiimperial, and a meeting of minds between prime minister and president was therefore always unlikely. But, then, the late President Roosevelt had been of a similar mind on these matters, and Churchill had nonetheless established an excellent rapport with him during at least the first two or three years of their alliance. However, the new president had been extensively prebriefed by diplomats like Joseph E. Davies, the former U.S. ambassador in Moscow, about what many in positions of power in Washington perceived to be Churchill's disarming charm, his eloquence, his negotiating wiles, and his perceived aspirations for Britain and its empire after the war. Davies now sat alongside Truman at the Potsdam conference table as one of his principal advisors, and, in light of his inexperience, Truman's consistently cautious if cordial approach to his dealings with Churchill was perhaps understandable. Churchill perceived that the Soviets were moving forward rapidly to achieve virtually all of their objectives; his former ability to influence the U.S. president was now largely negated; he was very conscious of the fact that British military power now fell well short of that of the Soviet

Union and the United States; and, finally, the announcement of the result of the general election in Britain was imminent. With these factors in mind, it was perhaps not wholly surprising that Churchill's legendary energy, acumen, and negotiating skills were not as often in evidence during his short time at Potsdam as they had been in former times.

Finally, Truman had come to Potsdam with a mix of uncertainty, inexperience, and preconceptions. Although he had been advised of Stalin's ability to renege on matters that had already been agreed with Roosevelt, the president, himself impatient of the need even to be at Potsdam at all, and impatient to conclude the summit's business, found Stalin's directness and desire to reach decisions speedily very akin to his own (very American) approach to politics and to doing business. This directness contrasted with the often less straightforward lines and negotiating positions adopted by the members of the British delegation.

Despite Churchill's sometimes lackluster performance at Potsdam, Truman did not possess the experience and depth of knowledge (and therefore the subtlety) either to counter Stalin's well-honed skills or to impress a British prime minister extremely well-versed in the complexities of international diplomacy and well aware of the special talents needed to conduct such weighty negotiations. However, the U.S. lead for much of the negotiating was perforce delegated by Truman, and Stalin quickly gained the measure of the new president.

Accordingly, the Soviet leader continued his already well-established ploy of highlighting the U.S.-British differences over colonialism, empire, and democracy in the postwar world, while at the same time exploiting Truman's relative inexperience and lack of expertise on European issues. At the same time, he pandered to Truman's desire to achieve quick results. Thus Stalin established a position which enabled him to influence the new president, and this was often by sidelining Churchill. The inevitable result of all this was that Stalin not only ensured that the Soviet delegation would leave Potsdam with virtually all of its goals achieved, but also that the U.S. president would be to a great extent convinced of the Soviet Union's benign political intentions and future international goodwill.

Churchill attended the first week of the conference, but then returned to England in time for the announcement of the result of the 1945 general election. Bizarrely, this was a political battle which he lost, and on July 26 a Labour government took office in Britain. In consequence, Churchill's departure from Potsdam with Eden on July 25 marked the sudden end of their long involvement with the war summits process. It also precipitated the arrival at Potsdam, on July 28, of Churchill's successor, the newly installed British prime minister Clement Attlee, together with his new foreign secretary Ernest Bevin, to conclude the business of the summit on behalf of Britain and its empire. However, aside from the fact that several observers had noted that Churchill's performance at Potsdam had fallen well short of that seen in earlier times, Attlee, like Truman, was more a national politician than a great statesman. Therefore, despite his role within the British coalition wartime government as Churchill's nominal deputy throughout the war years, he made little personal impact upon this crucial summit. He was, nevertheless, an astute politician, and was already much more aware than the Americans of the very real and developing threat posed by the communist Soviet Union. In 1954 Attlee recalled that he had then "thought that the Americans had an insufficient appreciation of this and indeed of the whole European situation. They suspected us of being old-time Imperialists, and were inclined to think of Russia and America as two big boys who could settle things amicably between them."[9] In any event, of the three delegations, only the key members of the Soviet negotiating team remained unchanged from those who had represented their country during most of the earlier such meetings with the Western allies— although it must be said that the British maintained to the end the foreign policy positions that had originally been established by Churchill and Eden, despite the coming to power of the new government.

European issues dominated Potsdam, and, quite properly, Germany was foremost amongst these. This in turn resurrected matters that remained unresolved from Yalta concerning Poland's western border. The conference focused on these vital issues in earnest from July 21. However, in the middle of the negotiations Churchill had flown back to London, never to return to the Potsdam summit, and this ill-timed change of Great Britain's national government and the two key members of its delegation at Potsdam, together with the final departure of

Churchill's still-redoubtable presence from the war summits scene, left the United States and the Soviet Union virtually unconstrained to complete the task of shaping postwar Europe between them.

The Council of Foreign Ministers

At the very beginning of the conference, Truman, as chairman, had tabled a proposal intended to speed up the drafting and implementation of the formal peace treaties with the defeated Axis countries, specifically Italy, Romania, Bulgaria, and Hungary. Washington was determined to avoid the delay that had occurred between the armistice and the Treaty of Versailles at the end of World War I, and the inefficiency that would be unavoidable if all interested parties were involved in such deliberations. Consequently, the U.S. proposed the creation of a Council of Foreign Ministers, with the United States, the Soviet Union, Great Britain, France, and China all represented. This Council would consider the most important matters, deciding them or directing their further study as necessary. Stalin believed that China's inclusion on this Council was inappropriate (Churchill also believed this, but less strongly), given that the greater part of its deliberations would focus on Europe. However, its continued representation on the Council was achieved by several devices that in effect excluded it from any decision-making on European issues. France's inclusion also attracted debate, and it was agreed that its representative could be involved in decisions affecting Italy and Germany, but (in accordance with Soviet wishes) not in those affecting Romania, Hungary, or Bulgaria.

Although agreement on the first accord at Potsdam was fairly quickly achieved—in fact, by the end of the second plenary session— and while the Council of Foreign Ministers would indeed be established, the language of diplomacy meant that its text was acceptable to both Washington and Moscow. Accordingly, it could be interpreted in either of two mutually exclusive ways. On the one hand, it satisfied the Anglo-U.S. understanding that the treaties it produced would be submitted to the United Nations, with the implication that they would then be subjected to wider scrutiny and approval. However, it also satisfied Stalin's view that, irrespective of the United Nations, the settlement of important world affairs would henceforth be a matter exclusively for the United States, Britain and the Soviet Union. Based on this semblance of Alliance unity, and with the yet-to-meet Council of Foreign Ministers tasked to draft the formal peace treaties for Italy, Hungary, Romania, Finland, and Bulgaria, the "Terminal" summit moved on to other matters.

The future management, control and peace treaties of the former Axis minor partners had been discussed at some length, although these negotiations achieved little that was of benefit to the states involved, despite the Declaration on Liberated Europe which the "Big Three" had signed at Yalta. The failure of Britain and America to ensure that Romania, Bulgaria, and Hungary had an opportunity to determine their political futures by the democratic means agreed at Yalta, and the consequent submersion of these states into Soviet communist-controlled eastern Europe, was hardly surprising, but it exemplified just how far postwar Europe would fall short of Roosevelt's original vision of a better world and community of democratic nations, as well as demonstrating yet again the diplomatic acumen of Stalin, who had once more achieved all that he wanted but still without shattering the Anglo-U.S.-Soviet Alliance.

At Potsdam, a number of important matters were deferred for later action by the Council of Foreign Ministers. However, one of the short-comings of the "Terminal" summit was later shown to have been its reliance upon what turned out in practice to be an unworkable and therefore politically impotent organization to complete the work that should have been done by the three Allied leaders.

The Division of Germany and Berlin

Following the much earlier decision in principle of the "Big Three" that Germany should be divided and occupied by the three Allies, the first Protocol on Zones of Occupation had been signed in London in September 1944. This provided for the country to be divided into three zones, with Berlin divided into three sectors. Within Berlin, eight city districts or boroughs were allocated to the Soviets, six to the British and six to the Americans. At Yalta, it will be recalled, agreement had been reached on the allocation of a zone to France, to come from German territory originally allocated to the United States or Great Britain, or from both. Despite their intended inclusion with the United States, Great Britain, and the Soviet Union as the fourth controlling power in Germany, France was not represented at Potsdam. With hindsight, this was an unfortunate omission, and one that would sour Franco-U.S. relations in particular in the years to come.

By implication, the allocation of a French sector in Berlin would be achieved in the same way, but at Potsdam the Americans argued that the offset of territory should be from all three Allies. The Soviets refused to relinquish any of their sector, and the argument continued until July 26 when, with Churchill in London and Attlee not back at Potsdam until July 28, the British delegation announced that they would give up two of their districts in northwest Berlin (Wedding and Reinickendorf) to the French. The conference agreed this British concession with alacrity.

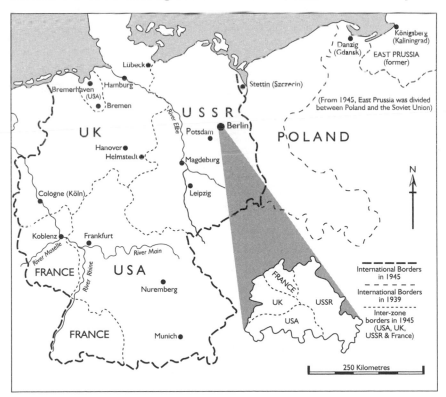

The Shaping and Control of Postwar Germany and Berlin

Allied control of Germany was to be vested in the Control Council for Germany, which first met on July 30. The broad political guidance for those who were now responsible for the control of Germany was laid out in a formal directive issued to Eisenhower in May.[10] In essence, its ten key points, or principles, were intended to promote German democracy, while totally extinguishing any and all residual traces of Nazism. The extent to which the U.S., British, and Soviet authorities subsequently adhered to the directive varied considerably: the U.S. commanders generally strived for the ideal, the British followed a rather more pragmatic and flexible line, and the Soviets implemented those policies that matched their national interests and ideology, irrespective of the directive (with aspects of which they had in any case taken issue).

Poland's Western Border and the Fate of East Prussia

Since Yalta, the debate over whether or not Poland's western border should follow the line of the western River Neisse or that of the Oder much further to the east, together with the eastern part of the River Neisse, had been overtaken by the fact that large numbers of Germans had already moved or been deported from the affected area, which had been repopulated by ethnic Poles. Therefore, although up to three million ethnic Germans still resided in the disputed territory, the humanitarian argument against the western Neisse option had been substantially undermined since Yalta. Moreover, despite the earlier difficulties over the establishment of a democratic and representative Polish government in Warsaw, the bilateral agreement brokered by Hopkins in Moscow the previous May had subsequently produced a Polish government that was at last recognized by all of the Allies. After a couple of days of inconclusive negotiations, the Allied leaders agreed that two or three representatives of the Polish government should travel to Potsdam in order that they should be able to express their views at first hand on these issues, which were once again proving so difficult to resolve.

The tortuous and convoluted process of negotiation and diplomatic coercion which had characterized the formation of the Polish Provisional Government and which had culminated in eight of its members and two deputy prime ministers attending the Potsdam summit from July 24 would provide the substance of a book in its own right.[11] Suffice it to say that the intrigue and suspicion that had attended all of the issues concerned with Poland during the earlier war summits, which then accelerated considerably through May and June 1945, were if anything now even greater, in order to produce an acceptably representative Polish government delegation at the "Terminal" conference that July. The new Polish government had taken office on June 28, and on July 2 Truman had proposed to Churchill that the two Western allies should recognize it. However, with the Polish government-in-exile and its staff

The Shaping of Postwar Poland

Note that the Curzon Line was set as the eastern border of Poland at the 1920 Paris Peace Conference. However, it failed to take account of the predominantly Polish city of Lvov, which lay to the east of the line. Subsequently the 1921 Treaty of Riga established the Polish–Soviet border much farther to the east. But this solution placed part of the Ukraine and Belorussia in Poland and laid the foundations of future controversy, as these territories were indisputably both culturally and ethnically Russian.

still based in London—and with a Polish national army of one hundred and sixty thousand men under the command of Gen. Wladyslaw Anders still engaged as part of the Western allied forces—the prime minister gained U.S. agreement to a short but essential delay. Then, on July 5, Washington and London announced jointly their recognition of the new Polish Provisional Government of National Unity, a government ostensibly dedicated to the tenets of democracy and liberal ideals, and to holding free elections as early as practicable, but which would ultimately prove, as Churchill had long feared, to be little more than a creation and puppet of the Soviet Union. Ever since 1939, Poland had occupied a unique place in the history of World War II and in the consciousness of the British people. Then, since 1941, this had been compounded by its enormous strategic significance to the postwar Soviet Union and therefore to the future shape of Europe. With the benefit of hindsight, these accidents of history probably always meant that the needs and wishes of the Polish people would inevitably be determined by a combination of political expediency and the perceptions of those in power in Washington and Moscow, however distasteful this might be to Churchill and the government in London.[12] Much of the more subjective debate over Poland was characterized by Britain and America seeking to ensure the safety and future wellbeing of those Poles who would soon be returning to Poland, together with ensuring that the Warsaw government would indeed hold free elections and that the Allied media would be able to monitor these elections without constraint. However, these wishes were countered by Molotov and Stalin saying either that the Anglo-U.S. position contravened that which had already been agreed (albeit imperfectly) at Yalta, or that it would place unreasonable and intrusive conditions upon the Polish government and the conduct of its internal affairs. A suitable form of words was contrived—one that was somewhat stronger than Stalin and Molotov had wished—but, as had been so when Roosevelt had made the point to Stalin before the 1944 U.S. election, Truman made the telling point that there were six million Polish voters in the United States and so it was necessary to present an acceptable solution for that audience as much as for the Poles in Poland. This was an argument that Stalin could understand, and in any case he well knew that any form of words devised at Potsdam could easily be rein-terpreted, manipulated, or disregarded once the pro-Moscow regime in Warsaw had been firmly established.

From the point at which the Polish frontier question was introduced by Truman at the plenary session on July 21, the arguments were clear-cut. Stalin contended that the matter had already been agreed at Yalta, that the Polish government view accorded with that of the Soviets, and that the disputed areas had for all practical purposes already become Polish due to the flight westward of most of their ethnic German popu-lations. The Soviet leader also rejected Truman's suggestion that Poland's extension west into Germany was, in reality, producing a fifth (Polish) zone of occupation within that country. He also rejected the suggestion that any reduction of the Soviet-occupied zone of Germany in favor of the Poles would reduce the ability of the Soviet zone to meet Moscow's reparation claims: if the reparations burden placed upon the remaining area of Germany were increased, the consequent hardship for the German population was not a matter of concern to Stalin.

Churchill disputed much of the Soviet case, not least the assertion that the affected territories had already lost most of their ethnic German populations. In any case, where they had moved, or might move, into Germany, these refugees would simply increase the practical problems for the occupying Allied powers, not least because the heavily industri-alized western zones would be dependent upon food supplied from the mainly agricultural eastern Germany and fuel from the coalfields of Silesia. Stalin remained unmoved by these arguments: the Germans could always purchase these essentials from the Poles. However, as Truman observed, with the punitive levels of reparations sought by Moscow, it was debatable whether the Germans would have the where-withal to make any such purchases. This point was entirely valid, as was the fact that Poland was unlikely to have any food and coal surpluses available for export in the first place. As the discussion became more animated, Stalin accused Truman and Churchill of wishing to create and safeguard a new Germany that would be able to threaten the security of the Soviet Union. This allegation was patently untrue in 1945, although Stalin may well have believed it given his by no means entirely unjustified experience of German militarism since 1914. However, with much more justification, Churchill certainly viewed Soviet control of Poland as a clear indicator of the westward advance of communism into central Europe. In any event, by the time that Churchill's involvement in the negotiations came to an end, the situation was one of stalemate.

Truman, much as Roosevelt would no doubt have done, tended toward deferring a decision on Poland until later. Stalin was prepared to defer the issue for a couple of months, when it could be dealt with by the new Council of Foreign Ministers in September. Churchill wanted the matter dealt with there and then. However, this was not to be: following further unproductive discussion of the border issue, it was agreed that representatives of the Polish government in Warsaw should be invited to Potsdam to put their case and views to the conference at first hand. The ten Polish delegates arrived at Potsdam on July 24, their presence having been facilitated by Moscow with alacrity, in the knowledge that the Provisional Government would support the Soviet proposals on Poland's frontiers and territorial gains. This was the day before Churchill's four-year role as a key player in the war summits process had come to an abrupt end, and the very day that he relinquished the post of British prime minister.

The negotiations about Poland, notably its future borders, had already occupied the best part of four days and would continue for a further five. During this time, the Polish delegation made a useful contribution, although the more pro-Western representatives such as Mikolajczyk had clearly been persuaded, or coerced, into accepting the line put forward by Moscow. With Churchill no longer able to champion the Polish cause after July 25 (although he did so with renewed energy almost until the moment that he left Potsdam for London), and because there was, it seemed, a meeting of minds by Moscow and Washington in prospect over Poland, Mikolajczyk's apparent agreement with Stalin and Molotov and with Boleslaw Bierut, the president of the Polish Provisional Government, was understandable. However, whether this was a consequence of the arrival of the Poles, or of the absence and change of key members of the British delegation between July 25 and 28, or of the Western allies' weariness with Polish issues, or simply of the pragmatism of the U.S. negotiators, on July 30 U.S. secretary of state Byrnes had a bilateral meeting with his Soviet counterpart, Molotov, at which they at last achieved a compromise agreement on Poland by linking it to another major issue that was then occupying the negotiators—German reparations.

Despite the ground given by the Soviets on this other matter, the accommodation on Poland none the less involved a major concession by the Americans on the delineation of the Polish frontier in the west. They agreed that, although the line of Poland's western border should be determined by a final peace settlement in due course, Poland should nevertheless gain administrative control of the German territory which extended to the line of the western River Neisse. Given the control that Moscow already exerted over Poland, and the fact that, in reality, once this line of control was established on the western Neisse there was little likelihood of its further modification, Washington had at last given Stalin precisely what he had so long sought—an effective buffer between the Soviet Union and Germany, a direct and secure land route into eastern Germany, Poland's western border as far to the west as possible, and the further punishment of Germany by the loss of territory. At the same time, but with no real dissent by Britain or America, the Allies had earlier agreed the division of East Prussia, with its territory going part to the Soviet Union and part to Poland. Although this attracted relatively little debate, it actually signaled a major change to the existing principle that the Allies would jointly occupy and control Germany: at a stroke, the Soviet Union had ceded a large part of its zone to Poland, thereby creating, in all but name, a fifth (Polish) zone of occupation. Meanwhile, as previously agreed, Lvov remained firmly within Russian territory. Although Bevin maintained the British opposition to the border on the western Neisse, rather than on its eastern branch and the River Oder, until the following day, he finally accepted the inevitable, and so the agreement of all three Allies to the U.S. proposal was achieved on Tuesday, July 31. Certainly, once the Americans and the Soviets were in accord, continued British objections would have counted for virtually nothing, and for no real advantage these might well have prejudiced the outcome of the wider conference.[13]

The Polish border issue had occupied a considerable amount of time throughout the war summits process. This had been unavoidable perhaps, given the mix of political and strategic factors that had affected it at various stages, but at Potsdam the issue had finally, if somewhat imperfectly, been laid to rest, as the remaining German population of Pomerania, East Prussia, East Brandenburg, and Silesia was condemned to relocate into the new, smaller Germany. Britain and its empire had originally gone to war over the issue of Polish freedom in 1939, and there was grim irony in the fact that, at the end of the war, the United States—for which Poland had no real significance other than the fact that American Poles were fairly numerous electors in some parts of the United States—had finally permitted the postwar freedom of Poland to be usurped by the Soviet Union for the next fifty years.

The Economic Status of Germany and the Reparations Issue

At Yalta the "Big Three" had disagreed over the size and management of the reparations due to the Allies from Germany. Although Roosevelt had smoothed the way with Stalin and Churchill toward deferring the resolution of this matter to Potsdam rather than Yalta, the Soviet leader and British prime minister had come to Potsdam with their positions largely unchanged from the previous summit. However, here also U.S. secretary of state Byrnes and the president were able to achieve an acceptable compromise by linking a resolution of the reparations issue to what Byrnes knew was of even greater importance to Stalin—U.S. (and therefore British) agreement to Moscow's wishes concerning Poland. In any case, as the U.S. and British delegations well knew, whatever might be agreed on reparations, the Soviets would in practice exact from their zone of occupied Germany the scale of reparations they saw fit. Indeed, the Soviet forces that were already in firm control of Romania, Hungary, and Bulgaria were comprehensively stripping those countries of a vast range of resources, as well as requiring them to sustain and support the Red Army units (a million Russian troops were in Romania alone) that now occupied them. However, in July 1945 the U.S. and British delegations were not fully aware of the true scale of this plundering.

With this reality in mind, on July 23 Byrnes had proposed to Molotov the idea that the three Allied powers should, as a matter of principle, each draw from their own zone of occupation the reparations they claimed. This was clearly at odds with the original intention to manage Germany as a single economic unit, a fundamental principle confirmed by the Allies at Yalta and one that had underwritten the follow-on work of the Reparations Commission thereafter. It did mean, however, that, in the short term, the fixed total sum and the Soviet Union's claim on the fixed percentage quoted at Yalta could now be abandoned, although in recognition of the need to rebuild its devastated industrial base and means of production it was proposed that amounts of equipment would be transferred to Russia from the German industrial heartland of the Ruhr, and possibly from elsewhere within the U.S., British, and French zones. However, whereas the United States and Great Britain were clear that the Allied reparations claims should not be settled at the price of starving the population of Germany— or of the Western allies therefore having to subsidize the Soviet claim—the Soviets had always accorded the payment of reparations a priority above the regeneration of Germany and the right to life of the German people.[14] Although not represented at Potsdam, the French view was also well known: although by no means wholeheartedly pro-Soviet, Paris viewed the removal or neutralization of the commercial competition provided by German industry in the Saar and Ruhr, together with its Rhineland agricultural capability, as commercially most desirable for the future health of the French economy. Amongst the three main Allies, there were signs of a growing division, with the Americans and British identifying signs of Soviet indifference to the future of western Europe, matched by a growing Soviet perception that the Western allies favored the wellbeing of the German population over that of the Soviet Union.

In any event, the U.S. negotiators made it plain to Stalin and Molotov that U.S. acquiescence over the Polish border issue was now entirely dependent upon Soviet acceptance of the U.S. proposal on reparations, and by bundling the two items together in this way both Moscow and Washington could each succeed with their priority issue while agreeing a suitable compromise on the other one. On Sunday, July 29, on

Truman's direction, Byrnes approached Molotov with the bundled proposals. These were duly put to Stalin, who then spoke with Bierut, who acknowledged the possible need for a territorial settlement which might fall slightly short of that upon which Stalin had thus far insisted. Both sides moved twice more from Byrnes' initial proposal, and that afternoon the combined proposal was formally tabled at a meeting of foreign ministers.

The discussion involving Byrnes, Bevin and Molotov centered on the assessment and source, or sources, of the industrial reparations, the means of their actual provision, and whether or not a fixed value for all these should be set. This last was of particular interest to Molotov, who argued that fixing the Soviet percentage was meaningless unless the total value was known. Despite some progress, the meeting was inconclusive, and the matter was deferred until the next day's plenary session, when its outcome was presented to the three leaders. That day, Tuesday, July 31, proved to be the most productive day of the conference, for that afternoon Stalin agreed to abandon the Soviet desire for the total amount of reparations to be set. He also accepted the principle that each of the Allies would take from its own zone the reparations it claimed. The percentage of industrial equipment that would be transferred to the Soviet Union from the Anglo-U.S. zones was also increased, although Bevin only accepted this increase reluctantly. Then, following some further discussion, the new line of Poland's western frontier was proposed by Truman and agreed by all three leaders. Right to the end, Bevin had maintained Churchill's concerns over Poland, but with Stalin's assurance that four fifths of the Soviet troops in Poland had already departed, with the withdrawal of the balance under review, he had followed the U.S. line. Finally, a third but less important U.S. proposal, concerned with Italy's postwar international status and the fact that it should not be required to pay reparations, was agreed by the Soviet delegation, having hitherto been strongly contested by them. Thus the unity of the Alliance was maintained and a successful outcome to the "Terminal" summit was assured.

On Wednesday, August 1, Truman informed the Polish government representatives of the conference decisions that had been made affecting their future frontiers and territorial gains. The decision on Poland's western border would give rise to other difficulties, as it was later viewed by France as precedent for a similar paring away of territory on Germany's western border. Here, Paris resorted to the all too familiar Soviet arguments about this being essential to the future security of Europe. These were of course largely invalid in the case of France, whose true aspirations were primarily commercial and—albeit on a lesser scale than those of Moscow—punitive.

In practice, the vastly different economic circumstances this repara tions solution imposed upon the separate zones of occupation undermined the Allies' ability to treat Germany as a single economic entity, and thus gave rise to many of the difficulties that the Western allies would encounter in Germany after 1945. Quite apart from industrial considerations, the traditional interdependence of the various parts of Germany—for example, much of the food for what were to be the Anglo-U.S. zones of occupation had traditionally come from eastern Germany before and during the war, while Germany's industrial base was firmly rooted in the Ruhr region—meant that the country could not be divided into viable, self-sustaining zones. Eventually, these practical economic problems, together with the increasing unrest resulting from the suppression of freedom and democracy in the Soviet zone and the widening gulf between Western capitalism and Soviet communism, precipitated the division of Germany, with the creation of separate East and West German states. In the meantime, the industrial and natural resources of eastern Germany lost to Poland meant that the economic balance between the eastern and western occupied zones of Germany, then between East and West Germany, and finally between eastern and western Germany would always be unequal, with the former area never able to compete satisfactorily with the latter, other than as a producer of food and a source of some natural resources, primarily coal.

Austria

If Germany and Poland had produced apparently insoluble difficulties, Austria was almost a model of the reverse. On July 24, in response to an Anglo-U.S. request during the seventh plenary session the previous day,

Stalin confirmed that the Red Army could, and would, provide food to the eight hundred and seventy-five thousand civilians within the British and U.S. sectors of Austria and its capital pending the arrival of the Anglo-U.S. occupation forces and the establishment of their own civil support arrangements. On July 27, Molotov raised the familiar issue of reparations claimed from Austria, but Truman and Attlee diverted this issue by agreeing that all German assets within the Soviet zone of Austria could be removed as reparations. They knew that the Soviets would have taken them anyway; indeed, not surprisingly, Moscow quickly determined that virtually every industrial complex in the Soviet zone had either been German-built or owned by a Nazi and accordingly removed them. Finally, the government of Dr Karl Renner proved, despite its early recognition by the Soviets, to be moderate, democratic, and multipolitical, and as such it soon won the trust of all the Allies. As in Germany, a control council was also established for Austria, although its first formal meeting was not until September 11, and this council's recognition of the Renner government in October paved the way for Austrian neutrality, its regeneration, the eventual withdrawal of the Allied occupying powers, and for the country to take its well-deserved place amongst the truly democratic nations of Europe. Austria's emergence from the war relatively unscathed has a certain irony given that, on April 20, 1889, at Braunau-am-Inn on the Austro-German border, to an Austrian minor customs official and his young peasant wife was born a son, whom they named Adolf.

Spain

Another matter raised by Stalin was his suggestion that the United Nations should sever all relations with General Franco's regime in Spain and engage itself positively to remove him. During the Spanish Civil War, from 1936, Italy and Germany had supported Franco's nationalists, while Soviet Russia had provided matériel support to the republicans; furthermore, a Spanish division had fought alongside the Germans on the eastern front, although Spain had not opposed the Western allies. Stalin argued that Franco's government owed its very existence to the Axis powers which the Allies had recently defeated, and that it was therefore inappropriate for Spain to be treated in the same way as those nations that had remained neutral during the war. However, while confirming his dislike for the nature of the nationalist government in Madrid, Churchill declared himself to be against Stalin's proposal actively to remove Franco, on the grounds that it might unite Spanish public opinion against foreign interference and so actually increase support for the Spanish leader. This in turn could lead to a second Spanish Civil War. Churchill also foresaw that the removal of Franco would create a power vacuum in Spain that could very easily be filled in due course by the communists. Although not as vehement on the issue as Churchill, Truman supported the British line, which in practice matched Roosevelt's long-held belief in the need for states to determine their own destiny through the democratic process. While the original Soviet proposal was not agreed, the conference did include in the Protocol a note of censure which highlighted the fact that the then Spanish government had been founded with the support of the former Axis powers, which meant that it did not therefore possess the necessary qualifications for membership of the United Nations organization. This compromise solution satisfied the Allies and the summit moved on to other matters.

Other Issues

A number of lesser matters were discussed during the conference. These ranged from the disposal of the German navy and merchant marine to the developing turmoil in the Balkans centered on Yugoslavia and Greek Macedonia, where Tito was rapidly imposing his authority over all of Yugoslavia, and where neither Britain nor the Soviet Union knew the extent of this or possessed the power to affect it. Nothing substantive emerged concerning either Yugoslavia or Greece. However, when Stalin had turned the conference's attention to Turkey, and in particular his wish for access to the Black Sea to be secured jointly by the Soviet Union and Turkey, he opened the way for Truman to introduce a proposal that could have led to all of the world's major inland water-ways that bordered on two or more different states being opened to unrestricted navigation, regulated and guaranteed by international authorities representative of all interested parties. This somewhat idealistic proposal may never have been seriously intended, but its rejection did nonetheless serve to expose the more limited desire of the Soviets to control access to the Black Sea and the fact that neither Britain nor the United States were prepared to allow Turkey to be so dominated.

And so the negotiating went on, sometimes at head-of-state level and at other times by meetings of foreign ministers, sometimes in plenary sessions but on other occasions bilaterally. The discussions encompassed such diverse matters as the future of the Italian colonies, Persia, Tangier, Syria, and the Lebanon, in all of which places one or more of the Allies still had forces at the end of the war in Europe. In most cases decisions were deferred, or statements of intent on the withdrawal of Allied troops were made. However, these matters fell mainly into the margins of the summit meeting.

The Japanese War

Surprisingly perhaps, one item not on the main agenda dealt with by the three national leaders at Potsdam was the war against Japan—but "Terminal" had always been conceived as a last chance to resolve the future of Europe. Consequently, the need to maintain the unity of the Alliance and the Soviet commitment to enter the fight against Japan were really the only matters concerning that campaign that might have been affected by the events at Potsdam. Nevertheless, while their principals considered the European and other issues, the U.S. and Soviet military staffs and senior commanders—which included both General Marshall and General Eisenhower on the American side—continued their planning for the imminent entry of the Soviet Union into the war against Japan. These discussions were almost exclusively military rather than political in nature, and therefore took little account of the postwar future of Japan, or indeed of Korea, Manchuria, or China itself. The relatively low profile accorded to the Japanese war at Potsdam may have been due to the fact that a number of the most senior Americans were by then very aware that the availability of the atomic bomb would, in all probability, render further work on planning the U.S.-Soviet attack against Japan largely nugatory. Conversely, by not overstating the urgency of this work, the U.S. delegation would have conveyed the impression that a conventional attack against the Japanese homeland was still some time away—a line that might have been taken deliberately, in order to divert any Soviet speculation about the fact that the U.S. atomic bomb was already operational, prior to Truman's disclosure of the fact to Stalin.

"Terminal" and Termination

On Thursday, August 2, the "Terminal" summit ended, and with it a process that had, for all its imperfections and setbacks, paved the way for the defeat of Germany and its Axis allies and provided an opportunity for the victorious Allies to shape a better postwar world. However, even as the three leaders returned home—and Stalin would never again to leave his Russian homeland—other events in the Pacific were shaping that postwar world in quite another way.

In the evening of Sunday, August 5, a B-29 Superfortress took off from the U.S. airbase on Tinian island, the name of the American pilot's mother, "Enola Gay," emblazoned on its nose. After a sixteen-hour flight the aircraft, shadowed by two others which had joined it en route, was flying in clear blue skies high above the Japanese city of Hiroshima, an industrial center that had not previously been subjected to any significant Allied air bombardment. "Enola Gay" dropped only one bomb that morning, Monday, August 6, 1945, but it was the first of the only two atomic bombs that have ever been used against an enemy in war. At Hiroshima there were almost one hundred and fifty thousand casualties, 78,150 of whom died that day. Three days later, on August 9, a further sixty-five thousand casualties were caused by the second atomic attack, launched against Nagasaki, where forty thousand died.[15] Ever the opportunist, the Soviet Union declared war on Japan on August 8 and the Red Army invaded Manchuria the following day. Then, on Tuesday the fourteenth, the Japanese government, mainly upon the insistence of Emperor Hirohito but against the advice of many of the Japanese military leaders, informed the Allies that Japan was now prepared to surrender unconditionally. World War II was over, the world had entered the nuclear age, and the "Cold War" was about to commence.

20

Quo Vadis?

War Summits and the Postwar World

T HE "TERMINAL" SUMMIT AT POTSDAM not only signaled the end of World War II in Europe and the beginning of the "Cold War" that followed it, it was also the final act in the remarkable process of war summits that had bound together the disparate ideologies, cultures, and national aspirations of the United States, Great Britain, and Soviet Russia in a common cause, in order to defeat an evil which transcended the individual national interests of these three countries and threatened the security of the whole world. Conversely, at the same time, it marked the end of any remaining illusions on the part of the Western allies that Europe—and specifically eastern Europe and the Balkans—was about to embark upon a new age of peace and stability, freedom, and democracy. It was also the point in history at which the age of the great statesmen was, with very few exceptions, increasingly replaced by the age of the professional politicians: few of whom, within three or four decades, would have had any direct experience of war or even of any form of military service. Nonetheless, some of these often ill-prepared leaders would in due course be required (or choose) to commit their nations to various conflicts, and once again to send their countrymen to a host of new battlefields about the world.

Self-evidently, the greatest single success of the war summits was the fact that the Allies won the war. Whatever may have occurred thereafter, the military victory achieved against the three principal Axis powers and their allies by the United States, the Soviet Union, and Great Britain and its dominion forces—all assisted to varying degrees by China and the military contingents of some of the occupied European nations (such as Poland and France) operating under Allied command—was unequivocal.

A prerequisite for this success had been the maintenance of Allied unity, and here the regular face-to-face gatherings of chiefs of staff, ministers, and national leaders promoted, and then assured, the meeting of minds, the discussions, the negotiations, the compromises, the agreements, and the decisions that at last produced the Allied victory. Irrespective of today's concepts of time management, perceptions of good government practice, and efficiency, and the developing capabilities of modern means of communication and data-processing, for those who were involved in assessing, planning, and directing the conduct of World War II, there was no substitute for meeting and dealing directly with their Allied opposite numbers. Throughout the war summits process the vital importance of this human contact was demonstrated time and again. While the formal business of the "Big Three" summits was clearly concluded during the main conference periods, the informal interchanges involving Roosevelt, Churchill, and Stalin at their evening dinner parties and other social occasions were in many ways just as crucial to the success or otherwise of the main proceedings. Similarly, the bilateral meetings of Churchill with Roosevelt or Stalin, and of Roosevelt with Stalin, were key elements of the wider process, as were the bilateral meetings conducted by their respective ministers and chiefs of staff. Moreover, certain matters could really only be dealt with on an exclusive and personal level for security reasons: for example, the decisions on the matter of "tube alloys" made during the bilateral summits of Churchill and Roosevelt at Hyde Park could not reasonably have been attempted or achieved at that time by correspondence, telegraph or telephone. If today's systems of video conferencing had been available in the 1940s, the need for the "Big Three" to travel at all could have been obviated entirely, with clear benefits in terms of time management, security and efficiency. However, it remains highly questionable whether or not even such state-of-the-art video conferencing facilities could have permitted Roosevelt, Churchill, and Stalin the standards of interpersonal communication and simple human understanding achieved through their many face-to-face meetings during World War II—the critical meetings that underwrote the wider success of the whole East-West alliance and laid the foundations for its final victory.

Once the process of war summits was under way, events showed that the longer the time that elapsed between Stalin's meetings with his Western allies the greater were the strains on Allied unity, as the levels of suspicion and perceived mistrust, especially on Stalin's part, grew, although this threat to the Alliance was usually dispelled, or effectively ameliorated, once the leaders met. Churchill's role here was crucial, and, irrespective of the diminishing power and influence of Great Britain after 1943, there is little doubt that Churchill more than anyone else was directly responsible for keeping alive the war summits process. Despite Washington's misgivings about his bilateral meetings, whether with Roosevelt or with Stalin, and almost irrespective of the actual substance of his discussions with the U.S. or Soviet leader on these occasions, Churchill ensured—at no little cost to his own health, owing to his willingness to travel to these meetings—that Allied unity perpetuated, and that it retained a human dimension during a succession of absolutely momentous world events, due to the direct involvement of the three remarkable men who were internationally the political giants of their time.

The beliefs of, and differences between, the "Big Three" leaders could not have been more diverse. Stalin was very aware of Russia's historical weaknesses and future strategic needs, and consequently he pursued his aspirations for the Soviet Union singlemindedly and irrespective of their wider implications beyond what he perceived to be the Soviet sphere of interest. Had he not needed the Western allies in order to defeat Nazi Germany, the East-West alliance would never have existed. Just as Hitler's invasion of Russia provided Britain with a welcome if unlikely ally in Moscow, so Japan's attack on Pearl Harbor finally sealed Germany's fate when Roosevelt took the politically courageous decision—American public opinion and much of the early military advice in Washington notwithstanding—that the U.S. contribution to Allied defeat of Germany should take priority over that required to defeat Japan. Had Roosevelt not directed this policy, all or most of the U.S. resources so desperately needed by Britain and the Soviet Union in 1942 and 1943 would have gone to the Pacific theater. Then Germany might well have fought the

Red Army to a standstill and an armistice and territorial settlement generally favorable to Berlin, even if such proved to be only temporary. In these circumstances, following a U.S. defeat of Japan and without a continuing campaign by the Soviets on the eastern front, a war-weary United States might well have opted for isolationism rather than a commitment to the opening of a new front against Germany in Europe.

Roosevelt's decision reflected his ability to take the broad view, and throughout the war he tended to consider the general rather than the particular, and to keep open as many options as possible for as long as possible. At the same time, he firmly maintained the focus of U.S. power in Washington—the White House map room was invariably the epicenter of U.S. strategic decision making throughout the war—and by his direct personal involvement. In parallel with this centralized control, he sometimes tested possible solutions by deliberately developing contradictory policies, thereby creating divisions and uncertainties among those who worked for him.[1] Consequently, the very visible audit trail of key decisions or fundamental policy issues that attended Stalin's and Churchill's positions during the war summits is less easily discerned in Roosevelt's case. His clear views on the need for, and the shape of, the future United Nations organization, together with his decision to make the defeat of Nazi Germany the first priority of the United States, were therefore all the more evident. Certainly he was an important leader of his nation, but, while his place in American domestic political history was already assured, Roosevelt's international stature as an individual was possibly rather less than that of either Stalin or Churchill, as his position in history had resulted primarily from the sheer military and industrial power of the country he headed rather than from the force of his own personality and wider leadership qualities. Had the United States not become directly involved in World War II—and Roosevelt was of course already resident in the White House before December 1941— the prominent place occupied by Franklin Delano Roosevelt in world history might have been less certain. Without doubt, several of his views on France and China were flawed, his understanding of certain German and Polish issues appeared on various occasions to be somewhat superficial, and his critical position on the old European colonial empires increasingly distanced him from Churchill once the seamless unity of the Anglo-U.S. military alliance became less essential.

However, against these observations, sight should never be lost of the fact that this man had not only been elected by his countrymen to serve four presidential terms, he had also led his nation to victory in a world war while all the time suffering the debilitating and painful effects of a crippling illness that had, by early 1945, developed into a terminal condition. Indeed, had Roosevelt survived the war, the political gulf between the two leaders would undoubtedly have widened, as indeed it did between his successors and successive British prime ministers, culminating in the 1956 Suez crisis, and then exacerbated much later by Prime Minister Harold Wilson's refusal to commit British forces to America's war in Vietnam. Arguably, it was not until Prime Minister Margaret Thatcher was resident at No 10 Downing Street and President Ronald Reagan was in the White House that the Anglo-U.S. "special relationship" established by Churchill and Roosevelt in 1941 and 1942 was once more restored to something akin to its original status.

In Churchill's case, the war years unquestionably provided his "finest hour": as he had noted in his diary on the night following his appointment as Britain's prime minister, "I felt as if I were walking with Destiny, and that all my past life had been but a preparation for this hour and for this trial."[2] Throughout the war years, Churchill had been able to draw on a wealth of experience gained in public office and as a soldier in various conflicts, as well as his extensive knowledge and understanding of history—that of Europe in particular. He was in many ways a prisoner of that history, and yet on balance, while this undoubtedly led to the pursuit of several less sound enterprises and policies, he also benefited enormously from it. Despite his awareness of empire, he was less strong on China and other Far Eastern matters, where he was perhaps somewhat more dismissive of the emerging military power and importance of a non-European enemy. Certainly his shock at the fall of Singapore to the Japanese in 1942 was palpable.

He undoubtedly established a high level of mutual respect and understanding with Stalin: the Soviet leader's apparent dismissal of Churchill's views on various occasions during the later war summits was indicative

of Britain's declining stature as a world power rather than of a diminution of Stalin's view of Churchill the man; and Stalin also used
Churchill's discomfort to promote the Soviet position in U.S. eyes. Both
men understood the vital importance of history as an aid to those who
needed to understand and conduct the international affairs of state, and
both were very familiar with the often traumatic history of the European
continent. Stalin respected Churchill's robust and expansive demeanor,
and admired his record as a competent and experienced soldier. He also
recognized a fellow pragmatist, one who could be every bit as devious
as he when the situation so demanded. Roosevelt, with his more laissez-
faire position on postwar Europe and lesser concerns over the spread of
Soviet influence, felt able to be magnanimous, to a degree, in his dealings with Stalin over the Polish and German issues. Churchill, on the
other hand, was all too aware of the future threat posed by Soviet
communism, and so was rarely in a position to match or sanction unreservedly the extent of give-and-take that finally existed between the late
president and the Soviet leader when they met for the last time at Yalta.

Churchill's time as a war leader guaranteed his place in world history
and earned him the well justified and grateful thanks of the British
nation. However, as the 1945 general election demonstrated, very many
British people had already decided that the sort of national leader and
the nature of the government they had so needed and appreciated ever
since the dark days of 1940 were now inappropriate for what was generally, if naively, assumed would be the period of peace and prosperity
that was to come; and it may be borne in mind that Churchill—unlike
Roosevelt, who had been elected and reelected to the presidency both
before and during the war—had been appointed prime minister in May
1940 and had not been elected to that office.[3]

In considering the more obvious successes and personality-driven
aspects of the war summits, it is possible to overlook the part they
played in shaping the international security organizations that were
designed for, or which developed in, the postwar world. Establishing the
United Nations had been Roosevelt's dream ever since his first meeting
with Churchill in 1941, and the emergence of that organization from the
San Francisco conference and its development from 1945 was in large

part a personal success for the late U.S. president, albeit aided by the support of Churchill and the relative passivity of Stalin on this matter. Although the resultant United Nations organization fell well short of that which Roosevelt had intended, its inability to take armed action against aggressors and other threats to international security (with the notable exception of Korea in 1950) was probably inevitable, given the huge ideological gulf that existed between the Soviet Union and the West in 1945, which then widened rapidly as the "Cold War" gathered pace.

Ironically, the rise of Nazism in Germany and its expansionist results had created the need for the Alliance, first that of Britain and the Soviet Union and then of both these nations with the United States. So long as Nazi Germany existed, it was the glue which indirectly cemented the Anglo-Soviet-U.S. Alliance together. Once the Anglo-U.S. campaign in northwest Europe was well established, the glue softened, more noticeably that which bound together Britain and America. Then, once Germany had been defeated, the glue began to dissolve rapidly. Thus it was in many ways remarkable that the Potsdam summit took place at all, or that it achieved as much as it did. By July 1945, Stalin had all but set the shape and political arrangements of eastern Europe. Britain had been more or less sidelined, while the by now supremely powerful United States had acquired the atomic bomb, and the capability to end the war against Japan almost at a stroke. This new Western superpower had also achieved the military capability to subjugate or destroy any other nation that might threaten America, an observation which remains valid almost sixty years later.

Although it might, therefore, have been naive to expect great things of the Potsdam conference in particular, there were nevertheless two areas that could and should have been addressed by that final summit in considerably greater depth or perhaps—with what might have been a much greater chance of substantive progress—at one or more of the earlier war summits. The first of these was the whole subject of Germany and that country's long-term future. From the failure to deal adequately with this matter later flowed many of the "Cold War" crises, with Berlin remaining the epicenter of that follow-on conflict from its beginning in 1945 until its end in 1989. In retrospect, given the importance that had been accorded to the defeat of Germany by the Allies and the well-known history of that nation since 1870–71, the amount of time allocated to this matter by the three leaders in particular was remarkably small. Throughout the war summits, only Stalin took a truly long-term view of the future strategic and geographical significance of postwar Germany and its indivisibility from the question of Poland and its frontiers, albeit from an entirely Russian perspective.

In the meantime, Roosevelt, and to a much lesser extent Churchill, often appeared to overlook or acquiesce in the activities of the Soviet ally, usually in the interests of harmony, upon which the continued unity of the Alliance so regularly depended. Churchill's view of Europe was largely influenced by a combination of history, an array of subjective and moral obligations, a well-founded suspicion of Soviet communist aspirations, and the need to preserve the British Empire. In the meantime, the U.S. president was preoccupied with the Pacific war; notwithstanding the events that had occurred in Singapore, Hong Kong, Burma, and China. Ever since Pearl Harbor and the "Day of Infamy," the war against Japan had undeniably been very much America's war. He was also driven by his vision of a postwar world united in peace and harmony (but controlled primarily by the United States and the Soviet Union), while at the same time he was influenced by an American view of history, which castigated Europe as the principal source of imperial and colonial ambitions, of devastating wars, and of aggressive and reactionary governments. Small wonder, then, that Roosevelt tended to take broader views, circumvented U.S. involvement in the detailed consideration of European issues, and sought (unsuccessfully, as it would soon prove) to disengage the United States from Europe in the postwar era. Nevertheless, while it is arguable that a more direct U.S. involvement in the European political debate might have resulted in a more equitable solution for Germany and Poland, it could also be argued that this might well have brought the United States into direct conflict with the Soviet Union, thereby destroying the Alliance and the war summits process, and even precipitated the war that some American military and political leaders urged should indeed be fought and won before the Soviets also acquired the atom bomb.

The decision of Roosevelt and Churchill not to widen consideration of the nuclear dimension beyond its more immediate potential as an exclusively Anglo-U.S. weapon system was another lost opportunity at the war summits. As is now clear, Stalin was very aware of the Manhattan project through the Soviet spying activities of the time. Consequently, although, obviously, he could not reveal this fact to his Western allies, this knowledge set against the failure of Roosevelt and Churchill to share their secret with him must have fuelled his suspicions concerning their real motives and future intentions. While it would probably have been unreasonable for the United States and Great Britain to have shared their nuclear technology with the Soviet Union in an unrestricted manner in the 1940s, it might have been prudent for the war summits to undertake a wider consideration of the control and management of nuclear energy while East and West were still of necessity bound together in the fight against the Axis powers.

Conversely, of course, had he been officially and fully included in the "atomic club" by his two Western allies, Stalin could, with some justification, have demanded early access to the new wonder weapon for the support of the Red Army. Alternatively, armed with this information from America, Soviet scientists might have been able to accelerate their own development of atomic weapons within Soviet Russia, in order to deal in short order with the German armored formations on the eastern front. There, much of the terrain, the strategic situation, and the then prevailing Soviet attitude to casualties (those of their own forces and of the enemy) could have allowed the atom bomb to be used to particularly good military effect. In these circumstances, the Soviet nuclear capability at the end of World War II and at the start of the "Cold War" might well have exceeded that of the Anglo-U.S. allies. In any event, this widening of nuclear knowledge did not take place, and any criticism of the fact that it did not must be set against the circumstances of the day. This was still a time when few really understood the potentially awesome implications of atomic weapons and nuclear energy. Moreover, the centuries-old concept of "the secret weapon" and the consequent need for states jealously to safeguard such weapons in the interests of their national security was still paramount.

The war summits of 1941 to 1945 were unique, and so any attempt to compare the process directly with modern practice may be ill-founded. Nevertheless, certain parallels can be identified, particularly during the immediate postwar decades. These war summit meetings were the product of the international situation that had developed from the consequences of German aggression in 1939, which in turn produced the Alliance of Great Britain, the Soviet Union, and the United States and others from 1941. For the Alliance to succeed in its aim of defeating the Axis powers, its members clearly had to coordinate their various campaigns effectively, and so the creation of a means of doing this was both inevitable and essential. The sheer scale of World War II took this process well beyond the needs of the battlefield, however, and so the deliberations of the war summits delegates between August 1941 and July 1945—notably the several meetings of the "Big Three" leaders—necessarily also encompassed consideration of the major political issues of the time.

In terms of its overall duration, the sheer scale of the Alliance it supported, and the nature of the global conflict it sought to resolve, the process of meetings and conferences which together comprised the war summits was without precedent, and it remains unique in the history of warfare and of international grand strategy and politics. Nevertheless, the need for the leaders, ministers, and military chiefs of sovereign nations to support alliances and to develop the necessary policies and plans to do this has always existed, and no doubt it always will.

From these thoughts two forums emerge that could perhaps qualify, at least in part, as the modern equivalents or successors of the former war summits process. The first of these flowed directly from the summits of World War II, and Roosevelt would no doubt have been able to identify the threads that linked the two processes. When the concept of the United Nations was devised, it had been intended that the new organization would, if necessary, be able to direct armed force to preserve or impose peace. In fact, due mainly to the postwar split between East and West, and then to that between the developed world and its Third World counterpart, the United Nations never achieved the necessary degree of consensus or a standing military force that would enable it to do this.

Nevertheless, in some respects the United Nations Security Council has taken forward the role envisaged by the "Big Three" during the 1940s. Indeed, it was actually able to fulfill that role in 1950, when it launched the war to counter North Korean aggression against South Korea. However, this action was virtually unprecedented, and had only been possible due to the fortuitous absence of the Soviet representative to the Security Council at the time the decision to counter the invasion was taken. Only in 1990–91 did a comparable situation exist, when the United Nations condemned Iraq's invasion of Kuwait and sanctioned the counteraction by a U.S.-dominated coalition.

The collapse of the Soviet Union from 1989 may yet, in the fullness of time, permit the Security Council to fulfill the role that was originally visualized for it more than half a century ago. Although, as Korea and Kuwait (and a very few other minor conflicts) have demonstrated, unless the potential threat posed to world peace is unequivocal or a major act of aggression has already been committed, the United Nations Security Council can probably never be more than a very pale imitation of the negotiating and decision-making organization that shaped and won World War II.

Nevertheless, if the achievements of the U.N. Security Council have fallen somewhat short of those of the war summits, perhaps one other postwar organization has managed to come somewhat closer to them. Certainly, this other organization was formed to support an alliance of equal and sovereign nation states; certainly, it also existed to support the military forces engaged in a form of warfare against a very visible, sizable, and potent military threat, though not a war such as that which had so recently preceded it. Nevertheless, during a protracted conflict that lasted for almost half a century, this organization directed the forces of the alliance it headed to achieve a total victory. The conflict was the "Cold War," the "war summit" organization in this case was the North Atlantic Council, together with the Defense Council and the Military Committee, and the alliance it supported was the North Atlantic Treaty Organization, or NATO. Given that the Americans and the British were the principal members of NATO from the outset, it is hardly surprising that its structure and way of doing business drew heavily upon the 1941–45 experience, particularly during its formative years. Indeed, the North Atlantic Council's dealings with the "Cold War" issues of Germany, the several crises in the states of eastern Europe, the inexorable expansion of Soviet power and influence, and the nuclear dimension surely had a resonance that would have been familiar to Roosevelt and Churchill had they still been in power throughout the "Cold War" years.[4]

The similarities between the broad subject matter of countless NATO planning meetings designed to counter the Soviet and Warsaw Pact threat in Europe and the matters debated by Washington and London during the 1940s concerning the war against Germany and the cross-Channel invasion are striking. The NATO strategic imperatives—control of the Atlantic seaways and the English Channel, the vital role of the British Isles as a secure forward mounting base, the intention to fight and win the ground war in mainland Europe, and an absolute dependence upon U.S. military involvement—all mirrored the fundamentals of the 1941–45 situation that had shaped the war summits. Even the two principal allies on the NATO side, the United States and the United Kingdom, were the same. Only the dominant role of nuclear weapons characterized the uniqueness of the "Cold War" conflict and separated it conceptually from World War II, particularly after the Soviet Union acquired its own nuclear capability. Indeed, while a very few of the armed conflicts between 1945 and 1990 were undoubtedly aberrations—for example, Britain's war to recapture the Falkland Islands from Argentina in 1982—virtually every campaign and conflict that flared up during the period fell directly or indirectly within the overall ambit of the "Cold War," the great struggle between East and West, between communism and capitalism. Here, the threat posed by the Soviet Union and the Warsaw Pact from 1945 and 1955, respectively, provided a focus that was at least the modern equivalent of that which had been posed by the Axis powers in former times.

The "Cold War"—arguably "World War III" in all but name—was the last great conflict of the twentieth century and, following so closely upon World War II and focused upon a probable ground war in Central Europe, it was hardly surprising that its high-level command and control drew, even if only if subconsciously, upon many of the arrangements that had produced the Allied victory in 1945. Perhaps the single greatest lesson that NATO—the United States and Britain especially—drew from the experience of the former World War II alliance was the crucial need to compromise and to achieve acceptable solutions to what were often potentially irreconcilable problems, despite the very different views and needs of its many member nations. Following on from this, the war summits had also provided lessons on the various ways in which accept-able forms of agreement might be achieved. Thus, in many ways, the war summits of 1941 to 1945 underwrote, and provided the learning experience for, the leaders and military commanders of the NATO alliance that was formed in 1949, which then went on not only to avoid a potentially apocalyptic clash of arms in Europe and to manage successfully the awesome power of its nuclear arsenal, but also to win a decisive but bloodless victory in 1989.

However, although NATO still exists today, it has increasingly become an historical anachronism since the end of the "Cold War." From 1990 its well understood and highly visible reason for existence diminished and very soon ceased to exist altogether, and, as every serv-iceman knows, where no credible and well-defined military threat exists or is deemed to exist, history has shown time and again that the armed forces of sovereign nations (especially democracies) can quickly become unfocused, disillusioned and vulnerable to cost-cutting exer-cises or, worse still, to their misuse on politically ill-judged enterprises. Predictably perhaps, the U.S.-led "war on terrorism" that has been ongoing since the Al-Qaeda atrocity in New York on September 11, 2001, has thus far produced no unified front to counter the asymmetric threat posed by the disparate but, to date, mainly Islamist terror groups. The nature of this war is such that, although it has now been waged for some three years, the sort of comprehensive international consensus and alliance needed to deal with it is apparently still some time distant.

Ironically, Al-Qaeda and other such terrorist organizations today represent just the sort of modern threats to world peace and security that Roosevelt and Churchill might reasonably have expected to be dealt with resolutely and in short order by the United Nations. However, the diverse national, political, and ideological composition of that organization—and often very parochial national political agendas of many of its members—indicated very early in its existence that it would never be able to assume this responsibility in practice.

In the meantime, following the demise of the Soviet Union and the Warsaw Pact, NATO quite bizarrely and with great haste began to welcome several of its former Warsaw Pact enemies into the organization, first by association through the Partnership for Peace program but later with a view to their full membership of NATO. The organization has also increasingly emphasized and developed its peacekeeping and humanitarian capabilities rather than its traditional war-fighting role. Self-evidently, these are laudable new activities in presentational and political terms, but it is debatable whether they should really be the core business of a major military alliance—currently the only such militarily viable alliance upon which the world, or possibly even the United Nations, could call if the need to do so should arise at some future date. In any event, these changes of operational emphasis will increasingly provoke an identity crisis over NATO's future role, together with the progressive politicization of the organization and the diminution of its war-fighting capability. At the same time, with European dependence upon U.S. military might now much diminished, NATO has been further weakened by the development of the Berlin- and Paris-inspired Euro-corps, which owes more to the personal aspirations of some European Union politicians than it does to the needs of European military security, and this has inevitably undermined the links between the United States and several mainland European states.

What, then, is the future, if indeed any such future exists, for the sort of military alliance and the consequent strategic negotiating machinery that existed and functioned so successfully during World War II and the "Cold War"? First and foremost, without the existence of a military threat, no need for such mechanisms exists. However, it is an undeniable (if sad) fact that throughout the history of the human race such threats have always existed, and it would therefore be most naive to assume that this situation will not exist in the future.

Perhaps the greatest lesson of the meetings that took place from August 1941 to July 1945 is that, when the nature and scale of the evil that presents itself as a threat is sufficiently great, the need to defeat it will transcend the cultural, ideological, religious, and political differences of nations as diverse as those of the capitalist United States, of the communist Soviet Union, of the imperial and colonial powers such as Britain and France, and of those of the most populous nation of all, China. In 1941 the Axis threat was abundantly clear. From 1945 to 1989, the global threat posed to the West by the Soviet Union and the Warsaw Pact was undeniable. Now, since September 11, 2001, another threat has emerged—one that is yet again global in nature but which targets neither West nor East exclusively and threatens the security of the entire civilized world. The new evil that has emerged as a legacy of the "Cold War" is terrorism, present in various forms throughout history but, since September 2001, in scale and nature unprecedented because of the escalating activities of various Islamist terror groups, and in particular because of their callous but devastatingly effective policy of using suicide bombers as the weapon of choice.

The inherent vulnerabilities of modern everyday life have combined with the disproportionately destructive capabilities of today's technologically and scientifically aware terrorists to create potentially catastrophic situations on a scale unprecedented other than in the course of waging total war. The U.S.-led "war against terror" has now been ongoing for some three years, and its major military campaigns thus far have, for better or worse, included those in Afghanistan from 2002 and—albeit with doubtful justification[5]—in Iraq from 2003, together with a number of lesser counter-terrorist operations, but, as yet, no meaningful global alliance against this asymmetric threat has emerged. Elsewhere, Israel has long been countering acts of terror inspired by the Palestinian situation, both within that country and emanating from the territories bordering it, while more recently the terror campaign and insurrection mounted against Moscow by the predominantly Muslim separatists of the Russian southern province of Chechnya have continued, Russian claims to the contrary notwithstanding. In the meantime, the series of devastating terrorist attacks across the world since the destruction of the World Trade Center in New York in September 2001 have, in virtually every case, been attributed directly or indirectly to Islamist extremist groups.

Consequently, the global war to remove the blight of terrorism has—entirely incorrectly, but for what are unfortunately all too understandable reasons—been perceived by many Muslims to be a religious conflict, a sort of modern-day crusade between the West and Islam. The close links between the United States and Israel and the long-running and bitter campaign by the Palestinians to regain an independent homeland have served indirectly to exacerbate and reinforce this misperception, while some of the war-fighting techniques adopted by the United States in Iraq since the overthrow of Saddam Hussein in March 2003 have also tended to fuel and harden such views within the Islamic world. However, the world is now approaching the abyss; and just as the "Cold War" might quite appropriately have been accorded the title "World War III," so the "war against terrorism" may yet attract, even more accurately, the title "World War IV."

Chemical weapons were used in World War I and nuclear weapons were used in World War II. Thereafter, nuclear weapons were deployed and utilized—as a deterrent—throughout the "Cold War." During the "Cold War" the anticipated tactical use of chemical weapons by the Soviet and Warsaw Pact forces also posed an ever-present threat. Since September 11, 2001, several instances of the use, or intended use, of chemical weapons by terrorists have already occurred. However, the "war against terrorism" may yet prove to be the first to involve the use of biological weapons, potentially turning today's conflict into what could literally become a war for the survival of large numbers of the human race.

Nevertheless, there is still time for an overwhelming majority of the world's leaders to recognize and agree that the elimination of the growing evil of terrorism must now be accorded the highest priority, just as Roosevelt, Churchill, and Stalin recognized that the defeat of Nazism was paramount in 1941, when they submerged their many differences in the interests of the greater good. In exactly the same way, it is already past time for certain nations of the world to subordinate their narrow, parochial and self-serving political, ideological or religious agendas, in order to enable the defeat of terrorism by providing the counter-terrorist police and security forces with the accurate intelligence that is so essential for this task. Just as importantly, they must also remove the political support (whether active or passive), funding, and safe havens upon which the terrorist invariably depends.

At the same time, other nations, especially in the developed world, must recognize that terrorism feeds upon disaffection, poverty, oppression, disenfranchisement, loss of hope, and the economic exploitation of disadvantaged peoples, and that they will therefore need to address these matters pragmatically and expeditiously. The oft-quoted adage that "one man's terrorist is another man's freedom fighter" remains as true as ever, so that discrediting and exposing the flaws in the cause of the terrorist operating in the guise of a "freedom fighter" is therefore every bit as important as his physical capture or elimination. There is nothing new in this.

Once the malignant threat of international terrorism has finally been excised from everyday life, it is just possible that the dream of a secure, stable, and better world which Roosevelt and Churchill discussed so many years ago aboard the USS *Augusta* and HMS *Prince of Wales* at Placentia Bay, Newfoundland, in mid-August, 1941, at the very outset of the war summits process, might yet be achieved during the first part of the twenty-first century. If a principal purpose of the study of history is that human beings may learn both from the failures and from the successes of the past, then surely the broad lessons and examples of the war summits that shaped World War II should provide the grounds for a degree of cautious optimism concerning the resolution of today's very different but equally dangerous conflicts?

Notes

1. World in Turmoil

1. Emil Hácha continued as the puppet leader of German-occupied Czechoslovakia until the Soviet invasion toward the end of the war. He died in a Prague prison on June 27, 1945.
2. Bender and Law, *Afrikakorps*, 20. Some other accounts (Macksey, *Afrika Korps*, 15) place this first clash at Nofilia on February 28.

2. Genesis of the Warlords

1. Churchill had previously, but on that occasion unsuccessfully, stood for Oldham in July 1899.
2. Tblisi was known as Tiflis at that time.
3. The British attempt to gain control of the Dardanelles, first by naval action and then by the Gallipoli landings, was a defining moment in Churchill's life. Later, during World War II, it would directly influence the views he expressed and the decisions he made during the war summits on the strategic importance of winning over Turkey to the Allied cause, and on the use of the Aegean as a "back door" route to attack Germany. However, the clearest evidence of the legacy that Gallipoli had left to Churchill would be seen both in his enthusiasm for the potential benefits of the Allied landings at Anzio and in his caution over the plans for, and timing of, the invasion of northern France in 1944.
4. Both of these provinces were linguistically, culturally, and ethnically Russian, rather than Polish.
5. In fact, Lenin had apparently indicated (in the "Krupskaya will") that he did not believe that Stalin was suitable to succeed him as leader, but without providing a clear indication of who he did wish to do so.
6. Having previously identified two events

or issues from the past—Gallipoli and Poland—that influenced Churchill and Stalin, respectively, during their later involvement in the war summits, the equivalent core issue for Roosevelt was probably his belief in, and determination to create, a viable international security organization, in which the United States would, by default, have a controlling role. The earlier failure of the League of Nations was firmly imprinted upon his consciousness. This vision of the future says much about Roosevelt, for it demonstrated both his breadth of vision and his idealism, but also, arguably, a degree of naivety about the world of international politics and the history of Europe. This in turn reflected the largely isolationist position that the United States had maintained prior to World War II.

3. The Road to "Arcadia"

1. Placentia Bay appears as "Argentia Bay" in some U.S. accounts of this meeting.
2. See Thompson, *I was Churchill's Shadow*, pp. 71–4.
3. Stalin had badly miscalculated the German intentions. Following the Operation "Barbarossa" invasion, he suffered a severe breakdown, retired to his *dacha*, and was not seen for a number of days. In mid-1941 Stalin undoubtedly viewed a second front in Europe as the only thing that could restore the strategic situation and thereby safeguard the Soviet Union and his own position as its leader. Subsequently, this theme dominated his thinking and priorities throughout the rest of the war summits process.

4. The "Arcadia" Conference and the Pacific Dimension

1. Given that such issues were clearly already being actively considered at the

highest level in Washington by November 1941, the complete lack of preparedness of the U.S. forces at Hawaii when the Japanese attacked Pearl Harbor the following month was surely both inexplicable and negligent. The removal of Adm. Husband E. Kimmel and Lt. Gen. Walter C. Short, the senior navy and military commanders, respectively, at Hawaii on December 7, just ten days after the Japanese attack, was viewed by many as Washington's abrogation of its own responsibility for the debacle. The first commission of inquiry, the Roberts Commission, stated on January 24, 1942, that both these officers had failed to take the necessary actions and properly evaluate the seriousness of the situation, and that these errors of judgment were the effective reasons for the success of the Japanese attack. Despite numerous inquiries and investigations into the attack—there were no fewer than nine between 1942 and 1946—it was perhaps significant that neither Kimmel nor Short were ever subjected to court-martial proceedings.

2. HMS *Prince of Wales* was the same warship that had conveyed Churchill to Placentia Bay just four months earlier, and he was much affected by the loss of so many crew members, of all ranks, that he had come to know personally during that Atlantic crossing and the conference period.

3. Yamashita's attack from the Malay peninsula succeeded in large part due to Singapore's main defenses and heavy artillery emplacements having been configured to defeat a maritime threat from the south.

6. In the Bear's Lair

1. Churchill's military advisors, traveling on a different aircraft, did not arrive at Moscow until the following day after a small fire broke out on their airplane shortly after its departure from Tehran, when it had to turn back. Such were the vagaries of air travel in the 1940s (quite apart from the threat of enemy action), and the additional stresses and strains imposed upon Churchill in particular by an extensive program of air and sea travel to meet Roosevelt, Stalin, and a host of other political and military leaders was considerable.

2. However, the story of PQ.17 is not as straightforward as it was reported in 1942, as it was in fact apparently linked to an abortive intelligence operation mounted by the British Admiralty with MI5 to use the convoy as bait to lure the German battleship *Tirpitz* from her lair at Altafjord, near Trondheim, into an ambush by a strong force of RN warships near Iceland. The ruse failed and the convoy was left unprotected from an incorrectly assessed imminent attack by *Tirpitz*. This led to the fatal order being given for the convoy to scatter. See also the account of this operation on p. 12 of *The Sunday Times*, May 25, 2003 ("Failed MI5 Tirpitz Plot Cost 24 Ships," by Peter Day, Jack Grimston, and Robert Mayes), based on a Public Records Office document released on May 22, 2003. Possibly Roosevelt, but certainly Churchill, would have been aware in advance of the intention to use PQ.17 in an attempt to entrap the German raider.

3. The statistics for Allied convoy losses are taken from Montgomery, *A History of Warfare*. By the end of the war the Kriegsmarine had lost 785 of 1,162 U-boats, and the U-boats had in turn sunk 2,828 Allied vessels (some 14,687,230 tons). The heaviest Allied losses were borne by the Royal Navy and British merchant fleet: some eighty-two thousand British seamen had been lost at sea by the end of the war against Germany in May 1945 (Montgomery, p. 517).

4. In practice, when Roosevelt renewed the Operation "Velvet" offer in December, the Soviets found that the extensive resources and Soviet support that the force would need were such that Stalin declined the offer of direct Anglo-U.S. air assistance in the Caucasus.

7. End of the Beginning

1. Despite this, Rommel's qualities as an outstanding military commander should neither be understated nor misunderstood. However, by the time that the Afrika Korps was confronted by Montgomery's revitalized Eighth Army, a combination of overextended lines of communication, inadequate logistic resupply, and a lack of reinforcements (due in large part to competing priorities for Germany on the eastern front) had all combined to seal the fate of the German forces engaged against the British and

Dominion forces at Alam Halfa and El Alamein in late 1942.

2. In February the following year, Rommel inflicted a telling reverse on the U.S. troops at Kasserine Pass in Tunisia, where the American military commanders at all levels learned a number of salutary, if costly, lessons about the war in which their nation was now very fully engaged. Despite early German successes, the Allies subsequently restored the situation at Kasserine and throughout Tunisia.

3. Darlan was later assassinated, on December 24, 1942.

4. The Germans never captured Stalingrad, despite Hitler's exhortations to do so. Initially, the Sixth Army at Stalingrad attempted to fulfill its mission to seize the city. Once that became unachievable, it sought to hold that ground which it had taken and within which it became encircled. Finally, without relief, reinforcement, effective resupply, or the opportunity to withdraw, the newly promoted Field Marshal Paulus bowed to the inevitable and surrendered the German Sixth Army to the Soviet forces.

8. Global Strategy and Unconditional Surrender

1. In any case, Churchill and the British chiefs of staff still maintained the position which they had held since the previous year—that any sort of Allied cross-Channel invasion in 1943 was unlikely to succeed.

2. The U.S. Air Force (USAF) was not formed until mid-1947. Throughout the war the U.S. Army, U.S. Navy (USN) and U.S. Marine Corps (USMC) maintained their own dedicated combat air and air transport support organizations.

3. The strategic bombing campaign against Germany had in fact been ongoing ever since May 15, 1940, when ninety-nine Royal Air Force bombers had struck oil production facilities and railheads in the Ruhr. However, as a matter of principle, the RAF conducted such raids only by night, in order to minimize what was a steady toll of aircraft. The introduction of the particularly robust four-engine Lancaster bomber into RAF service from March 1942 improved both the capability and survivability of RAF Bomber Command, which had by then just come under the command of Air Marshal

Arthur "Bomber" Harris. Once the United States entered the war and sought to coordinate its bombing raids on Germany with those of the British, its high command opted for its strategic bombing missions to be conducted in daylight, while the RAF continued its attacks by night. Although this was a conscious decision by the U.S. high command—one that enabled twenty-four-hour strategic bombing by the Allies—the consequent U.S. losses of Flying Fortress and Liberator bombers to the Luftwaffe air defense fighters and to antiaircraft fire while carrying out daylight raids in 1942 were very heavy, until the introduction of the P-51 Mustang long-range fighter some two years later redressed the situation substantially by providing a much enhanced level of close protection for the U.S. bomber forces.

4. The Turkish government remained fearful of the powerful German and Bulgarian forces deployed close to its borders. It was also concerned that direct involvement in the conflict might create or exacerbate territorial disputes and problems with the Soviet Union. Historically, Turkish-Russian relations had always been uneasy and, in view of the strategic importance of the region (notably the Dardanelles, which provided access from the Black Sea to the Mediterranean) to Russia and Turkey alike and of Soviet suspicions about the steady flow of arms from Britain to an as yet uncommitted Turkey, the Turkish leadership chose to follow the line of least risk by maintaining its neutral status. This issue was raised again by Molotov at the Moscow meeting of foreign ministers in October 1943, when the Soviets proposed that all three Allied powers should jointly persuade Turkey to enter the war on the Allied side forthwith.

5. When considered some sixty years later, this view—which certainly matched that of Roosevelt and very many others in the U.S. administration of March 1943—is seen to have been especially significant. Hull's various proposals expressed to Eden encapsulated U.S. opinion of America's future dominant role in the world, and the declining role and importance of Europe. Here, also, was clear evidence of Washington's irritation with and dismissal of France in particular, and

with the other old colonial imperial powers in general. In hindsight, Eden's political demise following the humiliation of France and Britain by the United States at Suez in 1956 might have been avoided if Eden had grasped the true import and significance of that which was put to him in March 1943. Certainly, several key traits of U.S. foreign policy that were now emerging from the war summits have influenced U.S. international and security perceptions and activities right up to the present day.

6. See Herbert Feis, *Churchill, Roosevelt, and Stalin: The War They Waged and the Peace They Sought*, pp. 119–26, for a detailed account of these discussions, including the Anglo-U.S. view of postwar Europe and Soviet territorial aspirations.

9. Sicily, Italy, and the Second Front

1. As the Allied campaign progressed, the French perspective returned time and again to frustrate the broad aims and intentions of the Alliance. Ever since Casablanca, the aims and vested interests of the Free French organization had been contrary to Washington's view of the way ahead for France and its overseas territories once the war had been won. At the same time, Washington had pragmatically supported General Giraud's administration in North Africa with the intention that he would bring increasing numbers of French military assets into the war on the Allied side. However, London had tended to favor de Gaulle's vision of postwar France and French interests overseas. The internal squabbling between Giraud and de Gaulle revolved around which would have control of the French armed forces, and not even the establishment of a French Committee of National Liberation—with both men as cochairmen—resolved the matter. A compromise arrangement involved de Gaulle having control over French forces other than in Africa, while Giraud retained control of the latter. The true extent of de Gaulle's poor relationship with Giraud (and with Washington?) was illustrated by the fact that, even when it would undoubtedly have assisted his cause and that of France to do so, he chose not to rely upon a number of agreements that already existed involving Giraud, Roosevelt, and Churchill

concerning postwar France and the future status of its overseas territories.

10. Italy, the Pacific, and Operation "Overlord"

1. Specifically, that if the invasion were to take place as planned, there would be no more than twelve German armored or motorized divisions available to oppose the invasion in northern France, that the Luftwaffe's capability in the area would already have been significantly reduced, and that means had been identified to overcome the practical difficulties of mounting and sustaining an invasion subject to the seasonal tidal changes in the English Channel.

2. One of the more bizarre moments during the "Quadrant" meetings occurred when the Vice-Admiral Louis Mountbatten—recently promoted, at Churchill's instigation—proposed to a joint conference of the U.S. and British chiefs of staff that unsinkable air-landing platforms constructed of reinforced ice should be developed by the Allied high command. In order to demonstrate the supposed viability of this scheme, Mountbatten had a pistol brought into the conference room, together with two large blocks of ice: at each of which he fired one shot. The second of these bullets flew off the reinforced block of ice, ricocheted erratically all about the conference room, and finally inflicted a nonserious flesh wound upon an already somewhat bemused U.S. chief of naval staff! Unsurprisingly perhaps, Mountbatten's "iceberg aircraft carriers" scheme was not adopted.

3. The process by which the United States and Britain—at first separately and later jointly—developed the atomic bomb is beyond the intended scope of this work. However, it is generally true to say that, prior to the United States' entry into the war, Britain had led in the atomic research field. Then, on October 9, 1941, Roosevelt decided fully to support U.S. development of this weapon, a decision that was given a dramatic increase in impetus just two months later because of the Japanese attack on Pearl Harbor. Thereafter, what became the "Manhattan project" received the highest priority, with almost unlimited U.S. resources and funding. By mid-1942 the British research effort had dropped far behind that of the

United States. Despite this disparity, when Churchill and the president met at the Roosevelts' family estate, at Hyde Park on the Hudson River in New York state, during the Washington Conference on June 19, 1942, they had apparently agreed verbally upon a joint Anglo-U.S. approach to the development of this weapon, although there was subsequently considerable disquiet in Washington over what was viewed by some as an unnecessary need to share the rapidly progressing U.S. program with Britain. Churchill was determined to dispel this U.S. concern and ensure full British involvement in the development of the project. To that end, atomic matters were discussed secretly elsewhere, and in the margins of other meetings (such as that at Casablanca) when appropriate. These crucial discussions over almost a year culminated in the secret agreement made during "Quadrant," which at last formalized the joint and equal Anglo-U.S. participation in the U.S. based atomic weapon program.

4. The activities of Klaus Fuchs—the "Atom Spy"—in particular, which had continued undetected by the British security services (MI5) during the war and subsequently, were of enormous concern to the United States once he was caught in 1949, the more so in light of this clause of the Anglo-U.S. agreement. Although less directly involved with atomic weapons issues, the ongoing saga of the spies Philby, Maclean, Burgess, and Blunt have all caused considerable embarrassment to the British government in view of the unique sensitivity and nature of Anglo-U.S. atomic (and later nuclear) secrets.

5. Although, in the short term, a Soviet military collapse might well have resulted in the German army being drawn ever deeper into the Soviet Union, in order to consolidate and capitalize on its success.

11. Toward the Power of Three

1. Such instances increased after the failure of the Ardennes offensive of December 1944, and certainly once the Western allies had crossed the Rhine in 1945. However, the abortive July Plot to assassinate Hitler in 1944, following closely the successful Allied landings in Normandy on June 6 and the trials and tribulations of the Germans on the eastern front ever

since the loss of the Sixth Army at Stalingrad in February 1943, was probably the point at which increasing numbers of senior German officers and officials actively began to consider this option. See also Beevor, *Berlin*, pp. 148, 150 and 208 for other various specific examples.

2. Roosevelt's vision of a postwar Europe without U.S. military involvement, in which any such involvement would be determined principally by considerations of Germany's future military capability, underlined the preeminent position that Germany had achieved internationally during the seventy years from 1870 to 1940; at the same time, it demonstrated Washington's naivety over the postwar intentions of the Soviet Union. Today, even though the "Cold War" ended some fourteen years ago, there are still U.S. troops stationed in Germany—albeit in considerably smaller numbers than was the case prior to 1990.

3. Much later, it was proved that the Katyn massacre had indeed been carried out by the Russian NKVD security troops on the orders of Lavrenti Beria, who was then head of the Soviet secret police. Moreover, as the NKVD answered only to Beria and Stalin, there can be no doubt that the latter knew about, and sanctioned, the atrocity. Other mass graves containing Polish personnel who had originally been taken prisoner by the Russians in 1939 were discovered at Kharkov and Kalinin. Thus the several complex issues involved with Poland, with its territorial perspectives, and with Polish-Soviet relations in particular continued to pose significant problems for the Allies throughout the final years of the war and beyond. After more than half a century as a catalyst for conflict during World War II, and with its often uneasy relations with its eastern European neighbors during the "Cold War" that followed it—and, as elsewhere in the former Warsaw Pact states, with a high level of lawlessness and organized crime in the post-"Cold War" years—it remains to be seen whether or not Poland's historic "return to Europe" as a member of the European Union in 2004 actually meets the high expectations of its citizens, or whether Poland becomes a liability and burden for the EU.

4. The treaty was signed on December 12,

1943. By accepting the inevitable, Benes undoubtedly did Czechoslovakia a considerable service, notwithstanding the loss of Czech independence and sovereignty that this involved. In addition to an agreement that Czech military units would be permitted to liberate Czechoslovakia alongside those of the Red Army, Benes secured advantageous terms for the postwar development of Czech industry, agriculture, and social legislation, and a degree of autonomy, even though one fifth of the positions in the Prague government were to be allocated to communists. He also anticipated that Teschen—seized by Poland at the start of the war, and one of several reasons for poor relations between Poland and Czechoslovakia—would be returned. For almost twenty-five years of the "Cold War" Czechoslovakia maintained its favored position with Moscow, until the emergence of the movement for reform and the rise to power of Alexander Dubcèk, which culminated in the Prague Spring of 1968.

5. In early 1945 British troops decisively defeated an ELAS army, by then some forty thousand strong, when it attempted to take control of Athens following the German withdrawal. The ELAS survivors fled to the mountains, where they regrouped for a guerrilla campaign. In March 1946 the Greek people voted for the restoration of the monarchy and King George II returned to Greece in September that year. Thereafter, a civil war was fought out between the communist guerrillas and the Greek government forces, the latter aided with matériel first by Britain and later by the United States. The government forces finally defeated the communists in late August 1949.

6. Ironically, in the aftermath of the violent fragmentation of post-Cold War Yugoslavia in the early 1990s and the failure of the U.N. to resolve the conflict, a large force (IFOR) of predominantly U.S. and British troops operating under NATO auspices deployed to the Former Yugoslavia to restore order. Although much reduced in size and number, units of NATO and the EU are still deployed in the Balkans more than a decade later, with no clear date for a total withdrawal in sight.

7. Churchill necessarily imposed a caveat

that the convoys might need to be curtailed if the operational situation so demanded. He also seized the opportunity to seek as an offset the better Soviet treatment of, and support for, British personnel based in northern Russia to support the convoys on their arrival. Predictably, Stalin's reaction to both of these British qualifying requirements was initially unfavorable.

8. Despite this, Stalin did not visit the fighting front or his operational commanders in the field. While his preoccupation with the focus of Soviet political power in Moscow was one explanation for this, it may also have been that Stalin was simply not prepared to risk his own life by going that close to the battlefront.

9. In late 1943, both Roosevelt and—albeit with reservations—Churchill were still of the opinion that Chiang Kai-shek's nationalists would be the controlling power in China postwar, having triumphed over the emerging Chinese communist movement. As such, the two leaders considered that it was entirely appropriate to increase the regional power and influence of what they believed would be a postwar pro-Western Chinese state, although Churchill was less optimistic than Roosevelt about the real extent of China's potential contribution to fighting the war against Japan or its future influence in the postwar world. Subsequent events showed all too soon that their faith in Chiang Kai-shek had been very seriously misplaced: a full-scale Chinese civil war began in 1945, ending in a decisive victory by Mao Tse-tung's communist forces just four years later.

10. Although Hopkins and Roosevelt clearly could not have foreseen this in November 1943, this statement of intent on the future of Korea set the United States and the postwar United Nations on course for its involvement in the Korean conflict less than a decade later. At the same time, the future U.S. occupation of Japan—in place to ensure that there would be no Japanese military resurgence—also meant that it was U.S. military formations that were strategically best placed to intervene on the Korean peninsula when the conflict broke out following the North Korean communist invasion of the South

in 1950. The final irony was the subsequent deployment of what was by then the communist Chinese People's Liberation Army (PLA) against the U.S. and United Nations forces.

12. The Power of Three

1. Stalin's attendance was itself a considerable achievement. Fearful of flying and paranoid about security, he traveled to Baku by rail, thereby limiting the subsequent flight distance to just three hundred miles. Then, at the last minute he changed aircraft, completing the journey to the Tehran conference in the aircraft originally allocated to his security chief, Beria.

2. The various codenames used for the war summits were generally originated either by London or by Washington. While a routine procedure existed for the random selection of operational codenames and codewords, it is a matter of record that Churchill, employing his literary talents and his sense of history, played a part in the selection of some of these (for example, the choice of "Argonaut" for the Yalta summit in 1945), particularly where all or some of the "Big Three" were involved. The appropriateness of "Eureka" for the first "Big Three" summit was self-evident; some other examples were "Tolstoy" (in Moscow, October 1944) and "Terminal" (in Potsdam, July 1945), which names reflected to various degrees the location, specific significance, or place of these conferences within the wider context of the war.

3. Since the earliest days of the Alliance, a degree of parochialism, and in some cases a lack of vision, had been evident in the views and arguments of the staffs of all three nations, and this was probably inevitable. Nevertheless, Roosevelt and Churchill in particular managed to transcend such national considerations where this was essential to the wider alliance; and, while he was undoubtedly less conciliatory in his dealings with the other two leaders, Stalin also demonstrated, where necessary, the breadth of vision and pragmatism that, whatever his less attractive qualities, also made him a great world leader.

4. The U.S. president's accommodation was of course fitted with eavesdropping devices, and each morning at 8:00 Beria

briefed Stalin on the previous evening's "take" of information and intelligence. However, aware that this technical surveillance was in place, Roosevelt was apparently able to use it to advantage to utter statements designed to allay Stalin's suspicions of any Anglo-U.S. duplicity. The world of politics, diplomacy, espionage, and intelligence was ever thus!

5. The Suez operation in 1956 exemplified Washington's long-running phobia over Franco-British colonial and imperial policy, and wherever it emerged this aspect of U.S. foreign policy was to the detriment of the wider NATO alliance during the early years of the "Cold War." Predictably, this issue assumed less importance once America became extensively involved in Vietnam from the mid-1960s; and U.S. policies since the "Cold War" have, ironically, in very many cases attracted the accusation that they are "imperialist" in concept or the manner of their implementation.

6. W. H. Thompson, *I Was Churchill's Shadow*, pp. 123–4.

7. Herbert Feis, *Churchill, Roosevelt and Stalin*, p. 273.

8. For a fuller account of the dinner on November 30, 1943, see Thompson, *I Was Churchill's Shadow*, pp. 124–7. Thompson also recalled that as Stalin was proposing a toast, with Pavlov interpreting it into English, a waiter entered "carrying a magnificent ice-pudding, tripped and flung the lot over [Pavlov]. Drenched in pudding from the crown of his head, the little man solemnly finished his translation before he allowed the waiter to mop him down." Even at a prestigious social event organized for the leaders of Great Britain, the United States, and the Soviet Union the entirely unexpected and highly comical could still occur.

9. The Curzon line had been set as the eastern border of Poland at the 1920 Paris Peace Conference, although it failed to take account of the predominantly Polish city of Lvov, which still lay to the east of the line. Subsequently, however, Polish military successes and the 1921 Treaty of Riga in any case established the border much further to the east, facilitating the inclusion of part of the Ukraine and Belorussia in Poland even though both of these territories were ethnically Russian. The issue of Poland's eastern border,

initially raised by an unsatisfactory political solution arrived at in the 1920s, was destined to recur time and again during the war summits of World War II—notably in late 1943 and then from October 1944.

10. This was despite the strategically important fact that Chiang's nationalist forces were already tying down up to a million Japanese troops in China—troops which could not therefore be deployed against the U.S. forces in the Pacific area.

13. The Fruits of Their Labors

1. Notwithstanding this agreement and the oft-stated enthusiasm of the British prime minister for this project, Churchill's support for Operation "Shingle" was undoubtedly less than it would have been for a landing in the Adriatic, followed by an advance into the Balkans. However, the potential dilution of "Shingle" because of the needs of "Overlord" and the complementary landing in southern France ("Anvil"), over which Churchill did have reservations, suited Stalin particularly well in mid-1944, as it meant that the Red Army's advance into eastern Europe and the Balkans would be unconstrained by the presence of any of the ground forces of his Western allies in that region. Indeed, the commitment to Operation "Anvil" meant that Stalin could plan ahead for Soviet domination of these territories, confident in the knowledge that the Anglo-U.S. forces would be entirely committed at the western side of mainland Europe from mid-1944. The Anglo-U.S. decision to commit to these operations—which was, not surprisingly, supported by Stalin—was one of the several triumphs achieved by the Soviet leader at Tehran, and one that had enormous implications for postwar Europe.

2. Edmonds, The Big Three, p. 367.

3. This well-known quotation by Churchill appears in slightly varying forms, depending on the source chosen. The broad concept for Operation "Shingle" has a certain resonance with Churchill's vision for the landings in the Dardanelles in 1915, when he was first lord of the admiralty. The Allies' failure to break out from the Anzio beachhead shortly after the landings recalled a similar failure of command (though in different circumstances) of the British and ANZAC forces

at Gallipoli almost thirty years before, which was on that earlier occasion an important factor in Churchill's subsequent departure from his post at the admiralty. It might be added that many of the cautionary remarks made by Churchill at various war summits in 1942 and 1943 concerning the forthcoming cross-Channel invasion were undoubtedly prompted by his vivid memories of the failure of that much earlier "D-Day" operation in 1915—for which he had borne the primary responsibility.

4. While Lucas, as the ground force commander, must bear the major part of the responsibility for the failure of Operation "Shingle" to achieve its original objective in January 1944, the British theater commander in Italy, General Alexander, must also bear a measure of responsibility for his arguably ill-conceived enthusiasm for the project. See also General Bernard L. Montgomery's criticisms of the Operation "Shingle" concept in Nigel Hamilton, Monty: Master of the Battlefield 1942–1944, pp. 428–31.

5. The parallels between Operation "Shingle" in January 1944 on the west coast of Italy near to Rome and Operation "Chromite," the U.S. landing on the west coast of Korea at Inchon close to Seoul in September 1950, are striking. Had the degree of offensive spirit displayed by the senior commanders at Inchon in 1950 been replicated by their equivalents at Anzio in 1944, the campaign in Italy to mid-1944 might well have been much foreshortened.

6. Churchill's personal aspirations for the Balkans and his increasing concern over the rise of communism in the East were understandable, while on a more personal level his particular support for General Alexander (by then the commander in Italy), who favored the "Vienna Alternative," further influenced his determination to pursue this operation. However, while postwar history has showed that there might indeed have been benefits in imposing a Western rather than a communist influence in the Balkans and eastern Europe, in the time context of June 1944 the "Vienna Option" could have threatened the future cohesiveness of the Alliance as a whole and the interpersonal relationship of the "Big Three" specifically.

7. See Stephen E. Ambrose, *Pegasus Bridge*, p. xv.
8. Although May 1, 1944, had been the date originally set—and the Germans had expected that the invasion would come in mid-May, and then, when it did not, in August—the final choice of June was occasioned mainly by practical considerations, not least the tide times, moon phases, visibility and projected weather conditions, the last of which finally provided some of the greatest concern and uncertainty right up to the last minute. Indeed, unseasonably poor weather in the English Channel in early June resulted in the invasion being delayed for twenty-four hours from the planned D-Day of June 5, 1944. Had the Allies (notably Roosevelt and Stalin) not settled and insisted upon a fixed date early on, but simply agreed "mid-1944" or something similar, the room that this would have allowed for individual interpretation and modification, although no doubt welcomed by Churchill in view of his reservations at the time, would have made the subsequent COSSAC operational joint planning process unworkable in practice. The fact that the "Trident" summit decision had been translated precisely into that which had been agreed, and only a month later than the date originally planned for it, was a brilliant demonstration of the resolve and unity of purpose of the Alliance.
9. The near-disaster for the U.S. troops at "Omaha" was due in part to the failure of the American invasion force commanders to adopt the several very successful specialist armored assault and engineer vehicles—the so-called "funnies" of the British 79th Armoured Division—that had been specifically developed by the British for D-Day. Arguably, this decision reflected the U.S. high command's reluctance to adopt non-U.S. operational techniques, together with a persisting legacy of caution on the part of some U.S. military commanders that stemmed from 1917–18, but which still influenced policy in 1944. Much more surprising, however, was the apparent lack of account taken by the U.S. high command involved with D-Day of the wealth of practical experience in amphibious operations that American forces—primarily the U.S. Marines—had already gained combating

the Japanese in the Pacific, operations that had included the development and very successful use by the USMC of amphibious tracked personnel carriers (Amtraks).
10. The Allied deception operation supporting "Overlord" was termed Operation "Fortitude." Conducted at the strategic and operational levels, it maintained the illusion that a powerful Anglo-U.S. army group—no more than a "paper army," in fact—based in the southeast of England and the Thames estuary and commanded by U.S. Gen. George S. Patton would launch the main amphibious assault at the Pas de Calais, the earlier landings in Normandy being no more than a diversionary operation.
11. Nonetheless, it is noteworthy that even as late as the evening before the landings, Gen. Alan Brooke noted in his diary: "I am very uneasy about the whole operation. At the best, it will come very far short of the expectations of the bulk of the people . . . At its worst, it may well be the most ghastly disaster of the whole war." Brooke's degree of pessimism at such a late stage reflected the continued British caution about the cross-Channel invasion, something that Churchill had expressed consistently from an early stage in its planning, and much of which stemmed from the bitter lessons learned by the Anglo-Canadian forces during the failed cross-Channel raid on Dieppe in August 1942. It also illustrated the fact that the success of the Allies in Normandy in June 1944 was by no means certain, even in the minds of some of those senior commanders who were directly responsible for the operation's execution. In his later comment on the landings and the follow-on operations, Basil Liddell Hart noted that "The ultimate triumph has obscured the fact that the Allies were in great danger at the outset and had a very narrow [sic] shave." This observation by an eminent historian and strategist accurately indicated the true level of risk involved in Operation "Overlord."
12. The first Chindit operation or campaign had taken place from February 8 to April 10, 1943; the second was conducted from March 5 to August 9, 1944.
13. MacArthur subsequently clashed with Roosevelt's successor, President Harry S.

Truman, over U.S. strategic policy in the Korean War, specifically over the former's wish to carry out direct offensive action against the People's Republic of China in 1951. However, he failed to gain presidential support and was relieved of his overall command of the U.S. and U.N. forces in Korea by Truman on April 11, 1952.

14. The discussion involving Roosevelt, Nimitz, and MacArthur at Pearl Harbor was conducted in private, with no record taken. Consequently, the real impact of MacArthur using this domestic political argument to influence his strategic decision cannot be precisely quantified. However, Roosevelt certainly desired reelection and, as MacArthur was very aware, he was an astute and very seasoned politician. Therefore, the potential harm that this issue might have done to the president's reelection campaign was certainly a matter which needed to be taken fully into account by him.

15. Whereas Romania shared a border with the Soviet Union, Britain's strategic links with Greece were, at the very least, somewhat tenuous. Certainly, in the wider scheme of things, Stalin and the Soviet Union stood to gain far more from this quid pro quo arrangement than Great Britain.

16. However, full account was taken of the fact that Bulgaria had not taken up arms against the Soviet Union. It had also been a signatory to the Tripartite Pact of 1941 and had therefore been an ally of Germany at the same time that Germany and the Soviet Union had themselves been allies in 1941. Consequently, Moscow's treatment of Bulgaria was relatively lenient—although the fact of Moscow's power and influence in the country thereafter was not in dispute.

14. Idealism and Realism

1. In his focused approach to Allied unity, Cordell Hull seems to have been somewhat blinkered with regard to the Soviet Union. Certainly the U.S. ambassador in Moscow, W. Averell Harriman, had updated him on Soviet policy, reinforcing Washington's earlier unease over Soviet plans for Bulgaria, Romania, and Hungary. Harriman and George F. Kennan prepared a detailed analysis for Hull on September 19, 1944, which made

it clear that Stalin was content to consider and accede to matters not affecting the Soviet Union, but that he reserved to himself all matters and decisions affecting East-West relations or the future of eastern Europe—the latter falling firmly within the Soviet sphere of interest and therefore not for discussion with his Western allies.

2. This was during the Korean War in 1950, when the absence of the Soviet representative from a critical U.N. Security Council meeting permitted the dispatch of U.S. and other national forces to counter the North Korean invasion of South Korea.

3. It would be incorrect to imply that Roosevelt was entirely trusting of Stalin's motives and of the Soviet commitment to go to war against Japan. Washington was very aware that, as recently as March 30, 1944, the Soviet government had concluded a five-year agreement with Japan over fishing rights, together with a second agreement by which Japan had promised to end its concessions in northern Sakhalin. These were, arguably, actions not typical of two nations on the verge of all-out war. The nature of Soviet foreign policy had also been amply demonstrated by the matter of the German-Soviet nonaggression pact of 1939. By fall 1944, neither Roosevelt nor Churchill, nor their advisors, could be in any doubt that Stalin's continued support for his Western allies would always depend upon any such support being unequivocally in the national interests of the Soviet Union.

4. Feis, *Churchill, Roosevelt and Stalin*, p. 436.

15. Strategy, Economics and "Tube Alloys"

1. Interestingly, the U.S. Chief of Naval Operations, Admiral J. King, had argued strongly against any Royal Navy involvement in the final assault on Japan, but Roosevelt directed that this offer of British support was to be accepted.

2. In fact, Operation "Dracula" was overtaken by events and so was never carried out.

3. Nevertheless, some U.S. airborne combat units were involved in the Burma campaign for certain specialist operational missions.

4. Feis, *Churchill, Roosevelt, and Stalin*, p. 399,

footnotes 4 and 4a.

5. Much of the landscape of southern Germany comprises forested hills, high mountains, many large and small lakes, and rivers. The north, on the other hand, is largely flat or undulating, dominated in the north by the Hanover Plain. After 1945, with the rapid emergence of the Soviet and Warsaw Pact threat, the development of NATO, and the permanent stationing of U.S. and British forces in West Germany, Roosevelt's decision in September 1944 had the effect of placing the predominantly armored U.S. forces in what was patently not "good tank country," and the comparatively much less armor-orientated British in the "good tank country" of northern Germany, there to counter a Soviet and Warsaw Pact onslaught which would be based almost exclusively on an overwhelming superiority in armor. This "Cold War" misdeployment of forces, demonstrably a politically rather than a militarily driven strategic defense, would frustrate NATO's operational planning for almost half a century, and it was further compounded by the fact that U.S. lines of communication to Bremen and Bremerhaven crossed from north to south those of the British and other NATO nations which ran from east to west. The final irony of Roosevelt's decision in September 1944 would prove to be de Gaulle's withdrawal of France from the integrated military structure of NATO in 1966, when the late president's reservations over de Gaulle's attitude toward the United States and the other Western allies were shown to have been not entirely unfounded.

6. The Danish scientist Neils Bohr was the world's leading nuclear physicist of his time. In 1943 he was smuggled out of Copenhagen to Sweden by the Danish resistance. From there, the British arranged for him to come to Britain. Later, Bohr moved on to join the work being carried on in the United States.

7. See Edmonds, *The Big Three*, pp. 395–406, for a useful summary of the Manhattan project and the development of the atomic bomb up to the time of the September 1944 meeting at Hyde Park, together with an account of the issues affecting the United States, Roosevelt, and Churchill at that time.

8. See Chapter 10.

9. The full text of this document is included in Edmonds, *The Big Three*, Appendix IV, p. 491.

10. Despite this, by mid-1945 the Soviet Union's very extensive espionage machine was already providing the Kremlin with regular intelligence on U.S. progress with the atomic energy and weapons program, and on Anglo-U.S. policy for its wartime use and further development postwar.

16. The Bear and the Bulldog

1. The "Argonaut" summit meeting was originally, if somewhat unimaginatively, codenamed "Eureka II" when the planning for what would be the second such meeting to be attended by all of the "Big Three" leaders first began in July 1944. The first "Big Three" summit in Tehran had of course also been codenamed "Eureka."

2. One of the casualties of the presidential wind of change in Washington was secretary of state Cordell Hull. He had vigorously and successfully opposed Morgenthau's proposals at the "Octagon" summit, although he had been excluded from this and other key conferences, notwithstanding the important role he had played in the early days of the war summits process. Increasingly frustrated by his marginalization by Roosevelt, Hull resigned in November 1944 and was replaced as U.S. secretary of state by Edward R. Stettinius, Jr.

3. See also Chapter 13 for more details of the events and decisions taken affecting these and other occupied European countries in late 1944, many of which overlapped, ran parallel to, or overtook the discussions and intentions of the "Octagon" and "Tolstoy" summits.

4. The full story of the failed communist bid for power in Greece and Churchill's role therein is beyond the scope of this work. However, the conflict during December 1944 was nonetheless noteworthy for three reasons. First, Stalin's avoidance of supporting the Greek communists (ELAS) was both remarkable and scrupulous and, rather than simply showing him to be a man of his word, this provided yet more evidence of the vital importance he attached to Churchill's quid pro quo agreement to give Moscow a virtually free hand in eastern Europe. Next,

Churchill's personal intervention at Christmas 1944 in what had by then become a civil war underlined his continued preoccupation with the Mediterranean in general and Greece in particular. Although this intervention neither resolved the political impasse nor ended the conflict, it nevertheless contributed positively to the later achievement of both (see Jenkins, pp. 770–2). Finally, one of Churchill's telegrams to the British commander in Athens, General Scobie, in early December was inadvertently copied to the U.S. ambassador in Rome by General Wilson's headquarters in Italy; the message urged Scobie to engage the communist guerrillas directly if necessary, and included (Jenkins, p. 767) the instruction "Do not hesitate to act as if you were in a conquered city where a local rebellion is in progress." The U.S. State Department's reaction to this text was predictably hostile, and all the more so when the text was leaked and published in the *Washington Post* on December 11. Even Roosevelt, while not condemning outright the British armed action in Greece, indicated that this was an issue on which Churchill enjoyed absolutely no support from America. Thus, in the wider context of the war summits, the situation in Greece at the end of 1944 reinforced and perpetuated the suspicions in Washington over Britain's postwar international intentions and aspirations—perceptions that had grown just as British power and influence within the Alliance had been overtaken by the effects of the comparatively new relationship between Roosevelt and Stalin.

5. Churchill was up and about again by mid-morning on October 16, his robust constitution having once again allowed him to make a speedy recovery. On October 15, his personal doctor, Charles Wilson Moran, had already prepared three specialists and two nurses in Cairo to attend the prime minister in Moscow. However, with Churchill's temperature having returned to normal by October 16, the request for this medical and nursing assistance was canceled.

17. Matters of War and Peace
1. The division's gallant battle against the odds has rightly entered the annals of military history as one of the great airborne engagements, and has attracted much analysis as such. However, what was undoubtedly a bold and imaginative concept, and one which matched Montgomery's views for a concentrated Allied thrust in the north, was frustrated primarily by the combination of an intelligence failure (or of commanders unwilling to take due note of adverse intelligence reports on the German strength in the target area), by the use of British drop zones too far distant from the objective at Arnhem, and by the plan's dependence for success upon a single route for the movement of the armored ground forces (the British 30th Corps) tasked to relieve the airborne forces and exploit the intended breakthrough.

2. See Whiting, *The Battle of the Bulge: Britain's Untold Story.*
3. Ibid., pp. 188-200
4. Yet again Stalin had set the venue—as well as managing to avoid any need to travel there by air, as Yalta and the Crimea were served by a well-established rail link running into the interior of the Soviet Union.
5. Once they had arrived at Yalta, the delegates were accommodated in a number of disused palaces—Stalin at the Yusupov, Roosevelt at the Livadia and Churchill at the Vorontsov—dating from the days of the czars. These had been hastily refurnished prior to the meeting with cheap furniture sent from Moscow. Predictably, the Western delegations' accommodation was fitted with eavesdropping devices, plus directional microphones to monitor Roosevelt's wheelchair-based conversations. The Soviet surveillance operation was under the overall control of Beria's son, and Stalin was briefed on the previous night's "take" each day before the meetings began. Beria himself arrived at Yalta on the final day of the conference, when his shadowy and habitually covert existence was exemplified by the fact that apparently nobody at Yalta other than Stalin quite knew who he was. While staff and ministerial meetings continued throughout the day, the formal conference sessions generally began in the late afternoon, by about 5:00, and then continued for up to five hours, inclusive of a brief break for light refresh-

ments. Dinner was scheduled for 9:30, with a formal dinner hosted by each of the three Allied leaders in turn on separate evenings. These events usually continued until well after midnight, and included the consumption of a considerable amount of alcohol in the course of the obligatory official toastmaking. Although he had experienced a brief recurrence of an attack of fever while in Malta, Churchill's usual practice of working through much of the night (most of the key dispatches from London arrived each night at Yalta at about midnight) and rising late the next morning meant that he was nevertheless fairly well prepared for the work program at Yalta.

6. The choice of these three republics was significant: taken together they comprised the Soviet Union's territorial and strategic buffer along the entire length of its western flank.

7. As U.S. president, Roosevelt was also commander-in-chief of the U.S. armed forces, whereas Prime Minister Churchill was not the commander-in-chief of the British armed forces, this authority being vested in the monarch, King George VI. However, in both the American and the British cases, the day-to-day direction (apart from policy matters) and management of the war was in large part delegated to the chiefs of staff and senior field commanders, while in the Soviet Union this control was by and large retained at the very highest level.

8. Henry Morgenthau was the U.S. secretary to the treasury.

9. Feis, Churchill, Roosevelt, and Stalin, p. 533.

10. Contrary to Churchill's wishes, General de Gaulle had not been invited to attend at Yalta. Although Stalin and Roosevelt both had reservations about the extent of French involvement in the occupation and control of postwar Germany, by the end of the summit the two leaders had agreed that France should enjoy an equal involvement with that of the other Allied powers. This decision partly offset de Gaulle's resentment over his exclusion from the negotiations, while at the same time it allowed Churchill to achieve one of his conference aims. For Roosevelt, it meant that French troops would be actively involved in maintaining the

future peace of Europe, while for Stalin his acquiescence in this matter was a small price to pay for the significant gains he made at Yalta in respect of Poland.

11. Feis, p. 539.

12. Ibid., p. 537.

13. The agreement at Yalta that all Soviet prisoners of war would be returned to Russia subsequently provided but one more illustration of Stalin's true view of such humanitarian and democratic ideals. On the presumption that the Soviet former prisoners had inevitably been tainted by noncommunist Western influences while in captivity, and were in any case also "guilty" of having allowed themselves to be captured in the first place, most of these men were either summarily executed on their return to their homeland or were dispatched to perish in the gulag.

18. Götterdämmerung

1. Stalin's change of heart followed the death of Roosevelt, and was ostensibly a gesture of friendship and cooperation toward the new U.S. president. Molotov attended the San Francisco meeting; then, in May, Truman moved forward positively what had been initially his uncertain relationship with Stalin by dispatching Harry Hopkins to Moscow. There, he renegotiated—successfully but bilaterally—the "Argonaut" summit's earlier agreements on the composition and representation of the postwar Polish government.

2. On March 17, 1945, the Ludendorff railway bridge collapsed, with the loss of twenty-eight U.S. lives. Its collapse was due to a combination of the German demolition attempts prior to its capture and to air bombardment and sabotage attempts by frogmen after March 7, as well as to the regular overloading of the weakened structure by the U.S. forces from that date. However, by then it had done its job, and other (pontoon) bridges and ferry sites had already been constructed adjacent to it by the U.S. army engineers. Hitler ordered the execution of the five German officers judged by a summary court-martial to have been responsible for the failure either to defend successfully or to destroy the bridge. Meanwhile, after the war Lieutenant Timmermann returned home to

West Point, Nebraska; however, his wartime fame quickly faded, he did not adjust to civilian life, and he reenlisted just in time to fight in Korea. He subsequently contracted tuberculosis and died in a U.S. veterans' hospital shortly afterward, his involvement in the events of March 7, 1945, unmarked and largely forgotten.

3. Lt. Col. R. B. T. Daniell DSO, commanding the 13th Regiment, Honourable Artillery Company, Royal Horse Artillery, was the first British soldier to enter the camp sometime after April 12, but because his unit was at that stage in contact with the enemy he was able only to carry out a brief inspection and advise his commander, Brig. Roscoe Harvey, commander 29th Armoured Brigade, of that which he had seen. The date of Belsen's formal liberation is therefore set at April 15, 1945. See also *The Relief of Belsen, April 1945*, published by the Imperial War Museum, London, 1995.

4. Six million Jews died at the hands of the Nazis, together with twenty-seven million Soviet servicemen and civilians. The enormous loss of life and widespread devastation visited upon Poland and the Soviet Union by the Germans go a very considerable way toward explaining Stalin's obsession over the security of his western borders and his desire for punitive action and reparations to be imposed upon the defeated nation.

5. See Edmonds, pp. 437–8.

6. The power (or "yield") of the Hiroshima bomb was about 15 kilotons. It killed 78,150 and injured more than seventy thousand. The bomb dropped on Nagasaki was of about 22 kilotons. It killed forty thousand and injured twenty-five thousand. However, the residual effects of the radiation produced by these atomic attacks brought further casualties long after they had been carried out.

19. Anatomy of a War Summit
1. Tony Le Tissier, *Berlin Then and Now*, pp. 309, 315.
2. This airfield was later established as RAF Gatow, the airbase serving what would shortly become the British sector of Berlin.
3. France had not been invited to send a delegation to Potsdam.
4. A four-power (U.S., British, Soviet, and

French) grand victory parade was later staged in Berlin during the first week of September 1945 to celebrate the final defeat of Japan.

5. Some accounts indicate that Truman may have visited the U.S. 2nd Armored Division or attended earlier a third such parade by the division during his tour of the city on July 16. However, most accounts have him attending that on July 20, for which the July 18 parade—attended by General Marshall and, at his invitation, by the British chiefs of staff—was in practice a full-scale dress rehearsal.

6. The pianist was a young American serviceman, Eugene List, who performed in his military uniform. Truman's favorite musical piece was a particular but little-played Chopin waltz. However, the score was unavailable locally, and so, after a hectic search for a copy, one was located in Paris and especially flown to Berlin for the occasion. Apparently, as List was unfamiliar with the piece, Truman turned the pages of the score for him as the young serviceman played.

7. The inclusion at one session of a Polish government delegation even produced a four-way discussion during the summit's final consideration of the issue of Poland.

8. Le Tissier, p. 319.
9. *Ibid.*
10. Directive No. 1067/8, dated May 14, 1945.
11. A suitably full account of this saga and of the development of the Warsaw government is at Feis, *Between War and Peace: The Potsdam Conference*, pp. 203–17.
12. As at July 15, 1945, there were about two hundred and fifty thousand Poles on British soil and within the British armed forces. Many had come to Britain as refugees early in the war, and Polish aviators flying with the RAF had made a particularly important contribution to the Battle of Britain in 1940 and early 1941, when Britain had stood entirely alone against Nazi Germany.
13. As soon as he arrived back in Potsdam, the newly appointed British Prime Minister, Clement Attlee, was briefed by Truman on the desirability of linking a compromise solution on Poland to one that was acceptable to the Anglo-U.S. delegations on German reparations—a matter to which Washington attached

greater importance. Truman might have added the need to maintain Allied unity, as the war with Japan was still ongoing, the success of the Manhattan project notwithstanding. Despite their continued reservations over Poland, Attlee and Bevin acquiesced, and so the bilateral agreement between Byrnes and Molotov was finally translated into a protocol agreed by the summit as a whole. Had Churchill returned to Potsdam, it is most unlikely that he would have changed either Truman's or Stalin's position. Consequently, his well-meant but perhaps misplaced intransigence might have provoked a major rift among the Allies, of the sort that had been long-feared but had been avoided during all of the summits which had gone before.

14. It was stipulated that the industrial equipment was to be removed within two years of the amount for removal being decided, this decision being made within six months of the Potsdam summit. The Allied Control Commission was required to determine how much industrial equipment in the U.S.-Anglo French zones was available for reparations vis-à-vis the essential needs of those zones to regenerate and sustain themselves.

15. The casualty figures are taken from Miller, The Cold War a Military History, p. 373. Some other estimates suggest that a total of more than two hundred thousand immediate fatalities resulted from the two explosions.

20. Quo Vadis

1. Interestingly, this was a trait that also characterized the way in which Eisenhower (a product of the Washington military establishment) conducted his military command of the Allied forces from 1944.

2. The Churchill Digest, published by The Reader's Digest Association, London, 1965, p. 37.

3. A full assessment of the impact of Churchill's 1945 election defeat is beyond the scope of this work. However, the fact that the election took place while Japan remained undefeated, and that the prime minister was consequently forced to conduct a domestic election campaign while still leading a country at war was at the very least bizarre (although of course Roosevelt had done just that, in 1944).

Certainly his election defeat was premature, and the Labour party's pressure to hold the election so early did it little credit. However, had the election been postponed until the defeat of Japan—an eventuality that was then, in theory, still up to eighteen months hence—it is questionable whether its outcome would have been much different. In any case, the return to power of the Conservatives led by Churchill in 1951 allowed him to achieve his final goal, that of being returned as prime minister as the British people's choice of leader. However, by then his age and his declining health meant that he was unable to enjoy the fruits of his final political triumph for very many years. Ironically, Churchill proved that he was still very well up to dealing with the new challenges posed by nuclear weapons in the postwar era, when he actively promoted a concept of graduated nuclear deterrence (a concept subsequently adopted by NATO) over what was then the U.S.-preferred strategy of mutually assured destruction (MAD).

4. In fact, Churchill was prime minister for a final term from 1951 to 1955 when, already in ill-health, he resigned as prime minister in favor of Anthony Eden. Churchill died ten years later, on January 24, 1965. He had survived his two former "Big Three" colleagues Stalin (who died on March 5, 1953) by more than a decade and Roosevelt by almost two decades.

5. No direct link between the former Iraqi regime headed by Saddam Hussein, which was quickly overthrown by U.S.-led coalition forces in March 2003, and international terrorist groups (such as Al-Qaeda) has been established as at date. However, an unforeseen consequence of the demise of Saddam Hussein was the development of a burgeoning guerrilla or terrorist campaign against (primarily) the postwar U.S. forces in Iraq. In the meantime, although the removal of Saddam Hussein has no doubt benefited some numbers of Iraqis, the wider international justification for the U.S.-led invasion remains highly questionable. This has served to undermine the authority and credibility of President George W. Bush's administration in Washington and, to an even greater extent, that of Prime Minister Tony Blair in London.

SELECT BIBLIOGRAPHY

Alanbrooke, Field-Marshal Lord, (ed. Dancher, Alex, and Todman, Daniel), *War Diaries 1939–1945*, Phoenix Press, London, 2002.

Ambrose, Stephen E., *Eisenhower: Soldier and President*, Pocket Books/Simon & Schuster UK, London, 2003.

— *Pegasus Bridge*, Simon & Schuster UK, London, 2003.

Avon, The Rt. Hon. the Earl of, *The Eden Memoirs: Facing the Dictators*, Cassell, London, 1962.

Beevor, Anthony, *Stalingrad*, Penguin Books, London, 1999.

— *Berlin: The Downfall, 1945*, Penguin Books, London, 2003.

Bender, Roger James, and Law, Richard D., *Uniforms, Organization and History of the Afrikakorps*, California, 1973.

Black, Conrad, *Franklin Delano Roosevelt: Champion of Freedom*, Weidenfeld, London, 2003.

Bullock, Alan, *Hitler and Stalin: Parallel Lives*, Fontana Press/Harper Collins, London, 1998.

Channon, John, (with Hudson, Robert), *The Penguin Historical Atlas of Russia*, The Penguin Group, London, 1995.

Churchill, Winston S., (ed. Scotland, Andrew), *The Second World War*, Cassell & Co., London, 1961.

Cobban, Alfred, *A History of Modern France. Vol. 2: 1799–1945*, Penguin Books, Middlesex, 1963.

Craig, Gordon A., *Germany 1866–1945*, Oxford University Press, Oxford, 1984.

Dunn, Dennis J., *Caught Between Roosevelt & Stalin: America's Ambassadors to Moscow*, University Press of Kentucky, Lexington, 1998.

Edmonds, Robin, *The "Big Three": Churchill, Roosevelt and Stalin in Peace & War*, Hamish Hamilton, London, 1991.

Este, Carlo d', *Eisenhower: A Soldier's Life*, Weidenfeld & Nicolson, London, 2002.

Feis, Herbert, *Churchill, Roosevelt and Stalin: The War They Waged and the Peace They Sought*, Oxford University Press/Princeton University Press, Binghampton/New York, 1957.

— *Between War and Peace: The Potsdam Conference*, Oxford University Press/Princeton University Press, Binghampton/New York, 1960.

Gilbert, Martin, *Churchill at War*, Imperial War Museum/Carlton Books, London, 2003.

Glenny, Misha, *The Balkans 1804–1999: Nationalism, War and the Great Powers*, Granta Books, London, 2000.

Hamilton, Nigel, *Monty: The Making of a General, 1887–1942*, Coronet Books (Hodder & Stoughton), London, 1984.

— *Monty: Master of the Battlefield, 1942–1944*, Coronet Books (Hodder & Stoughton), London, 1985.

— *Monty: The Field-Marshal, 1944–1976*, Sceptre Books (Hodder & Stoughton), London, 1987.

Jenkins, Roy, *Churchill*, Pan Macmillan, London, 2002.

Jewell, Derek, (ed.), *Alamein and the Desert War*, Sphere Books, London, 1967.

Kershaw, Ian, *The Nazi Dictatorship: Problems and Perspectives of Interpretation*, Arnold (Hodder Headline Group), London, 1996.

Kochan, Lionel, *The Making of Modern Russia*, Penguin Books, Middlesex, 1962.

Koenig, William J., *Americans at War: From the Colonial Wars to Vietnam*, Bison Books, London 1980.

Le Tissier, Tony, *Berlin: Then and Now* (After the Battle Publications), Plaistow Press, London, 1992.

Loewenheim, Francis L.; Langley, Harold D.; and Jones, Manfred, (eds), *Roosevelt and Stalin: Their Secret War Correspondence*, Barrie & Jenkins, London, 1975.

Macksey, Major K. J., *Afrika Korps*, Macdonald & Co, London, 1968.

Miller, David, *The Cold War: A Military History*, Random House (Pimlico), London, 2001.

Montefiore, Simon Sebag, *Stalin: The Court of the Red Tsar*, Weidenfeld &

Nicolson, London, 2003.

Montgomery of Alamein, Field-Marshal Viscount, *A History of Warfare*, Collins,

London, 1968.

Pallud, Jean Paul, *Blitzkrieg in the West: Then and Now* (After the Battle Publications), Battle of Britain Prints International, London, 1991.

Roberts, Andrew, *Hitler and Churchill: Secrets of Leadership*, Weidenfeld & Nicolson, London, 2003.

Stone, David, *Wars of the Cold War: Campaigns and Conflicts, 1945–1990*, Brassey's/Chrysalis Books, London, 2004.

Thompson, R. W., *Battle for the Rhine*, Ballantine Books, New York, 1959.

Thompson, Sir Robert, (ed.), *War in Peace*, Orbis Publishing, London, 1981.

Thompson, Detective Inspector (Retd) W. H., *I Was Churchill's Shadow*, Christopher Johnson Publishers, London, 1955.

Whiting, Charles, *Battle of the Ruhr Pocket*, Pan Books, London, 1972.

— *The Battle of the Bulge: Britain's Untold Story*, Sutton Publishing, Stroud, 1999.

Wisniewski, Richard A., *Pearl Harbor and the USS Arizona Memorial*, Pacific Printers, Hawaii, 1986.

Index

Note that the index sub-references are generally arranged alphabetically. However, some references are shown chronologically as an aid to identifying their historical context.

ABC-1 plan (1941), 43–4
Adana conference, Turkey (1943), 76, 79
Afghanistan, war in (2002), 278
Afrika Korps, German: operations 1040 2, 16–17, defeat of, at El Alamein, 64–5; and Rommel, 16, 17, 46, 64–5
Alexander, Field Marshal Sir Harold, 80
Algiers meeting (1943), 80
Allied Control Council (Commission) for Austria, 260
Allied Control Council (Commission) for Germany, 250
Anders, Gen. Wladyslaw, 252
Anschluss (in Austria) (1938), 5
Antonescu, Marshal Ion, 103
Antonov, Gen. Alexei E., 202, 205
"Arcadia" conference, Washington (1941): Pearl Harbor, possible influence of, 44–5; second front, discussion of, 46, 47, 49; Pacific theater, U.S. policy for, 45, 47, 48; Eisenhower, influence of, 48; North Africa, discussion of offensive action in, 46; follow-on meetings and actions, 47, 48, 50–7
"Argonaut" conference, Yalta (1945): location, debate about and decision on, 211; preliminary meeting in Malta, 211–14; United Nations issues, discussion of, 215; eastern and western fronts, co-ordination of, 215–16; liaison, dissent over, 216; Germany and Prussia, discussion of, 217–19; Morgenthau plan, discussion of, 217; reparations, issue of, 217, 219–20; Polish borders, issue of, 221–2; Joint Declaration on Liberated Europe, 222–3; Japan, Allied campaign against, 223–4; U.S.–Soviet secret accord, 224; overall significance of, 225
Atlantic Charter (1941), 37 42, 56, 76, 174, 222
Atlantic conference, Placentia Bay, Newfoundland (1941): Churchill, sea journey to, 36; peripheral activities, 36; matériel support for the Soviet Union, 37, 39–40; vision for the postwar world, 37–8; development of Atlantic Charter, 37–9; follow-on activities and meetings, 40–2
Atlantic convoys, Allied: convoy PQ.17, destruction of, 62–3, 282; German U-boat campaign against, 61, 62–3; losses during, 63, 67, 73, 74; policy for, 63, 64, 73
Attlee, Clement, 246, et seq.
Atomic bomb (see also "Manhattan" project): Anglo–U.S. policy on, 88, 189–91, 234, 272, 284–5; international control of, 88; Quebec Agreement (1943), 88; Stalin informed of, 235–6; test at Alamogordo, 234; Truman and, 234–6; use of against Japan, 234, 236, 263
Austria (see also Anschluss), division and control of (from 1945), 259–60
Axis Powers: allies of, 15, 160; formation of (1940), 15, 33

Badoglio, Gen. Pietro, 90, 172
battles (and other military actions) of: Alam Halfa (1942), 64–5; Anzio, Allied landing at (1944), 151–2, 288, Ardennes (the "Bulge") (1944), 208–10; Arnhem (1944), 192, 208, 292; Atlantic (1941–2), 61, 67–8; Berlin (1945), 232; Bismarck, sinking of (1941), 18; Britain (1940), 13; Crete, German invasion of (1941), 18; Dunkirk,

evacuation from (1940), 12–13; El Alamein (1942), 64–5; Guadalcanal (1942–3), 54; Hong Kong, fall of (1941), 47; Kohima (1944), 158; Kursk (1943), 90, 147; Monte Cassino, 1944, 151; Normandy (1944), 155–7, *289*; Okinawa (1945), 223; Pearl Harbor, Japanese attack on (1941), 33, 43, *282*; Philippine Sea (1944), 158; Remagen, capture of the Rhine bridge at (1945), 227–9; River Plate (sinking of the *Graf Spee*) (1939), 9–10; Salerno, Allied landing at (1943), 85, 89, 93, 147; *Scharnhorst*, sinking of (1943), 146; Singapore, fall of (1942), 47, *282*; Stalingrad (1942–3), 59, 67, 126, *283*; Taranto, British landing at (1943), 89; *Tirpitz*, attacks on (1943 and 1944), 146, *282*; Tobruk (1941), 16, 54

Beaverbrook, Lord, 37, *et seq.*

Belsen concentration camp, 230

Benes, Eduard, 100, *286*

Beria, Lavrenti, 117, 238–9

Berlin, division and control of, from 1945, 248–9; see also battle of Berlin

Bevin, Ernest, 246, *et seq.*

Bierut, Boleslaw, 199

"Big Three": bilateral meetings of (other than during war summits), 150, 180–9, 189–93, 194–207, 211–14; creation of, 45, 91, 115, 266; first meeting of, at Tehran, 115–42; last meeting of, at Yalta, 215–25; and successors of, at Potsdam, 237–63

Blitzkrieg, 5, 11

Bohr, Niels, 189; see also atomic bomb and "Manhattan" project

Bradley, Gen. Omar N., 186, 209–10, 229

British armed forces (including imperial and dominion forces): Royal Navy (RN), 8–10, 15, 18, 40, 62–3, 75, 146; army, 12–13, 64–5, 155, 157, 192; Royal Air Force (RAF), 13, 67, 74

British Expeditionary Force (BEF) (1940), 8, 12–13, 92

Brooke, Gen. Sir Alan (later Field Marshal Lord Alanbrooke), 80, 194, 203

Bulgaria, 160, 161, 165

Byrnes, James F., 243, 257

Catroux, Gen. Georges, 80

Cecilienhof, Schloss, see "Terminal" conference (1945)

Chamberlain, Neville, 5, 11

Chetniks, 101, 167; see also Yugoslavia

Chiang Kai-shek, Generalissimo, 107, 108, 110, 113, 177, 224

Chiefs of Staff, Supreme Allied Command (COSSAC), formation of (1943), 74, 79

China: Allied air support for, via "The Hump", 73, Churchill's opinion of, 109; civil war in (1945–9), 76; Japanese campaign in (from 1937), 6–8; quality of Chinese military forces, 157, 158, *286*; Roosevelt's opinion of, 110, 124; Stalin's opinion of, 96, 109, 117, 124

Churchill, Sir Winston Spencer: early life and career, 1874–1941, 20–22, 25–6; family members of, 20, 86, 134; Gallipoli (1915) landings, later influence of, 25, *281*; as prime minister, 11, 25; at war summits, see references to specific conferences

Clark, Gen. Mark, 151

Clark-Kerr, Archibald, 195

Clemenceau, Georges, 221

"Cold War" (1945–90), 61, 88, 122, 178, 189, 264, 270, 274–6, 279, *291*

Council of Foreign Ministers (1945), see "Terminal" conference

Cripps, Sir Stafford, 34

Cross-Channel invasion (of France), see operation "Roundup" and operation "Overlord"

Cunningham, Adm. Sir Andrew, 80

Curzon Line, 221; see also Poland

Czechoslovakia, 5, 6, 100

Daladier, Édouard, 5, 6

Darlan, Adm. Jean François, 66, 72, *283*

Davies, Joseph E., 81, 244

D-Day (1944), see operation "Overlord" and battle of Normandy

Deane, Gen. John R., 102–3, 195, 203, 204

Declaration of the Four Nations on General Security (1943), 95–6

de Gaulle, Gen. Charles, 72, 80, 82–3, 172–3

Deutsches Afrikakorps (DAK), see Afrika Korps, German

Dumbarton Oaks Conference, Washington (1944): United Nations, shaping of, 174–8; key issues raised at, 176, 177–8; news release at end of, 178; analysis of, 179

East Prussia (Germany), see "Terminal" conference and Poland

Eden, Sir Anthony, 34, 40–2, 76, 94 *et seq.*, 161, 193, 194, 204, 211

Eisenhower, Gen. Dwight D., 65–6, 72; views on prioritizing of U.S. strategy (1942), 48; as supreme Allied commander, 141, 185–6, 210, 229

"Eureka" conference, Tehran (1943): significance of, 115–16; agenda for, 116; accommodation arrangements for, 116–17; bilateral meetings of Roosevelt and Stalin during, 117–18, 123–5, 135–6; strategic overview and discussion, 118–19; Mediterranean theater, Churchill's proposals for, 119–21; divergence of views, 121, 129, 131; Germany and Prussia, discussion of, 121–2, 136–7; Poland, discussion of, 123, 135–6; China, future role of, 124; U.S. future role in Europe, Roosevelt's views on, 125; Sword of Stalingrad, presentation of, 125–6; second front, discussion of priorities, location and timing, 126–7; execution of German officers and military experts, views on need for, 128–30; celebration of Churchill's birthday during, 131, 134–5; bilateral meeting of Churchill and Stalin during, 131–3; Three Power Declaration, signing of, 135, 137–8; analysis of, 138–40

"Eureka II" conference (1945), see "Argonaut" conference

extermination camps (Nazi), discovery of, 230–1

Falkland Islands, war to liberate (1982), 275

Finland, 14, 170–1

France: collapse of (1940), 13, 25; Germany and Berlin, allocation of zones of occupation in (1945), 248–50; postwar plans for, 171–3; Vichy government of, 13, 18, 66, 82

Franco, Gen. Francisco, 5, 260

Franco-Prussian War (1870–1), 3, 13, 98

general election, British (1945), 241, 246, 295

George VI, King, 36, 125

German-Soviet Pact (1939), 6, 14

Germany: defeat of, 233; division of, in 1945, 248–50; rise of Nazis in, see National Socialism; Allied strategic bombing campaign against, 74; and unconditional surrender, 71, 97

German armed forces: Wehrmacht (and Reichsheer), 16–17, 18, 63, 64–5, 75, 97, 102, 129, 232; Kriegsmarine, 61, 62, 67–8, 75, 146; Luftwaffe, 13–14, 51, 62; Waffen-SS, 129, 167, 232

Giraud, Gen. Henri, 72, 80

Goebbels, Joseph, 97

Göring, Reichsmarschall Hermann, 13, 233

Greece, 17, 100, 168–9; King George II of, 100; ELAS guerrilla campaign in, 100–1, 286, 291–2

Gromyko, Andrei A., 176

Groves, Gen. Leslie R., 214, 234; see also "Manhattan" project

Gustav line, German, in Italy, 147, 151

Hácha, Emil, 6, 281

Harriman, W. Averell, 37, 58, 106, 193, 195, 204

Himmler, Heinrich, 233

Hiroshima, atomic attack on (1945), 263

Hitler, Adolf, 5, 18–19, 208, 209; birth of, 260; as German Chancellor, 4; reaction to death of Mussolini, 233; suicide of (1945), 233

Hopkins, Harry, 35, 51, 55, 76, 211, 222

Horthy de Nagybanya, Nicolas V., 166

Hull, Cordell, 18, 76, 94, et seq., 161, 175, 291

Hungary, 160, 165–7

Hyde Park conference (New York) (1944), 189–92

Iraq, war in (2003), 278, 279, 295

Islamic extremism, threat posed by, see terrorism, post-1945

Ismay, Gen. Sir Hastings Lionel, 102–3

Israel, 279

Italy: as Axis power, 15; declares war on Britain and France, 13; postwar plans for, 171–2

Japan: atomic attacks on, 205, 236, 263; as Axis power, 33; defeat of, 263; situation in, pre-war, 8, 44; surrender of, 263

Jews, German persecution of, 5–6; see also extermination camps and Belsen

Joint Declaration on Liberated Europe, see "Argonaut" conference

"July plot" (against Hitler) (1944), 208

Katyn forest massacre (1940), see Poland

Keitel, Field Marshal Wilhelm, 233

Kennan, George F., memo by, 179

Kesselring, Field Marshal Albert, 151
Korea, 111, 224
Korean War (1950–3), 270, 274, *290*
Kosoglyad, Col. G. D., 238
Kristallnacht (1938), 5
Kuwait, liberation of (1990–1), 274

League of Nations, 174
Lend-lease, U.S. aid by: extent of, 15; ending
of, postwar, 188–9; and transfer of U.S.
destroyers to Britain, 15

MacArthur, Gen. Douglas A., 87, 110, 159,
290
Maisky, Ivan, 219
Malta, meeting in (1945), 211–14
Manchuria, 7, 111, 205, 263; see also China
"Manhattan" project, 189–90, 205, 214–15,
234, *284*
Mao Tse-tung, 7, 177
Mareth line, German, in Italy (1943), 70
Marshall, Gen. George C., 44–5, 47, 49, 50,
51, 53, 55, 68, 72, 80; and Marshall Aid
Plan, 189
Michael, King, of Romania, 164
Middleton, Maj. Gen. Troy, 209
Mihailovich, Gen. Draja, 101–2, 167
Mikolajczyk, Stanislaw, 198, 227
Molotov, Vyacheslav, 29, 39, 53, 82, 94, *et
seq.*, 205, 219
Montgomery, Gen. (later Field Marshal)
Bernard Law, 63, 64–5, 80, 155, 183, 186,
209–10, 229
Morgenthau, Henry, 187
Moscow meeting (1941), see Atlantic
conference follow-on activities and meetings
Moscow conference (1942), 58–62
Moscow conference (1943), 94–106;
importance of, 106–7
Munich Agreement (1938), 5
Mussolini, President Benito, 5; as ally of
Hitler, 13, 85; death of, 233

Nagasaki, atomic attack on (1945), 263
National Socialism, in Germany, 4, 98, 270
Nationalsozialistische Deutsche Arbeitpartei
(NSDAP), see National Socialism
"naughty document"(1944), 196, 226, see
also "Tolstoy" conference
Nazi Party, see National Socialism
Nimitz, Adm. Chester W., 159
NKVD (Soviet secret police), 238–9

North Atlantic Treaty Organisation (NATO),
274–6, 277

"Octagon" conference, Quebec (1944):
strategic situation, summary of, 181–3;
Japan, planning timeframe for defeat of,
184; Japan, projected campaign against,
185; western Europe, policy for future of
campaign in, 185–6, 187; Allied military
commanders, views of, 183, 186;
Germany, discussion of, 186, 187–8;
Morgenthau plan, origins of, 187; France,
zone of occupation in postwar Germany,
188; lend-lease, Anglo-U.S. decision on
ending of, 188–9
operations (all are Allied operations unless
shown otherwise): "Anvil" (landings in
southern France, 1944), 133, see also
operation "Dragoon"; "Avalanche"
(landings at Salerno, Italy, 1943), 85, 89,
93; "Barbarossa" (German invasion of
Soviet Union, 1941), 18, 33–4, *281*;
"Battleaxe" (counter-offensive in North
Africa, 1941), 17; "Bolero" (U.S. build-up in
Britain from 1942), 51–3, 54, 55;
"Buccaneer" (proposed offensive at
Andaman Islands, Bay of Bengal), 111, 113,
132, 139; "Cobra" (U.S. breakout to St. Lo
from Normandy beach-heads, 1944), 157;
"Dracula" (proposed assault on Rangoon,
1945), 185; "Dragoon" (landings in
southern France, 1944), 133, 152, 154 see
also operation "Anvil"; "Dynamo"
(evacuation of Dunkirk, 1940), 12; "Epsom"
(attack on Caen, Normandy, 1944), 156;
"Fortitude" (deception activities supporting
"Overlord", 1944), *289*; "Goodwood"
(British breakout from Normandy beach-
heads, 1944), 156; "Gymnast" (codename
for action to occupy French North Africa,
1942), 55, 65; "Husky" (invasion of Sicily,
1943), 72, 75, 85; "Jupiter" (proposed
offensive in northern Norway, 1942), 60;
"Market Garden" (airborne assault to seize
Rhine crossings, 1944), 208; "Neptune"
(assault phase of cross-Channel invasion,
1944), 155; "Overlord" (cross-Channel
invasion, 1944), 79, 83, 85, 104, 133, 155–6,
289; "Plunder" (Rhine crossing, 1945), 227,
229; "Roundup" (planned invasion of
Europe in 1943), 54, 74; "Sealion" (*Seelöwe*)
(planned German invasion of Britain,

1940–1), 13, 92; "Shingle" (landing at Anzio, 1944), 139, 147, 151–2, *288*; "Sledgehammer" (planned invasion of Europe in 1942), 51, 55; "Torch" (invasion of North Africa, 1942), 55, 60, 63, 65–6; "Velvet" (proposed Anglo-U.S. air support for Soviet forces in the Caucasus), 63

Pacific theater: major U.S. offensives in, 54, 148, 157–8, 223; prioritization of U.S. support for, 44, 159–60
Patton, Gen. George S., 183, 209–10
Pétain, Marshal Henri Philippe, 18, see also Vichy government
Peter II, King, of Yugoslavia, 102
Placentia Bay, see Atlantic conference
Poland: borders, issue of, 99–100, 135–6, 162, 199, 221–2, 250–6, 258, 259, *287*; German invasion of (1939), 3, 6, 8; government of, 99, 199–200, 227; Katyn Forest massacre (1940), 99, *285*; Polish-British Treaty (1939), 6, 8, 99; and Soviet-German non-aggression pact (1939), 6

"Quadrant" conference, Quebec (1943): British delegation, travel arrangements of, 85–6; operation "Overlord", discussion of, 86–7; Far East and Pacific campaigns, future strategy for, 87; Quebec Agreement, 88; follow-on activities and meetings, 89–93; Stalin's reaction to outcome of, 90, 92–3
Quebec Agreement (1943), see "Quadrant" conference and atomic bomb

Reagan, Ronald, 268
Red Army (Soviet), major offensives and actions of, 67, 90–1, 147, 154, 203, 208, 232–3
Reynaud, Paul, 13
Ribbentrop, Joachim von, 29
Rommel, Gen. (later Field Marshal) Erwin, 16, 17, 46, *282*, *283*
Romania, 160, 161, 163–4
Roosevelt, Franklin Delano: early life and career, 1882–1941, 24, 29–30; attitudes to Europe, 15, 162–3, 271; concern over German aggression, 14–16; declining health of, 30, 148, 226; death of, 231; and U.S. preparations for war, 15, 34; at war summits, see references to specific conferences

Runstedt, Gen. Gerd von, 209
Russia (see Soviet Union)

"Sextant" conference, Cairo (1943): Chinese delegation, presence of, 107, 109, 110; Far East and Pacific, discussion of Anglo-U.S. campaigns in, 110, *et seq.*; Japan, plans for dismantling its empire, 111; Anglo-U.S. tensions at, 110, 112, 113; Japan, increased U.S. prioritization of war against, 113; dilution of Anglo-U.S. special relationship, 113–14
Sforza, Count Carlo, 172
Soviet Union, 4; collapse of (1989–90), 274, 277; occupation of Estonia, Lithuania, and Latvia (1940), 14; U.S. and British aid to, 34–5, 39–40, 61, 62, 77, 105, see also Lend-lease; war against Finland (1939–40), 14; plans for war against Japan, 205–6, 224, 263
Spaatz, Gen. Carl, 235
Spain, 260–1
Spanish Civil War, 4; and German, Italian and Soviet involvement in, 5
Stalin, Joseph Vissarionovich: early life and career, 1879–1941, 22–4, 26–9; exploitation of Anglo-U.S. differences, 61, 118, 125, 245, 269; Germany, attitude to, 29, 122, 130; preoccupation with need for Anglo-U.S. second front, 56, 57, 60, 67; reluctance to travel beyond Soviet Union, 107–8, 180, *286*; at war summits, see references to specific conferences
Stettinius, Edward R., 215
Stimson, Henry L., 50, 53, 55, 234–5
Suez crisis (1956), 268, *284*, *287*
Sword of Stalingrad, see "Eureka" conference
"Symbol" conference, Casablanca (1943): unconditional surrender, disclosure of requirement for, 70–2; Mediterranean, campaign in, 72; cross-Channel invasion, aspects of, 73–4, 75; Far East and Pacific, increased importance of campaign in, 70, 73; COSSAC, formation of, 74; reaction of Stalin to, 75; follow-on activities and meetings, 74, 76–7

Tedder, Air Marshal Sir Arthur, 80
"Terminal" conference, Potsdam (1945): Allied victory parades during, 241; atomic bomb, perspective of, 262–3; Attlee at,

246, *et seq.*; Austria, discussion of, 259–60; Berlin, discussion of, 248–50; Black Sea, access to, 261; Churchill at, 243, *et seq.*; Council of Foreign Ministers, creation of, 247–8; East Prussia, discussion of, 255; Germany, discussion of, 248–50; Japan, war against, 262–3; organization of, 242–3; other issues, discussion of, 261–2; Poland, discussion of, 250–6, 258, 259; preparations for, 237–40, 242; reparations from Germany, discussion of, 256–9; security arrangements for, 238–40; social events during, 241–2; Spain, discussion of, 260–1; Stalin at, 243, *et seq.*; Truman at, 243, *et seq.*; visits to Berlin by Truman and Churchill during, 241; Zhukov, role of, 237

terrorism, post-1945, 276, 278–80,

Thatcher, Margaret, 268

Thompson, Detective-Inspector W.H., 125, 240, *287*

Three Power Declaration (1943), see "Eureka" conference

Tito, Marshal Josip Broz, 101–2, 167–8, 261

"Tolstoy" conference, Moscow (1944): background to, 192–3, 194; arrangements for, 193, 195; division of Allied responsibility for postwar Europe, 195–6, 197; Poland, discussion of, 197–200; Polish delegates, intransigence of, 198, 199; Anglo-U.S. campaign in Europe, future strategy for, 200–2; Eastern front, Soviet future strategy for, 202–3; Far East, Allied future strategy for, 203–6, 207; Pacific theater, U.S. future strategy for, 204–5; Japan, future involvement of Soviet forces against, 205–6, 207; Churchill, illness at, 204; analysis of, 206, 207

"Trident" conference, Washington (1943): cross-Channel invasion, discussion of, 79; Italy and Sicily, future campaign in, 78–9; subsequent directive to Eisenhower, 79–80; reaction of Stalin to, 80, 81–2; analysis of, 83–4; follow-on meetings and activities, 80–4

Truman, Harry S., 222, 231–2

"Tube Alloys", 88, 189–91, 214, 265; see also atomic bomb and "Manhattan" project

unconditional surrender, issue of, 70–2, 96

United Nations: issue of Security Council composition (1944), 172, 177; issue of voting rights, representation and veto (1944), 176, 177–8, (and 1945), 215; origins of, 174, 227, 273–4; see also Dumbarton Oaks conference

U.S. armed forces, 15; army, 155, 157, 227–9; navy, 157; U.S. Marine Corps (USMC), 148, 157; air force, 74, *283*

V-E Day (1945), 233

Versailles, Treaty of (1920), 3, 9, 131, 247

"Vienna Alternative" (1944), 152–4

Vishinsky, Andrei, 214

V-J Day (1945), 263

Voroshilov, Marshal Klimentii E., 103

V-weapons (German), 112, 181, 209

Warsaw Pact (1955), 277, 279

war summits 1941–5 (in chronological order): Atlantic conference, August 1941, 136–42; "Arcadia" conference, December 1941, 144–9; Moscow conference, August 1942, 58–62; "Symbol" conference, January 1943, 68–9, 70–7; "Trident" conference, May 1943, 77, 78–84; "Quadrant" conference, August 1943, 85–9; Moscow conference, October 1943, 94–107; "Sextant" conference, November 1943, 107–14; "Eureka" conference, November 1943, 115–42; Dumbarton Oaks conference, August 1944, 174–9; "Octagon" conference, September 1944, 179, 180–9; Hyde Park meeting, September 1944, 189–93; Tolstoy conference, October 1944, 193, 194–207; Malta conference, January 1945, 211–14; "Argonaut" conference, January 1945, 214–25; "Terminal" conference, July 1945, 237–62, 270; post-1945 analysis, 264–80

Welles, Sumner, 76

Wilson, Harold, 268

Wilson, Field Marshal Sir Henry Maitland, 234

Winant, John Gilbert, 34

Yugoslavia, 17, 101–2, 161, 166–8, 261

Zhukov, Marshal Georgii K., 233, 237–8, 243